AF449344

CASHING IN ON THE AUCTION BOOM

CASHING IN ON THE AUCTION BOOM

****

JAMES WAGENVOORD

****

Rawson, Wade Publishers, Inc.
New York

Copyright © 1980 by James Wagenvoord Studio, Inc.
10 East 49th Street, New York, N.Y. 10017
All rights reserved.

Published simultaneously in Canada by McClelland and Stewart, Ltd.

Manufactured in the United States of America

An Oak Alley Book Created and Produced
by James Wagenvoord Studio, Inc.

EDITOR—James Wagenvoord

WRITERS—James Wagenvoord, Douglas Colligan,
Jeffrey Hogrefe, Edward Stevenson

ILLUSTRATIONS—James Jones

COPY EDITOR—Ted Johnson

EDITORIAL RESEARCH—Cory Alperstein,
Scott Hudson, Megan Marshack, Amelia Wood

ASSISTANT EDITOR—Anne Dodd

ART ASSISTANTS—Lorna Beiber,
Carol Hamoy, Lisa Albert, Jerry Harding,
Rita-Sue Bell, Jo-Lynn Crabs

ACKNOWLEDGMENTS

Our deep thanks to the many people who gave invaluable assistance in the preparation of this book. A special thanks to:

Marie G. Dodd; Nancy Thompson; James Boswell, member of the Certified Auctioneer's Institute; Bowers and Ruddy Galleries; Frank Campbell, the American Numismatic Society; Al Diedro, the Bank of New York; Max Dreisner and Sidney Dreisner, Tepper Galleries; Warren Beatty; Roland Edelstein, the Pawn Brokers Association; Keith Harmer, Harmer's of New York; Bernard Hart, the National Auto Auction Association; William Godfrey, country auctioneer; Seymour Kirshner, Jewelry Auction Marketplace of America; Russell Kruse, Kruse Auction Company; Joseph Liebson, Astor Galleries; Diane Markes, Golden Movement Emporium Auction; Pete Murray, appraiser and real estate broker; Alexander McNally and Peter Egan, Heublein Inc.; Fred Reisner, Fred Reisner Inc.; Hubert L. Reape, Heany-Koski; Marcia Shafer, Martha's Vineyard General Services Association; Max E. Spann, Max E. Spann Inc.; Stack's, New York; Robert Strauss, David Strauss and Company; Lewis Trainman, Lewis Trainman Real Estate; James Williams, the Keeneland Association; David Bathurst, Christie, Manson & Woods International Inc.; William Doyle, William Doyle Galleries, Inc.; Peter Fairbanks, Robert Gowland and Paul Viney, Phillips, Son & Neale, Inc.; Hugh Hildesley, John Marion and Elizabeth Robbins, Sotheby's Inc.; Kathleen McFadden-Guzman, Plaza Galleries; Jim Graham, Jim Graham Auction School; Richard W. Dewees, Missouri Auction School; Bill Josko, auctioneer and teacher; Stephen J. Martin, the Certified Auctioneers Education Institute, Inc.; Gordon Taylor, World Wide College of Auctioneering, Inc.; Doctor Bruce Allen, the University of Louisville; Gary Carmichael, the National Auctioneer's Association; Charles Benner, Walter Grancher, David Leonard, Roy Marken, Russell Mclain, Kay Tinsman and Richard Vawter, the General Services Administration; Dick Rosencrants and Paul J. Tuliano, the Department of Defense; Captain Robert Truax; Bill, Terry and Sheila Schwedes; George Fay, Bertha Merriman and John Whitehead, the U.S. Postal Service; John Driscoll, Karl Girardi, Diane Harvey and Neil Lageman, the U.S. Customs Service; George Coakley, Gerard Ennis, Eve Miller and Gary Prutsman, the Internal Revenue Service; Sergeant Roy Clary, the Nashville, TN Police Department; Sergeant Edward Cowhey, the Chicago, IL Police Department; Captain Thomas McAndrews, the New York City, NY Police Department; Sergeant Robert Sanford, the Minneapolis, MN Police Department; Sergeant Dewitt Smith, the Atlanta, GA Police Department; Mr. Dempsy, the U.S. Marshal's Service, Washington, D.C.; Deputy Segerer, the Los Angeles County Marshal's Department; and Mike Kogan, Action Photo.

CONTENTS

CASHING IN
ON THE
AUCTION
BOOM

THE AUCTION ARENA

The auction arena is the oldest marketplace in the world, and it continues to be the most active. If you are prepared to trade there seriously, auctions can serve as the first place to shop for nearly everything that adds up to your personal inventory: furniture; rugs; cars, vans, trucks; land; houses; appliances; housewares; general collectibles; fine art; books for collecting; everyday tableware, fine china; cameras; musical instruments . . . the list goes on and on. And the savings, the bargain buying go on and on.

If you approach auction shopping with patience and inquisitiveness, no little humor and some determination, it will work for you. And the cost of your purchases should average only 50 to 60 percent of retail replacement cost.

I know that this bargain figure holds up, on the average—and is actually conservative—because for the past fifteen years I've been doing nearly all my shopping at auctions. Virtually the only things I haven't bought at auction are food, bed linens, and clothing. (I did, however, bid for and get a sable parka for a friend at auction a year ago for $350. The coat was appraised later that week at $2,000.) Some other personal examples: A Nikon camera with a 105mm lens. The replacement cost at the time was $725. I got it for a $150 bid at a pawnshop clearance auction. Reconditioned and cleaned, it cost me a total of $225—a saving of $500. And a 9- by 18-foot wool rug, in mint condition. My winning bid at a general merchandise and estate auction was $80. Another $40 for cleaning, $15 for delivery—the total lay-down cost was only $135. And also at an estate auction, in early January 1980, 24 Baccarat crystal wineglasses (8 all-purpose, 8 white, 8 red) at $4.50 a glass. They currently retail at $22 to $28 each.

I am not a collector, and certainly not a dealer, but I've become an unreconstructed auction shopper. Moving frequently is one reason. Having been burgled more than once is another. But the fascination of the flow of merchandise, the excitement of an active auction room, and the search for bargains add up to the real motivation.

At the first auction I ever attended I bought a small bust—a likeness of a Masai warrior—for $3. I thought it was carved from ebony. It was plaster. I don't think I even took it home. At the second auction I ever attended—it was a year later—I bought a carved oak chess table for $25. It was not made out of plaster. It remains one of my favorite pieces of furniture. It was that buy that really started me shopping the auction markets. And in the years since, I have furnished several apartments and done nearly all of my gift shopping at auctions.

My auction experience has centered around general merchandise and estate auctions—the middle-level auction houses that can be found in most cities and towns (detailed in the chapter that follows). I've also followed and shopped at (to name a few) police auctions, post office sales, the various federal government auctions, and on occasion the international houses. And this experience has convinced me that to shop auctions is to shop the world's finest marketplace.

Anyone can bid at auction. But getting the greatest value for your dollar and enjoying the experience takes more than just putting your hand up in the air. This book is designed as a resource for the auction shopper who is searching for good buys (and who can, when the occasion arises, benefit by using auctions for selling). You need to know how to locate and sort out the various auctions, how they work, how to recognize the competition, what your rights are as a buyer, and—perhaps most important of all—how to plan and control your bidding.

This last point is, I feel, the key to successful auction shopping. Without self-control you will have, at best, limited success in buying bargains. Dr. Bruce Allen, associate professor of marketing at the University of Louisville, calls the response that challenges a bidder's self-control "the competitive factor." As the heat of the auction (or for that matter any situation involving a concentrated bargaining process) builds up, the need to close the deal can become overpowering. Beating out the competition, winning the item, can be a momentary obsession. The other factors—the price to be paid for the item, the functional reason for wanting it—diminish in significance. "You can get to feel like you're running in a race," says Dr. Allen, "and you must win, you must come in first."

How else could one explain why, without exception, the most common mistake people make at auctions—according to auctioneers, who should know—is overbidding? Many an auction shopper sets a bidding limit, or at the very least has an approximate idea of what something is worth, and in spite of that bids the item through the ceiling.

At a recent Sotheby auction a bidder relentlessly went after a rare piece of fabric appraised at $3,000 and took it at a knockdown price of $11,000. More than mildly curious about the particular bidding sequence, the auctioneer later asked the bidder why the price had risen to nearly four times the value of the fabric. The answer was short: "I just had to have it." The competitive factor in action.

This emotional element is not something to take lightly. But it is a problem only if you allow it to take hold and obscure the other aspects of auction buying. The feeling of winning is—and should be—one of the rewards of shopping at auction. But it's important to remember that a "win" is a purchase made carefully and at the right price.

You will not overbid if you follow the guidelines offered in this book. Auction shopping is an economical and exciting way to buy. The bargains are out there. They can be yours.

There is repetition throughout this book. This is because there is a great deal to say about auctions that bears repeating—particularly the steps and guidelines that should be followed by any bidder who intends to shop the market seriously and buy well. It really is necessary to view the merchandise prior to the sale, to set bidding limits and to stick to them, to get out of the action if you feel at all uncomfortable, and to remember, if something you're interested in gets past you, that another auction will be coming up soon. This world is not about to run out of people selling and people buying.

It is, of course, much easier to write or repeat guidelines than to follow them. For example, a few years ago my wife and I were furnishing a new apartment. It was early in the "live in your own urban garden" era. Pure white walls, thick green carpeting, garden-style (yet comfortable) furniture, hanging plants, some glass, some chrome, a few favorite pieces such as the already mentioned chess table—and the fact that we were living some 200 feet above the street with a hermetically sealed view would be less apparent. We had the white paint and the carpeting; what we lacked was the garden-style furniture.

Part of the excitement of the move was that we were now only two blocks from an auction house I had been shopping for years. And on the first Saturday morning in the new apartment we walked through the door of the already crowded gallery as the unforeseen answer to our needs was being placed on the block at the far end of the room. Five pieces of white-painted wrought iron garden furniture—a loveseat, two side chairs, a coffee table, an end table. Touch up the paint, upholster and lay down a few cushions, and one of the fastest and trendiest decorating jobs in history would be complete.

The lot number was called, the bidding began, and less than a minute later I had bought the lot for $270. A floor assistant took my deposit, and we turned and went back out the door—and on to lunch to celebrate our luck. Later we made arrangements for delivery over the phone. Lot number 192 was delivered the following Tuesday.

There is a style of miniature garden furniture that was popular at the turn of the century. Its perfect proportions created an illusion of depth when the pieces were placed at the rear of a garden, or of an auction gallery. In the apartment they offered the reality of tininess. Normal chair height is 18 inches; the seats of the loveseat and the chairs were exactly 12 inches off the floor. Both my wife and I stood six feet tall. We hunkered in the tiny chairs for a few moments, trying not to bruise each other's feelings. I broke the silence: "Maybe if we get some really thick, firm 10- to 12-inch cushions, it will be fine." (As is mentioned several times in the pages that follow, imagination and adaptability are important factors in auction shopping.) My wife's four-year-old nephew and two-year-old niece had this classic example of trompe l'oeil furniture in their yard at the end of the week.

It was embarrassing, but not embarrassing enough to make me miss an auction the following weekend. However, I have never since bid on any item I haven't looked at during a presale exhibition. And I did price the miniature buy at retail. The same mistake from the far end of a huge retail showroom would have cost me three times as much. The bargains are indeed to be found in the auction rooms.

GENERAL MERCHANDISE AND PERSONAL ESTATE SALES

Of all the marketplaces discussed in this book, the general merchandise auction probably has the most opportunities for true bargains. It is also the best training ground for the auction shopper. There is a vast diversity of goods—everything from grand pianos to cocktail coasters—and it is all knocked down at a breathtaking tempo, with a new item under the hammer every 40 seconds or so. Usually it's an entertaining affair, an arena in which both the slick and the gentlefolk lose their civilized veneer and compete head to head. And there is always a chance to save—to pick up what you need, or what you just want, at an average savings of 40 to 50 percent of what you'd have to pay retail. And surprisingly often it's a chance to strike it rich—to get an item for a tiny fraction of its worth.

Yet most people, whether they admit it or not, are at least a little fearful of general merchandise auctions at first. I certainly was.

Perhaps you fear that the passion to buy—something! anything! —can overpower your native good sense, leaving you bewildered, embarrassed, and overextended. Auction horror stories abound; everyone has heard tales of auction goers who bought things they did not want or need, bidding sums they could not hope to pay. Or perhaps you think you don't know enough about merchandise to compete with dealers and experienced auction goers.

Mistakes happen. As mentioned, I've made plenty, from ignorance or excitement or both. But oddly enough I've found in my own experience and from talking to both frequent and occasional auction goers that the mistakes you remember the longest are not the times you paid a little more, or even a lot more, than what you later discovered was the item's true value. It's the times when you *didn't* make the winning bid—when you let an opportunity go by and later discovered that the actual bargain was tremendous—that linger. I'm not saying you should bid on everything you see and never let yourself be outbid—in fact, a large part of this book concerns careful evaluation of merchandise and calm, deliberate bidding. I am saying that if you're careful, you can be a bargain buyer from your very first auction.

There is no secret to becoming a successful auction shopper. All you have to do is learn what to expect and what to do when the expected occurs. In the following pages, I'm going to provide you with a guided tour of the general merchandise auction, including a close look at its procedures and rhythms, the sources of the merchandise it auctions off, the categories of merchandise you'll see offered, the types of buyers you'll meet, the bidding you'll encounter, and the ways in which you can prepare yourself to buy successfully.

AUCTION RHYTHMS

Auction sales tend to be carefully choreographed. Merchandising principles are indeed important to the auction marketplace.

There are a number of reasons for organizing an auction in a particular way. Some have to do with practical considerations, some with psychological factors. Different auctioneers will handle the same problem in different ways, each according to his or her theory of how to do a better business, but there is no disagreement on the fact that the sequence in which goods hit the auction block has an influence on the sale outcome.

Here, for instance, is how the general sales run at the auction gallery I attend most regularly. It is a fortnightly sale that always begins at 11:00 a.m. First comes the silver, always sold in one sequence. If there is no silver, there is usually jewelry, or—occasionally—rare coins. Anyway, the sale is always launched with the disposal of the

```
 4 GILT ...
 5 DECORATED COLO...
36 WROUGHT IRON 3 LIGHT ...
87 SET 10 BLACK LACQUERED ARM CHAIR...
88 3 PANEL CHINESE DECORATED SCREEN
89 2 GILT METAL WALL DECORATIONS
90 DECORATED BOW FRONT CABINET
91 CARTON & CONTENTS
92 ZENITH COLORED T.V. ON STAND
93 KING SIZE HEADBOARD
94 4 PIECE DECORATED CHILDS BEDROOM
   ENSEMBLE
95 PAIR TWIN BEDS
96 DECORATED CONSOLE MIRROR
97 BRASS BENCH
98 UPHOLSTERED SIDE CHAIR
99 PAIR PROVINCIAL BEDSIDE CABINET
100 TRI-POD BASE CIGARETTE TABLE
101 DECORATED SHOE RACK
102 PAINTED CABINET, DRESSER & 3 BEN...
    ...EATHER TOP POE COMMODE
    ...TING-THE GUITAR PLAYER
    ... GIRLS ...
```

intrinsically valuable items first, and this segment of the sale seldom lasts more than half an hour.

Following the opening segment come 50 to 75 lots of inexpensive furniture followed by 50 to 75 lots of moderate-value decorative items. Furniture and decorations are far and away the largest categories of goods in terms of number of lots in the sale, and they will therefore take up the bulk of the time.

In the early afternoon, at exactly 1:00 p.m., session after session, the alternating batches of furniture and decorations are interrupted. It is rug time. The rugs, usually coming up around lot number 200, are sold in one unbroken sequence—not intermixed with the other goods in any way. (Most auctioneers feel that professional rug dealer/buyers are so disruptive that the best solution for everyone is to hold that portion of the sale at one time and get the major rug buyers in and out as quickly as possible.)

Following rugs, there are further groups of furniture alternating with decorations increasing steadily in quality. Then come the paintings and other graphic arts, sold, like the silver and rugs, in one continuous group. The art is usually the last significant special portion of the sale—though there may, on some days, be books or similar goods —and the auction usually winds down gradually from there, ending with miscellaneous smaller decorative objects, glassware, porcelains, fans and miniatures.

Another middle-level gallery, one of the more prestigious ones, does not mix its merchandise at all. Instead, it sells all the decorative arts, then all the silver, all the furniture, and all the rugs, finishing with 100 to 200 lots of paintings, prints and drawings. Within each grouping, however, individual items may be carefully placed. This is because it has become more and more important in today's world of merchandising expertise to place the most important goods, those expected to bring the highest prices, to their greatest advantage. There are different theories on how best to accomplish this.

Some general auctioneers intersperse the important items periodically within the flow of more ordinary goods. The idea is that including an interesting, unusual, or costly piece at frequent intervals will keep the crowd's attention focused fairly consistently throughout the auction. This avoids the doldrums or dead spots that plague some sales.

Other general auctioneers organize the flow of goods so that excitement reaches a climax at a specific point during the sale, usually either in a "bell curve" with interest and tension building slowly to a peak in the middle of the sale and then relaxing slowly to the end, or in a series of smaller ups and downs escalating to a peak at or near the end. Each pattern has its own advocates.

But whatever the pattern, if you recognize it and understand what is going on, you can anticipate the general course of events and be better prepared for them. For one thing, having a sense of when the merchandise you desire will come up in the great scheme of auction choreography can help you anticipate the price competition you'll face. At the very least, recognizing the general pattern of the sales at the houses you frequent can enable you to schedule your buying time more efficiently. Once you are an old hand, you will develop a pretty good sense of when you should make your appearance to bid on the things that interest you.

SPECIALIZED GENERAL AUCTIONS

What I've been describing so far might be called the old style in auction selling, which is to put up for sale the merchandise that has accumulated since the last sale, knock it down, clear it out, and make room for the new merchandise. This is the auctioneer acting as sales agent in the classic manner. Many houses do the bulk of their business in this way. I feel it is the most satisfying kind of auction to go to. The sense of the possibility of discovery, of bargain finding, is much greater. Only the roll of the celestial dice determines what goods will come up from sale to sale.

Sharply contrasted with this is the modern merchandising approach, characterized, above all, by specialization. The specialized sale is the most effective tool that auctioneers have exploited for raising the prices of auction goods and creating new specialized markets.

Special auction sales were originally generated as a reaction to the needs and interests of collector/buyers. The concept made—and still makes—perfect sense. Individuals shopping for certain kinds of goods —such as African art objects, or German porcelain figurines, or 19th-century American tin toys, are much more likely to attend a sale devoted entirely to their specialty than to attend one in which only one or two items of interest to them are offered. By accumulating merchandise in the various areas of collecting and specialization, and by targeting specific advertising to the specialized customer, the astute general auctioneer can, in addition to general merchandise selling, bring together rich collections of goods and rich collections of customers in the same time and place. The result? Better selection, more competition, higher prices. A service is being performed for the buyer; a reward is earned by the seller.

Specialized sales are definitely the wave of the future in the auction business. The idea has already been used to generate new special markets—areas of collecting that were not defined and really did not exist before the sales that created them. This is not to say that old-style auctioneers and auctions will disappear. They will remain because they serve the interests of the general auction buyer. As time goes on and auction sales secure an even firmer foothold in American commerce, however, they will become increasingly overshadowed by the aggressively innovative specialized marketers.

A good example of the lengths to which this special-sale principle can be carried out is New York Americana week. Every spring in New York City, the great international auction houses hold their annual sales of American antiques (very much sought after, these days, and very costly). These sales are scheduled to coincide with the biggest and most important antique show of the year, also devoted to American furniture. All the smaller general merchandise houses that do specialized sales also hold their Americana sales during this period. Even the museums get into the act, offering lectures and symposia on the many subject areas that fall within the general heading of Americana. It is a lot of market hype, and it generates an unbelievable amount of activity, interest, and business.

Meanwhile, the debate rages quietly among the different styles of auctioneers about the relative merits of the two different approaches. Those who are committed to the special-sale approach say, "How can you argue with success? We're getting higher prices than ever before. We're in a customer service business. It's an expanding market." Those who operate in the old move-it-in, move-it-out style say, "I sell twice as much merchandise in two weeks here as they do in two months. My bank balance proves it. I can't be bothered." There is room for both approaches, and there will continue to be customers for both kinds of sales.

WHERE THE MERCHANDISE COMES FROM

Any business that styles itself an "auction gallery"—a permanent place of business with a steady clientele—requires a reliable source of supply. Indeed, one of the things that continues to impress me at auction is the apparently inexhaustible flow of merchandise that passes through the rooms of the country's general merchandise houses. Where do all these goods come from? The explanation is as simple as it is sobering. To be blunt, most of the personal property marketed on the auction block—the furniture, the pictures, the rugs, the glassware, the enamel and bronze clocks, the brass-bound campaign chests, the appliances, the ashtrays, the television sets—arrives there because of death.

Personal estates: Sidney Dreisen, proprietor of New York City's Tepper Gallery, says that 85 percent of the items he sells fall into this category. Kathleen McFadden-Guzman of Plaza Art Galleries, another New York auction house, reports that while 80 percent of their goods used to be estate-generated, that figure is now down to about 40 to 50 percent. At any rate, all this merchandise comes to the various galleries through the process of settling people's estates. The quality of the goods reflects the wealth and tastes of the original owners.

Although most decedents bequeath much or all of their personal property specifically to their assorted heirs, sometimes no such specific bequests are made. In such a case, the estate must be liquidated—turned into readily available cash—before it can be disbursed or divided. In other instances, the heirs may have no particular use for the bequeathed possessions and choose to liquidate them.

In either case, the executor's responsibility is to sell the effects in a manner most advantageous to the heirs.

The experienced executor, who is usually a lawyer or a banker, knows the auctioneers in his town or region and knows who is "right" for the disposal of various types of property. His contacts and connections may often reach over quite long distances; if he is doing his job conscientiously, and the estate is important enough, he will see to it that the property reaches the most advantageous market, no matter how far away.

Sometimes the executor merely has to get the goods to a market in which the buyers are accustomed to dealing at a high level of value. Sometimes he must take into account regional biases affecting the prospects of getting a reasonable price. Until recently, for example, fine Victorian furniture was a drag on the market in New York. In Atlanta, however, Victorian furniture has been popular for a long time, and good pieces have brought high prices there. Again, in New England, buyers of antiques are extreme purists. Everything must be in original condition. Restoration, refinishing, or alterations of any sort reduce the value of a piece drastically. But in St. Louis, an auctioneer reported to me that he can't sell a piece of fine furniture unless it glows and sparkles and looks as if it just left the original cabinetmaker's shop. These are a few of the possible considerations that account for the cases in which estate property travels long distances to be sold.

Finally, an executor may simply turn over the entire liquidation process to a single auctioneer or auction house, which will handle the entire job from examination to appraisal to transportation to selling.

Other legacies and gifts: Due largely to the ways tax laws are structured, schools, museums, charitable and other institutions receive many donations from private individuals, either as legacies or as gifts from the living, in the form of valuable property. In the past, these bequests were often accompanied by covenants that required the institution to retain ownership. But in recent years because of the burden and expense of dealing with such gifts, institutions frequently accept bequests only on the condition that they have the option of converting them into money (which is usually in short supply). Here again the auctioneer comes into the picture.

Moving—Must sell: Another source of personal property that doesn't involve death is the many people who are relocating, who periodically move and want to liquidate their households. In these days of corporate and governmental gypsies, a lot of moving goes on. Increasingly, the idea of packing an entire household of belongings into a truck and carting it hundreds or thousands of miles to a new house (in which it may be totally unsuitable) is more than many care to face.

Solicited merchandise—off-the-street business: Most auction dealers, especially those who have permanent galleries, solicit merchandise from the general public. You will find ads in every classified telephone directory (usually under "Antiques") from the auctioneers in your town or city saying "We Buy All Sorts of Household Goods—Highest Prices Paid." These ads are answered by people who, either to raise cash, to simplify their lives, or unclutter their living spaces, wish to dispose of one or more of their belongings. The transaction can take the form of a consignment or an outright sale.

Collections: As more and more people get into the wheeling and dealing of the ever-growing list of things collected, auction houses are using private collections as a merchandise source. As I have explained, some houses have learned that they do even better business if they hold occasional specialized sales in specific areas of collecting. Entire collections come up for auction regularly both as estates liquidate and as collectors sell off and move in new directions.

Grab bags: There is a final category of merchandise that comes to the general auction house because the question of its ownership is—for one reason or another—unclear. I am talking about such things as the unclaimed contents of safe-deposit boxes and property left in storage warehouses. In selling this kind of merchandise, the auctioneer is fulfilling his historic role of serving as a conduit to channel back into circulation things that have somehow escaped from or fallen outside of the traditional patterns of commerce.

What is it? Anything; everything; nothing. Whatever people stash, store, hide, lose, forget about. Coins, jewelry, documents, love letters, clothes, pots, pans, many, many things of no value whatever except to the person who put them where they eventually turn up.

SELLING YOUR OWN GOODS AT AUCTION

If you should ever consider selling possessions of your own at an auction, you will have to consider whether to consign the goods or sell them outright to the auctioneer. (Virtually all auction houses will handle them either way.)

Consigning goods to auction sale is tantamount to finding the true market value of the merchandise. That value may be high, in which case you will receive a high price and be pleased, or it may be low. Another way of looking at it is you take a risk, in a sense, in exchange for the possibility of gain. With experience, it is possible to predict a reasonable market price for any item offered at auction, and the bidding estimates in auction catalogs are just that. But it is the bidding mechanism at the moment of sale that determines the true price.

If the auctioneer, the middleman, buys your goods from you outright, the element of risk—having your goods sell for a very low price—is eliminated, but so is the possibility of gain. The auctioneer who seeks to buy may offer a good price, but obviously he will never pay a price that he feels endangers his chances of making a profit on the public sale of the goods. In other words, when you sell outright to an auctioneer, you are almost certainly taking less than you would realize from auction consignment.

For many people this is perfectly acceptable. Not everyone is interested in realizing the highest possible price for their things. You may simply want to dispose of your goods in a convenient way, and selling to an auctioneer is likely to be simpler and quicker than many of the alternatives.

If you prefer to consign your goods rather than sell them outright, the fastest way to get your money is to find an auctioneer who sells regularly, who puts goods up promptly, and who pays within a short time of the sale date. The fastest that you can reasonably hope for payment by this "conventional" route is three to four weeks from the time the goods are delivered to the auctioneer.

The length of selling time can become a problem when you're dealing with an auctioneer who has a large backlog of goods or who plans to hold the items in question for a special sale. In these cases you must decide whether the wait is likely to be compensated for by a higher sale price in the end. It is a matter of choice.

WHAT'S FOR SALE

Now is the time to take a closer look at just what exactly is up there on the block and how it measures up against what's available in the national chainstores, the local thrift shop, retail stores in general, and that antique shop across town.

Usually it measures up very well. But before going on to discuss what is for sale, you must put to rest any illusions you have about acquiring really fine antiques for next to nothing at a general merchandise auction. From time to time, a piece from this vanishing species may appear on the general merchandise auction block, and there are special sales such as those during New York Americana week. But most houses agree that fine antiques—particularly 17th and 18th-century furniture—are all but unobtainable on today's general middle-range market. It is pretty much all in the hands of collectors and museums.

Free from false expectations, you can focus on what *is* available. It is a tough task to give a meaningful rundown on the offerings of the general middle-level auction. It is, in fact, impossible to enumerate more than a small proportion of the possible items, and regional considerations may contradict or nullify some of the information I do venture to offer. But with these reservations in mind, let us take a look at some of the many bargains to be gained.

FURNITURE

Probably the single most important category of goods at the general auction is used furniture. Most popular today are the pieces in the *styles* of the 18th-century cabinetmakers Sheraton, Chippendale, and

Hepplewhite, as well as the 18th-century English genre known as Queen Anne and the French style known as Regency. Needless to say, the original products of these makers and eras are rare and very valuable, but fine reproductions of all of them have been produced in European and American shops since early in the 19th century. The continuing popularity of these styles today is in keeping with a general trend favoring lightness, elegance, adaptability, and moderation in size. This is perfectly understandable, since most of us find living space diminishing as we crowd into the 21st century. So, well-wrought reproductions dating from the 19th century are much in demand.

463 REGEN... TABLE
464 SET 4 REGENCY STYLE MAHOGANY...
CHAIRS
465 CHINESE CHIPPENDALE STYLE LIFT TOP
CONSOLE TABLE
466 QUEEN ANNE STYLE CHINOISERIE
LACQUERED CHINA CABINET
467 PAIR CHIPPENDALE STYLE LEATHER
UPHOLSTERED LIBRARY CHAIRS
...DECORATED CONSOLE MIRROR
...LISH PORCELAIN DESSE

There is no set price ratio between a reproduction piece and the antique original. Many factors of craftsmanship and condition determine the prices of specific pieces. There is a sort of sliding scale that operates relative to the demand for a certain type of piece. A nice modern reproduction of a Regency drop-side dining table might sell for something in the vicinity of $200, while its antique equivalent in good condition might bring anywhere from eight to ten times that. Good reproductions of classic 18th-century English three-pedestal dining tables will bring anywhere from $1,000 to $2,000, while the antique equivalent would be likely to draw three to four times that price—a smaller multiple in the case of the larger, more costly item.

One notable exception to the rule on 19th-century furniture is the genre known as American Empire. These adaptations of the furniture of France from the period starting around 1760 were made in the United States throughout the middle of the 19th century. They are currently selling for quite reasonable prices in many areas of the country.

On a more general level, any furniture that contrasts with the true antiques mentioned above is likely to be relatively inexpensive. That is to say, relatively new pieces that are large, space-consuming, difficult to move, are likely to be bargains. Sofas are a good example. First of all, practically everyone has a sofa. It may not be loved, but it is *there,* and that counts for a lot. Apparently the job of moving the old sofa out and moving the new one in is more than most people care to face. Time and again, I have watched a sofa equivalent in quality to other pieces that are going in the same auction for many hundreds of dollars sell for $100 or $150. At retail the same sofa could cost well over $1,000. Thus sofas tend to be excellent buys, and the principle applies equally to other kinds of furniture. A large, handsome library table may sell for $100 or less, simply because it's difficult to move and too big for many homes; but a fairly ordinary drop-leaf dining table might bring $400 or $500.

Chairs are all over the lot. As with other furniture, genuine antiques in good condition invariably bring high prices (several thousand dollars each) if and when they turn up. Good reproductions of Regency, Hepplewhite, Chippendale, etc. bring high prices also (hundreds to thousands). Good late-19th-century and early-20th-century English and American side chairs or dining chairs bring variable prices. Very large sets (12 to 16) tend to be cheap by the piece, as few people have use for such a large number of chairs. There are always some bargains to be had. It is still surprisingly easy to find a decent side chair at auction for $10 or $15.

Chests, dressers, desks, and breakfronts are particularly vulnerable to the ins and outs of fashion. Breakfronts, for instance, are extremely popular right now, even up to gargantuan size (which proves once again that there are exceptions to every rule). But even with stiff competition the auction price still beats the dealer's price by a long shot. The breakfront you buy for $1,000 at auction might well go for four to six times that from a dealer.

American slant-front desks are skyrocketing in price. The pressure is so strong that unpretentious factory-made copies, less than 30 years old, are riding the same wave and are selling now for more than they did when new.

In stark contrast, anything that looks like an office desk (except for roll-tops) brings a low price unless it is very finely made.

Reproductions of dressers and highboys in the styles of the great 18th-century makers are costly, but 20th-century Arts and Crafts oak is cheap (in the cities of the East and Midwest, at any rate).

Among the available styles of used furniture that appear with reasonable frequency at reasonable prices are American Empire (already mentioned), both English and American Victorian (although, again, the finest pieces are already collector's items), English Tudor and Jacobean styles, American oak, and country pine and maple furniture.

Finally, on a lower level (which is also a newer level), there is a large quantity of factory-made furniture put out in this country beginning in the 1940s, in a variety of styles. There is a sizeable pool of this merchandise, and it thus constitutes the most promising fishing ground for younger buyers who are furnishing their homes.

BARGAINS TO LOOK FOR:

- ★ Bulky pieces
- ★ Sofas
- ★ Large sets of chairs
- ★ Beds
- ★ Single, orphaned pieces (such as one of a pair of armchairs or end tables)
- ★ Fully upholstered pieces
- ★ Newer, factory-made furniture

SILVER BARGAINS

Silver remains unquestionably one of the best auction buys—compared, at least, to the cost of buying at retail. Since silver (the metal) is an industrial commodity as well as a monetary standard, it has a market price that fluctuates daily with supply and demand. The price of silverware at auction fluctuates with and stays reasonably close to the commercial price of the metal. It is sold pretty much by weight. In the old days, a year or so ago, when the market price of the metal was relatively stable, the products of the various silverware manufacturers tended to sell at specific, reasonably consistent premiums over the bullion price. If the going commodity price was $X per ounce, the price of Gorham ware was likely to be $X plus 20 percent; Tiffany, $X plus 30 percent; International, $X plus 15 percent; Jensen, $X plus 30 percent; and so on. You could pretty much count on getting the item you desired by following these formulas.

Things have changed radically in some ways, stayed the same in others. The price of the metal has increased almost fivefold at its highest point. This created a situation in which the bullion or melt-

down value of the metal so totally eclipsed any aesthetic, craftsmanship, or prestige value that all silver was selling at virtually the
same price per ounce for a while. The sameness is that the price of
the ware was still tied closely to the commodity price. Virtually any
silver piece, excluding true antiques, could be bought at auction for
about 20 percent over the melt-down value of the metal. As a result,
a great many silver pieces were sold and indeed melted down and
had the effect of raising the long-term value of all that has survived
the panic.

Fortunately the tide is receding somewhat, and you can now expect a return to something like the old state of affairs in which
different qualities and manufacturers of silverware find consistent
premiums over the current commodity price of the metal. However,
the metal will doubtless settle at a stable level significantly higher
than the years prior to 1980. Fifteen to 25 percent over the bullion
value of the metal should secure most pieces, the higher prices going
for the work of the more prestigious makers. Compared to the prices
in retail outlets, it is indeed a bargain.

15   8   TASSE SPOONS
16   4 GEORGIAN SILVER
VICTORIAN SILVER CAKE KNIFE 4 OZ
17 PAIR STERLING SILVER CANDELHOLDERS
18 9 STERLING SILVER BOULLION HOLDERS
WITH 6 LENOX LINERS 12 OZ
19 STERLING SILVER ART NOUVEAU
SERVING FORK 4 OZ
STERLING SILVER CANDY DISHES

Most of the silver on the auction market these days dates from the
1940s to 1960s. Antique silver is both rare and costly. Art Nouveau
and Art Deco silverware is significantly more valuable than the "ordinary" run of silver, and is usually sold in special collector sales
where, along with other goods in the same styles, it commands relatively high prices.

Within the general field of silver, there is little or no price distinc-
tion between the various sorts of items. Flatware (eating utensils)
sells for about the same price per weight, maker for maker, as do
coffee and tea services, vases, serving pieces, ice buckets, decorations, and center pieces. There are no particular bargains in that

sense, nor are there particularly over-priced items. Things remain pretty close to the going bullion value of the metal.

In comparison with retail silverware prices, according to the estimate of one dealer I talked with recently, you would be paying about one-third at auction for the more ordinary pieces. For the products of the finer, more popular makers, which are sold at a higher retail markup, you may be paying as little as one-fourth or one-fifth of current retail prices. It is indeed a bargain.

RUGS

Rugs are a hot item at auctions. They have been so for quite a long time. But be warned. Probably 95 percent of all rugs sold at auction these days are so-called orientals: the Persian, Caucasian, Turkoman, and other tribal rugs, the traditional products of the Middle East. In no other area of home furnishing or personal property is there so much potential for deception, fakery, trickery, and general confusion. I am still smarting over having paid something over ten times the value of a plausible fake a number of years ago. If the bidding is running high, you'd better be knowledgeable about rugs or stay out of it.

There used to be a fairly steady flow of good used rugs from the Middle East into the markets of Europe and the United States, but now, virtually all of the loose rugs have been sought out and exported. These days, most of the genuine oriental rugs that come up for auction sale are from estates, and the professional dealers seem determined to corner the market—to buy up everything in sight, regardless of quality and condition. Rug dealers have a well-earned reputation for aggressiveness and tricky-dick tactics. Private buyers are justifiably timid about challenging them at their own game.

It is possible to buy a good oriental rug at auction at a fair price, but I, for one, would not undertake it without putting in much study and field work, attending numerous sales, inspecting the offerings minutely, and paying close attention to the bidding.

One hopeful note! Several auctioneers have reported to me sadly that the rug field seems to be "depressed." This may be true, but it does not seem depressed to me. Merely voracious. The one generalization it is safe to make here is that anything you buy at auction will be cheaper there than at the shop of the dealer who is bidding against you. In this case, however, for most value-conscious buyers, the security of dealing with a reputable merchant and the knowledge that the investment is solid may well be worth the extra dollars.

True bargains: The true bargain rugs in the auction rooms are the wool broadlooms. It wasn't so long ago that this was what most of America aspired to. Now that the admittedly beautiful artistic creations of the Middle East have captured the public's attention and imagination, top-quality broadlooms, although they do not turn up in large numbers, can be fantastic buys—selling for one-fifth or less of their original price. Even adding the cost of cleaning (usually necessary), find a broadloom of the right size and color to fit your living space and you will have won yourself a true trophy.

Other carpets that go for quite reasonable prices at auction these days are the modern, domestic, machine-made copies of the genuine Persians, as well as carpets, both new and old, that come from either India or China (and, too, the domestic copies of these). Auction prices for these rugs run around the standard 40 to 60 percent of the new equivalent.

JEWELRY

Lots and lots of jewelry is sold at auction—rings, necklaces, brooches, stickpins, hair ornaments, wristwatches and pocket watches, chains, bracelets, cameos, studs, cufflinks—and although perhaps 90 percent of it goes to dealers, the auctioneers I talk to claim there are fantastic bargains for the private buyer.

I agree. Private bidders should be able to pay more for the auctioned jewelry and still come out way ahead. If you learn to break into this market, you can pick up all this glitter for one-third to one-half retail.

Most of the jewelry that comes up at general merchandise auctions tends to be, if not antique, then certainly out of style. Not that it matters. Fashion doesn't seem to have a very significant influence on jewelry prices these days. The exceptions are Art Nouveau and Art Deco—very fashionable and very expensive. But usually it's the value of the metal and/or the gemstone that counts.

Gold, diamonds, and other precious goodies—such as rubies, sapphires, and emeralds—are unabashedly expensive. Gold sells pretty much by weight, gems by both weight and quality. Market prices for these substances are not retail jewelry prices though, so they remain bargains in the modern auction.

Pearls have just recently gone through the roof. A strand of pearls that sold for $100 a couple of years ago is now selling for $3,000. Most of the pearls on the current market are cultured, too. Still, the same principle applies as with gold and stones. You should do much better at auction than at the jeweler's. Savings should be at least 50 percent.

Other, less costly bargains in jewelry can be found in the following miscellaneous categories: wristwatches, cameos, corals and other trinkets made from less intrinsically valuable materials, gold-filled ornaments (especially Victorian pieces), and semiprecious stones (topaz, amethyst, aquamarine, etc.) in modern settings.

GLASSWARE BARGAINS

A wide variety of glassware turns up at auction. It's a rare sale in which a large selection of pieces is available, but over the long haul practically anything your heart desires will cross the auction block.

The possibilities run from the ordinary, such as anonymous highball glasses, 1950s martini sets, and pressed-glass berry bowls, to the extraordinary, such as enormous brilliant cut pedestal punch bowls, ruby overlay goblets, Lalique and Tiffany art glass, and other collector's items.

Like other items that come in sets, large sets of glassware frequently bring substantially lower prices per piece. The reason is obvious. Few people really have a use for 24 wine glasses and are reluctant to tie up their money in unused merchandise. If you can work out a deal with a friend to divide up a large set, you may be able to buy very cheaply indeed.

CHINA

Like glassware, quite a lot of fine china comes up at auction—again, never a lot at one time, but a good selection over the long run. And like glassware, the china that comes up spans a fairly wide range of qualities. Auction houses offer box lots out of the incomplete sets or miscellaneous groups of ware by lesser or unknown makers. Somewhat higher on the scale are the plentiful Czechoslovakian reproductions of classic French and English dinnerware patterns. But the real bargains of the auction china market are the sets of French and English porcelain and stoneware—with names like Spode, Worcester, Haviland, Royal Doulton, and Sevres—that grace almost every sale.

```
456 PAIR CRYSTAL DECANTERS  WITH
STOPPERS
460 PAIR FRENCH ENAMEL URNS
461 MEISSEN DECORATED PORCELAIN FI
FIGURE GROUP
```

The same principles that apply to glassware apply to china. Fairly complete settings for eight to twelve bring lower prices per piece than you might expect. The more highly decorated patterns will bring higher prices than the plainer ones. Prices for the most desirable sets run from $4 to $10 per piece these days. Taking into consideration all the variables mentioned, that can amount to between 40 and 60 percent of the current equivalent retail value, making china one of the potential bargains.

DECORATIONS

This is the largest and most varied category of auction merchandise, and it is difficult to generalize about it at all. It includes such things as clocks, porcelain figurines, art pottery and glassware, candlesticks, chandeliers, lamps of all kinds (the phrase "mounted as a lamp" preceded by a description of almost anything is one of the more familiar auction-room lines), fireplace fittings (andirons, fenders, fire screens, tools), trophies (animal and otherwise), weapons, bronze figurines, stone statuary and pedestals to stand them on, screens, quilts, samplers, tapestries—the list goes on and on, covering the myriad items and objects people use to adorn living spaces.

```
435 REGENCY STYLE CARVED &
UPHOLSTERED 4 CHAIRBACK SETTEE
436 2 BRASS DOORSTOPS
437 WOOD CARVED FIGURE LAMP
438 GILT BEVELED GLASS MIRROR
```

The only real place to shop for these goods, other than at auction, is the antique shop. In terms of prices and savings to be realized, there is little to add to the basic dictum that by buying intelligently and carefully at private auction you can usually count on picking up an item for a little more than 55/60 percent of what a typical dealer would charge you for it on the retail market. But it is important to remember that auction room competition in the area of decorative arts is perhaps more heated than in any other category of merchandise. This tends to raise prices a little.

COMPETITION

Occasional auction goers too often waste time and nervous energy worrying about the other buyers. "Those other people are *experts*," runs the internal monologue. "They know more than I do—how can I compete with them?" And the typical auction-room gossip can be disconcerting. "Those sharks out there will get anything they want!" I've heard words to this effect spoken (gleefully) by an old hand to nervous newcomers on more than one occasion.

You can relax. After you have witnessed several auctions, you will realize that the competitors at the typical sale are not nearly as formidable as legend would have it. Here they are; judge them for yourself.

THE DEALERS

My estimate—one that auctioneers tend to agree with—is that today there are more private buyers at the average general merchandise and estate sale than there are dealers. The ratio, in fact, appears to be about three to two throughout an auction program.

One reason dealers are in the minority is that auction houses often control their numbers through deliberate scheduling practices. Of the six or eight categories of merchandise that will be sold during the course of a general sale, two or three will be of interest primarily to professional dealers. It is useful to dealers to know that at X gallery's general sale, the rugs, the silver, or whatever will come up at a particular time. It allows them to schedule their day's buying activities without having to sit through a full 4 to 6 hour sale. These arrangements are not necessarily made entirely for the convenience of the dealers, however. Dealers in some of these areas can be disruptive, so it is really to everyone's advantage to get the dealer-oriented segments of the sale over with as quickly and expeditiously as possible.

But although the number of dealers is not relatively large, there are still quite a number of different *types* of dealers. Some are more regular general merchandise attendees than others. You'll see secondhand or junk dealers—they do turn up. And there are buying agents, operating for others, who scoop up quantities of various sorts of goods, such as clothing and office furniture. There are also proprietors of neighborhood "antique" furniture and furnishings shops. There are top level antique dealers who shop for and buy fine pieces of furniture, decorative objects and artwork at a number of different price levels. There are dealers who specialize in particular kinds of goods that fall within the general category of personal property, such as jewelry. There are retail specialists geared toward the many areas of "collectibles." There are proprietors of fine arts and antiques galleries (a number are auctioneers themselves). And there are large-scale wholesalers who deal in huge volumes of goods which they market over a wide territory.

Most of the fears about competing with dealers are based on two misunderstandings of the situation. The first is the idea that the dealer's knowledge gives him an advantage and this puts you at a disadvantage. True, a dealer's knowledge, experience, acumen is his or her stock in trade. The dealer must know the merchandise, recognize saleable pieces, be aware of the markets for the goods. In short it is the dealer's business to know what he's buying. Each potential find is a potential sale and a potential profit. If many unwise purchases are made, the dealer will be out of business. Each mistake is a threat to financial security. The advantage is yours in that you can follow the professionals' lead in indicating a worthwhile item.

The other misunderstanding is based on the feeling that the dealer's economic muscle gives him an advantage. False. The truth is —and this cannot be overemphasized—that as he is in business he is far more restricted than you in the ability to roll up bids. For him, the central economic reality is the fair market value that the goods command. The dealer has a very real price ceiling determined by what kind of a profit can be made on the immediate resale of the item in question. Different dealers, of course, operate on different degrees of markup, but it is safe to say that a person looking to resell at retail will have to get close to 100 percent more for an item than he pays for it in order to have a profitable transaction. Think about it. That leaves you, the private buyer, with quite a lot of leeway between the competing dealer's auction price ceiling and the price you would have to pay for the item at that dealer's shop. If you take a piece at one bid over a bidding dealer, the chances are that you have made a decent buy. The irony of the dealer competition myth is that nowadays many dealers are complaining bitterly about the competition from private buyers.

THE SPECULATORS

There are a few dealers whose prominence in the marketplace—their remarkable success—gives them an edge that many envy. If they occasionally indulge in what seems to be an extravagance—paying more than the current market price for a piece—they are gambling that by holding the item, they will eventually be able to resell at a sizable profit. Be prepared for the fact that on occasion items of immediate interest to you will be worth more to someone in trade. The fact is that in our volatile economy speculators have frequently enjoyed high returns on buys which have at the moment of auction seemed foolish.

THE PRIVATE BUYERS

The central reality about dealers is that they have to make resale profit to stay in business. That obviously does not apply to private buyers. The central reality about private buyers is perhaps best summed up by a notable Pogo quote: "I have met the enemy and they is us." It is difficult to generalize, because there are almost as many different types of auction shoppers as there are people, but one way to view the private competition is to consider others' reasons and your own reasons for being at the auction.

Stalking the wild bargain: By far the greatest number of private shoppers attend auctions for the same two reasons that I do: they are bargain hunters, and they enjoy the theater it provides. The immediate objective is usually to gradually upgrade or supplement their home furnishings. They are looking for good deals, and they pay sensible prices.

But there are also a certain number out there who will pay big prices for what they want.

Movers and shakers: One such type of buyer is the person seeking to furnish an entire house or apartment quickly. Their reasons for buying at the auction market place are different from those of most of us, and their buying habits reflect exactly that fact. People in this position tend to be less concerned with the prices of the goods they buy. Either they are not directly absorbing the expense, which may be carried or subsidized by a government or corporation, or they are rich enough so that they don't have to concern themselves with the item-by-item cost of their home furnishings. They therefore are able to act on whim, whatever the cost.

Collection buffs: Another group of private buyers that drives prices up is the collectors. There have always been collectors, but never as many as there are now. Collecting, once merely a personal and relatively private pastime, has become an important economic activity for many; it is, today, both a way of amassing wealth and a hedge against inflation. "Collectibles" (even the term is fairly new) are rising in value at several times the rate of general merchandise. This is not to say that collectors are not seeking bargains. But when it comes to something they really covet, they tend to pay whatever it takes to get it. Part of what makes this possible is the fact that the purchase itself tends to establish a new value and price, both for the item in question, and for other items within a collection. Thus the collector can be fairly certain, at the very least, of recovering the investment.

The Secret—Money: There is one final group that comes to auction with a different point of view from that of most of us. These are the people who are there for the simple reason that this is one of the few sources where the things they want are available. They are after first-rate pieces, and this, again, is a highly competitive market. True, most of their buying time is spent at the top-level auction houses, but not *all* the best merchandise goes that route. There are usually a few standout pieces at every general second-level sale, and there are always buyers fighting it out for them.

Good news—Bad news: It is because of the diversity of competing bidders that many items sell for bargain prices at auction while other items sell at highly inflated prices. There is really nothing you can do about the latter, except to prepare yourself to drop out of the bidding fast when things get out of hand.

BIDDING

Everyone has heard stories about unfortunate auction spectators who made an ill-timed but innocent scratch of the nose or pull of the ear and found themselves owners of fire engines, draft horses, windmills. In reality mistakes like this don't happen. Auctioneers, like the rest of us, don't need problems. When in doubt, they'll usually *ask* a person whether he or she is making a bid or scratching an itch.

THE SIGNALS

Straightforward bidding signals are always the best. A wave of the catalog, a raised hand, or a lifted paddle are the standard forms. Once you are in the bidding, a slight nod of the head is usually enough to indicate to the auctioneer that you're continuing in the race if the auctioneer has established eye contact. Conversely, a slight shake of the head informs the auctioneer that you're not going to answer an invitation to bid.

It is true that some buyers, wishing to remain anonymous, have been known to invent secret signal systems that allow them to participate inconspicuously. Some of these systems have been simple and practical—"As long as I'm standing, I am bidding," for example. Others have been so complex and involved that both the auctioneer and the customer himself have become confused. Such cases have contributed a number of amusing tales to the auction anecdote repertoire over the years, but secret bidding systems and their attendant foul-ups are pretty much limited to the rarified atmosphere of the international auction houses. You aren't likely to encounter such goings on in the lower order of general merchandise sales, where bidding tends to be very straightforward.

Getting noticed: One worry that plagues newcomers is the fear that their bids may be ignored or not noticed. This is unlikely. The auctioneer wants as many bidders in on each lot as he can get. While he may fail to notice you, the chances are that one or more "spotters" are on the floor—either in the aisles or grouped at the sides or in front of the auctioneer's stand—for the express purpose of alerting the auctioneer to bids. If you feel you are being ignored, you can always call out your bid aloud. This often brings you more general recognition than you want, however. One situation in which it may *seem* to you that you are being ignored is when, as a matter of style more than anything else, the auctioneer chooses to focus on only one pair of bidders while taking the price up. In the long run this does not affect you. As soon as one of the first pair drops out, the remaining competitor will be pitted against another individual, and so on, until there are only two bidders left who can then bid it out to the end.

OPENING BIDS

An experienced auctioneer, with a feeling for the crowd at a particular sale, usually has an accurate idea of the bottom opening bid price for a given item. In opening the bidding, he will smoothly glide down the scale: "Surely someone will offer me five hundred dollars for this unusual piece—three-fifty, three, two hundred, one-fifty, do I hear fifty?—I have fifty." And the bidding is under way. Other equally experienced auctioneers have a set policy on opening-bid calls, consistently asking 10 percent of the high estimate, two-thirds of the low estimate, or some other prearranged amount. Still others rely solely on intuition.

The auctioneer has two somewhat contradictory aims in calling for a particular opening bid. On the one hand, he wants to open the bidding quickly, to get on with it—for after all, in the auction business, time is indeed money. And, if a high opening bid is offered, this will tend to raise the final selling price. That means more money for the house. "Significant" items are often puffed in this manner—called into bidding at a higher percentage of the estimate than the more ordinary merchandise.

All bids off: The auctioneer may withdraw an item from the block if he fails to get what he considers a "reasonable" bid. Theoretically, if the auction is an "open" one with no reserves or minimums operating, this should not occur, but don't be surprised if you see it happen. There is nothing unethical about pulling one back. These days especially, no one is inclined to give merchandise away.

INCREMENTS

Once bidding is under way, it usually proceeds upward in predetermined increments. By tradition (and, in many states, by law) it lies in the discretion of the auctioneer, but most auctioneers have an established policy. Typical general merchandise bidding raises would be by $1 up to $10 or $15, by $5 up to $50, then $10 up to $100 or $150, $25 up to $500 or so, then $50 up to $1,000, and upward and onward. It is also at the discretion of the auctioneer to take "partial-increment" bids, but many establishments refuse to do so as a matter of policy. The rationale is that they "protect" each bidder whose raise of one increment forces a bid of twice that increment to raise him. It is a sound and fair policy.

WHOSE BID?

There are times, especially when things are moving rapidly, when it is unclear whose bid stands. A good, careful auctioneer will, at least as the bidding nears a close-out, generally take pains to identify the individuals whose bids he is taking—"Fifty dollars in back, sixty on the aisle, seventy by the post, eighty in back," etc. He will often do the courtesy of informing a confused bidder, "Yes sir, your bid." In case you are in doubt about whether or not you have the standing bid, it is perfectly legitimate to either ask or signal the question, "My bid?" To which you should get either the reply "Yes, yours at eighty," or "Against you."

In cases in which more than two bidders are vying for the item and hands go up simultaneously, it's up to the auctioneer to award the bid to a single party. Some houses have established policies (those wonderful dispute-settlers) for awarding bids arbitrarily in such cases. One such policy is to give the bid to the person closest to the auctioneer.

BY THE PIECE OR THE LOT?

Many auction lots consist of sets or groups of goods—anything from a pair of decorative urns up to a set of 16 side chairs or a complete dining room suite. In such cases, the auctioneer has two alternatives in terms of pricing. He can sell "by the lot," which means that the bidding determines the price of the entire contents of the lot, or he can sell "by the piece," in which case the bidding determines the price of a single item. When you bid on a lot "by the piece," you are contracting to take the entire lot at the price of the bid multiplied by the number of items in the lot. It is generally easier for the buyer to bid on an entire lot, but you will encounter "by the piece" lots frequently enough. It makes perfect sense in cases where the lot consists of a batch of identical items such as plates, glasses, chairs, and the like. It gets tricky only when a lot such as a bedroom suite contains both desirable and less than necessary merchandise. In this situation, all you can do is be cautious, decide on the value of the items you want and bid no more than that for the whole lot.

An honest auctioneer will leave no doubt in your mind as to the terms on which a particular lot is being knocked down. "Lot number three forty-three. A group of three crystal decanters. Bid by the piece. Take all three. OK, let's go."

BIDDING TACTICS

There are endless theories regarding bidding tactics. Most of them are too involved for me to follow. Quite a lot of manipulation does take place in the auction scene, but most of it happens at the presale exhibition and takes the form of customers bad-mouthing merchandise they covet in order to discourage other potential buyers' interest.

One subject on which there seems to be pretty general agreement is that of auction demeanor. Poker faces are the order of the day. Experienced auction buyers always remind me of bored but impatient commuters waiting with restrained nervousness for a train that may or may not be on time.

According to the popular wisdom, avid interest, clearly expressed serves only to stimulate bidding (or at least competitiveness) among the other buyers. It will also encourage the auctioneer to work a little harder. So the general rule for most is to play it low-key; don't get too excited or eager.

When to bid: As far as actual bidding strategy is concerned, there are two definite schools of thought and they are probably equally valid. The first says, keeping in mind the principle that it is unwise to show that you really want something, that making an opening bid, or at least getting in early, works to your advantage. After all, how else are you going to pick up a surprise bargain? Any fast knockdowns or sleepers tend to go to the first or second bidder. In addition, getting in early and bidding vigorously—crowding your competitors—is an aggressive style that may well contribute to your success by intimidating the less secure among the opposition.

The other side of the bidding strategy coin is the hang-back method. In this style of bidding, you relegate to others the task of running the bidding up to the drop-off level—the point at which bids and bidders thin out significantly. This is when the hang-back bidder will make his move, if he bids at all. He will often wait until the last possible moment before knockdown to get his bid in, in the hopes of breaking the spirit of the bidder who has fought it out thus far—

against a *known* opponent. This style gives you the luxury of seeing how the land lies before you commit yourself, which is definitely in keeping with the principle of remaining inconspicuous. If the bidding goes beyond your limit, you have revealed nothing about your desires or your pocketbook.

Shutout bids: Since the object of auction shopping is to get the merchandise for the least money possible, the usual scenario is to start low and head upward, nickel-dime, as the increments progress. This sets the stage for a high-powered, and I believe ill-advised, tactic: the shutout bid.

The shutout consists of making a significant jump in the bidding. Suddenly and loudly doubling or tripling the bid currently on the floor tends to be very disconcerting to the other bidders, throwing them off long enough for the item to be knocked down to you. It is usually the bidder's limit. I've seen it happen a number of times and I'm convinced it is a waste. In making a shutout, you relinquish the possibility of taking the item for a lower figure. Why would anyone do it? There is only one reason I can think of: that the bidder hopes, through bizarre behavior, to keep the bidding from going higher than what the bidder can afford.

ORDER BIDDING

An order bid is a bid that you can leave with the auctioneer or the house when, unable or unwilling to attend the sale, you still want to bid on an item or items. The order is actually a bidding ceiling. You authorize the house to bid up to the limit on your behalf.

The way it works (or the way it *should* work) is that someone from the auction house bids for you as though you were present, going as far as necessary up to the limit. If, for example, I leave a $150 order on an onyx-and-brass lamp, and the actual bidding runs out at $80, the auctioneer places my next bid, $90. If there is no answering bid, the lamp is mine. If anyone on the floor is willing to go above $150, he will take the piece. And if the auctioneer is holding a higher order than mine, then I am obviously out of the running before I even start. Auctioneers are usually skillful enough that they can give the limit bid to the order bidder. In other words, if the bidding on the lamp ran to $150, that would usually be *my* bid, not that of someone at the auction.

In many houses, the auctioneer has all the order bids in front of him and executes them himself. There are differences in style. Some auctioneers give the impression that it is someone on the floor making the bids. Some are quite straightforward about acknowledging order bids, making it perfectly clear to the crowd by means of such phrases as "To the order," "To my order," or "To the absent bidder."

Increasingly, auction houses are adopting the practice of having a separate person, or persons, on the bidding floor acting on behalf of the order customers, either from the crowd or from a special desk. I was once surprised to see the foreman of the moving crew bidding vigorously on a number of lots the first time I attended a sale at one of the sales rooms I now frequent. The fact was that some of the gallery customers preferred to deal with the foreman. They had been doing so for years.

LEARN AS A SPECTATOR

I've introduced a number of friends to auction shopping. Some have jumped straight in with both feet. Others gave up before overcoming their uneasiness about the pressure of bidding. A good way to begin is to attend one or two auctions without bidding for anything. Watch the bidding. Try pricing items that are of interest to you in your head. And chart the prices by recording them in your catalog. You might as well get started immediately developing your own price guides. As observer rather than participant, you'll be able to become attuned to the auction's flow of events free of charge; and you'll witness a good show. In addition, you'll begin to learn what is perhaps the most important single truth about auction buying: *There will be another sale,* and any item you long for is likely to come along again.

An alternative method for easing into the auction game without too much risk is to bid on one or two inexpensive items that have little importance to you. If you win, you can enjoy the taste of success. If you lose, you won't mind much. And you'll get valuable on-the-spot experience for the moment when you make your first bid for something you really want.

PREPARING YOURSELF

In order to get what you want out of an auction—merchandise at a considerable savings—you must prepare yourself before you actually begin to bid. Here are three guidelines. I didn't invent them: I simply follow them. They have kept me free from serious blunders.

1 Inspect the merchandise carefully before you bid on it.
2 Set a firm price or bidding limit before you go to the auction.
3 Stick to your limit.

INSPECT THE MERCHANDISE

Every reputable auction house has a preview or exhibition at which you are given an opportunity to view the merchandise offered in the upcoming sale and examine it to your heart's content. The exhibition is critically important to you for it is the one opportunity you will have to find out the exact condition of the item you are going to bid on. If you use the opportunity wisely, you will be a satisfied auction shopper. Examine the items. Otherwise, you may be charmed by the appearance of a lamp, a table, or a chair only to discover too late (after hearing your bid stated by the auctioneer as the winner) that it has flaws rendering it worthless. The piece then ends up a burden rather than a bargain.

The reason it is vitally important to know precisely what you are bidding on is that virtually all auctions are conducted on a *caveat emptor* basis: let the buyer beware. Unlike retail dealers, auctioneers will not usually take responsibility for the condition or authenticity of the goods they sell. That's not their business. Their business is that of moving merchandise along to the buyers. They function as agents only.

The first term of sale is "as is." Virtually every auction firm has written terms of sale, which are printed in every list and catalog, and right at the top of the list is the warning that goods sold carry no guarantee of quality, authenticity, or condition. Pay attention to this warning, they're not kidding.

However, as general merchandise houses have only in the past ten years overcome a reputation for slick dealings (deserved or undeserved, it has been a difficult one for them to shake off), auctioneers usually take considerable pains to avoid misleading anyone. Ultimately, though, the responsibility is yours. It is safe to say that any reputable auction house that sold you a piece as sterling silver, for example, would make some sort of arrangement if the piece turned out to be silver plate. However, you cannot expect a general auction house to care at all if you complain of previously undetected chips or hairline cracks in a piece of porcelain.

Many serious auction goers, including many dealers, will therefore turn up for the exhibition armed with a few simple tools that help them greatly in examining the merchandise. The basic set consists of a magnifier, a tape measure, and a notebook. The magnifier is invaluable for reading makers' names and hallmarks, examining details, locating chips and scratches, and looking into the grain of wood. The tape measure is, of course, for checking dimensions. It is an auction-house tradition to have a yardstick on the premises for that purpose, but there are often many people waiting to use it. Besides, for larger pieces, a tape measure is both handier and more accurate. The notebook serves as repository for all the notes, comments, observations, and price records that auction buying generates.

In addition to the above, some buyers carry a small magnet to distinguish iron objects from brass, bronze, and other nonferrous metals, and a penknife for discreet poking, prying, or occasional scraping to get a look at what a piece is really made of.

Catalogs: As a secondary source of information, you can also refer to the item-by-item catalogs offered by nearly every general merchandise auction house. These range from simple mimeographed sheets with the briefest capsule descriptions ("Seven colored crystal wine glasses; drop-leaf dining table; eight Renaissance-style velvet-covered side chairs . . .") to generously illustrated and handsomely printed booklets (often worthy of collection in their own right). The compilers supply accurate information to the best of their ability, but it is not guaranteed. Accept the descriptions and also the listed estimates of the prices the lots are expected to bring (provided by many but not all auction houses) only as points of reference.

It is also standard policy for most auction houses—that is, most reputable houses—to clearly indicate in their catalogs all those items that are being sold "subject to reserve." (A reserve is the price below which a consignor will not sell his goods.) An auction in its purest form, of course, would never have reserves. But even these days, when such predetermined minimum bids are a fact of marketplace life, there are still plenty of other items available for mere fractions of their original value. Besides, it makes perfect sense that the seller try to get a price for his goods commensurate with their value. However, in fairness to the buyer, the merchandise subject to reserve should be identified beforehand. Only in this manner will everyone at the sale—buyer, seller, and auctioneer, too (who stands to earn no commission if he can't promote a bid equal to the reserve price)—have a chance.

Thinking it over: Taking advantage of the exhibition and catalog (typically available to buyers at least a day or two before the auction itself) will gain you some precious time. And time, in turn, will provide you an opportunity to answer questions you should ask yourself about a possible purchase. Will you still love it once you get it home, or is this just a passing fancy? Is the color right? Will it go with your other similar belongings? Will it fit in the space you have in mind? Is it of standard dimensions? ("Normal" chair height is 16 to 17 inches; dining-table height is approximately 30 inches; coffee-table height is 15 to 18 inches; and so on.) If not, does it matter? Is it sturdy enough? Can you live with that chipped base? The list can be as varied as the people who compile them. The only generalization I feel I can safely offer you is this: When in doubt, let it go.

If, on the other hand, you asked yourself all the questions, found the right answers, and are now more determined than ever to bid for the item, you're ready for the next presale preparation.

ESTABLISH PROPER VALUE

Once you have decided that you want an item, the next decision you face is determining how much it is worth—*to you*. Your objective here is to establish a top price—a bidding limit—for each lot that interests you.

One way in which you can at least begin to get a handle on the question of value is to find out what similar items are worth to someone else. Comparison shopping is an obvious and straightforward solution. Browsing in the local antique dealer's showroom, for instance, will give you a chance to learn the price ranges of those items similar to the ones you're considering. Antique shows are also rich sources of price information. In the case of some items, such as appliances, china, and glassware, you should be able to compare prices with new merchandise of equivalent quality in retail stores.

Books are another source of price information, particularly for antiques and "collectibles." There are a number of books covering the different types of antique and collectible goods that frequently appear at auctions, providing not only prices but a wealth of information on the merchandise's background, history, identifying marks, etc. Two excellent general guidebooks are Warman's *Antiques and Their Current Prices*, E. G. Warman Publishing, Inc., Uniontown, PA 15401 and *The Complete Antiques Price List* by Ralph and Terry Kovel, Crown Publishers, New York. They are both periodically updated.

Condition: Once you've gotten an idea of the comparative value of the item in general, you should next consider the specific condition of the item. Are there any flaws, chips, or cracks, either obvious or hidden? (These may significantly reduce the resale value of ceramic or glass items.) Is the veneer loose, chipped, missing? Are the legs loose, are pieces missing? (The piece may be propped up on a brick —I've seen this sight lots of times.) Are the knobs or pulls original? Are they missing? Has the piece been cut down or otherwise altered? (Again, this significantly reduces both your purchase price and your resale value.) Does it (lamp, TV, blender) work? If not, or if you cannot find out, in which case assume the worst, how much could repair cost? Can you do the repairs yourself? If not, will you be able to find someone who can do them properly? You must consider the total cost of acquiring an item in usable or working condition. Costs that may accrue in addition to the hammer price include repairs, cleaning, refinishing, and moving or transport.

Mixed lots and sets: The circumstances and/or special conditions of the sale may also affect the value of the goods you desire. Will you, for example, be required to buy things you don't want in order to get the items you do want? This is a sales tactic used in many kinds of auctions to get rid of secondary merchandise by linking it with the more desirable items. Miscellaneous goods are thrown together into groups and sold together, either by the lot or by the piece. In such cases, base your limit *only on the value of the items you want* and bid no higher than that for the entire lot. If the other items turn out to be useful in some way—or if you manage to sell them or swap them to others for whom they possess some attraction—so much the better, you are ahead of the game. But don't make any allowances for such speculative deals in your initial pricing.

Is the merchandise you seek being offered in such a way that you can buy what you want in a single transaction? If, for instance, that service of Royal Doulton dinnerware you covet is being sold as one set of 12 dinner plates and a separate lot of 12 matching salad plates, you may buy the first lot only to find yourself competing for the second lot with some zealot who seems to eat only salad. Adjust prices accordingly. Note: One time-honored custom that operates at the discretion of the auctioneer is to sell one lot "with the privilege" of buying similar or complementary lots at the same price. Ask about this possibility in advance if it seems to be applicable to merchandise you desire.

Casual items: Up until now, I've been dealing with the objective determination of auction-merchandise value. There are also, however, a couple of purely subjective valuations that should also be taken into consideration.

The first belongs to a category I like to call "The No-Big-Deal Goods." Often, there may be items in a sale that interest you only casually. You can easily get along without them, but if the price is right—i.e., cheap—you'd like to have them. One recent example is a silver-plated champagne cooler I purchased for a bargain-basement $10 bid. When I first spotted the cooler in the preview exhibition, I decided that I'd bid up to $10, on the chance that no one else would be interested. If I got it, I'd be pleased. If I didn't, well, I hadn't gone to the auction for coolers anyway.

Buying items like this is fun, but I do advise setting bidding limits (see p. 3) even for these nonessentials. I also give myself a strict overall dollar limit on purchases of this kind at any one auction.

Life-or-death items: The other side of the coin concerns those items worth more to you than any market value you can establish. You are, in effect, creating a new market value for the goods in question. This should happen only in cases in which there is no retail source available to you. All the varied reasons that justify such purchases are variations on the theme "I can't live without it." The best you can hope for is that that tune will not play often enough to bankrupt you.

(Incidentally, the phenomenon of goods selling at higher than their established value or previous selling price—often several times higher—occurs most frequently at the highest levels of the auction world, as detailed in the next chapter.)

Adding it up: This process of deliberation will bring you eventually, inevitably, to the point at which you can sensibly decide how much of your cash you're willing to part with for the honor and privilege of carting away all the items on your want list. In general, the economic area you will now find yourself in will be what auction buffs describe as "reasonable price." This tends to be between 40 and 60 percent of the cost of the equivalent item, in equivalent condition, on the retail market. This does not mean that in the heat of actual competitive bidding every item will go for the "reasonable price." The great beauty of auctions is that you can frequently pick up an item for substantially less.

STICK TO YOUR LIMIT

It is admittedly hard to live with such a rule as this. It is so unfeeling, so rigid. The truth is that most people do hedge on it one way or another. I have more than once revised my bid limit on an item during the course of a morning's selling, sometimes upward, sometimes downward. This is either because I have gained some additional information or because I find my feeling has changed in some way. I see nothing wrong with either of these criteria for reevaluating a bid limit. Once the actual bidding starts on the item in question, however, I stick to my limit.

Other auction goers I know will occasionally go one bid over their limit, especially in cases in which there is reason to believe that that will be the winning bid. The situation can occur, for example, in a case where the house person executing order bids indicates that he or she has reached the absent bidder's limit—and they often do make it perfectly clear. If it has just been you and the order bidder, your next bid will take the goods. There are other personal hedges, but as mentioned, and stated throughout this book, the situation to avoid is going into an auction without an effective personal estimate and limit of any kind. You *can* lose your shirt.

HAVE THE CASH OR CREDIT

Typical auction-house terms are "cash or certified checks only; 25 percent deposit at time of purchase; balance to be paid on pickup and removal of goods." There are many houses that adhere to this way of doing business. After you have succeeded in wrestling your competition to the auction-room floor (i.e., won the bidding on a lot) you will be approached by a firm but friendly young man or woman and politely asked for a deposit. This is definitely the old-fashioned way of doing things. The growing trend is to ask each bidder to "register" before he or she participates in the sale. The buyer is usually asked for a nominal deposit, $20 or $25, along with some credit information that will aid the house in establishing the credentials of the individual as a long-term customer. You're then generally issued a bidding number, often in the form of a numbered paddle which serves as your identification for the duration of the sale. Each time you make a bid the paddle is held up. The number of the winning bidder's paddle is recorded by the clerk. This simplifies the paperwork (of which there is a great deal), and as one auctioneer friend pointed out, it makes it easier for people to buy. "If a guy has to reach into his pocket and pay every time he gets a piece, he's going to think twice about the number of pieces he bids on." There is a lot of truth in that.

It is wise to head for the auction rooms with cash or a certified check in your pocket, especially if it is your first or second time buying at that particular place. If they like your face, they may accept your personal check, but don't count on it. When they do get to know you, there should be no problem about payment by personal check.

THE INTERNATIONAL HOUSES

The first thing you will notice about it is its luxuriousness. It is *the* place for auctions of the rarest and finest things—everything from medieval tapestries to Sung Dynasty porcelain and Andy Warhol silk screens—and it is situated in major pockets of wealth, from New York to Los Angeles, Zurich and London. Outside the tony entrance, a pair of stiff uniformed guards portend what is inside—a setting of formality, wealth and gentlemen's sport. It *is* a game, not unlike racehorse breeding or Monte Carlo gambling, and since its prototype is London-based Sotheby's and Company, it is conducted with the heavily manicured ritual of a British courtroom. Decorous chambers, hushed by thick carpet, are graciously lit by rheostatically controlled crystal chandeliers, and are furnished with shimmering display cases and paintings exhibited museum-style. In fact, such auction houses really have become commercial museums. They are attended by scholarly art historians, and frequented by the most discerning connoisseurs in the world. And since exhibitions and sales are open to the public, free of charge, you may, in general, want to know more about the ultimate consumer sport or, in particular, how to venture a bid at the richest store in the world.

SELLING IN STYLE

There's a breathless sort of suspense in the final minutes before an important international auction. Sleek black limousines have deposited their passengers in front of the building. Small groups of pinstriped men and linen-clad women stand and mill in the entrance to the auction room and chatter about exhibitions, art gossip, next summer in Southampton or last summer's misadventures on the photo safari. Before the sale is over, millions of dollars' worth of oil paintings and inlaid furniture will pass across the draped stage in front of the auction room, and yet everyone seems composed, reserved and self-assured. A tall square-jawed man in a tartan plaid blazer and horn-rimmed reading glasses makes one final check in his catalog before sitting down in the section marked "Reserved", which is for insiders only.

All eyes are directed to the front of the room. It is a room about the size and scale of a hotel ballroom, complete with the trappings of institutional elegance—parquet floors, dark red carpet, Neoclassical cornices and a stage draped in brown velvet. As the auctioneer, a well-mannered man in his early forties, passes the rows of gold-and-black cushioned metal chairs, a hush begins to sweep over the room. Except for the rustling of the catalogs that everyone seems to be holding in his or her lap, there is a reverent silence as the auctioneer ascends the carved-oak canopied podium on the right side of the stage. The auctioneer checks the room to make sure the eight spotters, beige-jacketed men who will assist him during the sale, are all in their stations. He then acknowledges the associates who are lined up, seated and standing, on either side of the podium. With everyone's attention directed to the conditions of sale in the front of the catalog, the auctioneer announces, "The sale will begin for your competition."

The bidding: Then the sport begins. A large Hudson River School landscape is placed on the easel on the stage. The auctioneer calls out a lot number and pithy description—"Lot number one, Martin Johnson Heade, 'Sunrise' "—and then bellows clearly, "The bid is against the room, ladies and gentlemen. Five hundred dollars to start," which a blond woman in the front row immediately agrees to pay by raising her pencil. "In the front, thank you, madam," he replies.

In the next minute, a flurry of bids flies across the room, visible on an electronic digital "scoreboard" above the auctioneer, which converts dollars into yen, marks, pounds, francs. A man seated in the rear holds up a folded catalog, and in doing so, agrees to pay $680. The two bidders begin to battle it out. $700, $720, $740, $760, $780, $800. An associate to the right of the auctioneer, who is talking over the telephone, gets the auctioneer's attention. There is someone on the telephone who wants to bid $820. "Against both of you," he declares to the two bidders on the floor. $840, $860, $880, $900, $920. And then another man standing at the side of the room enters the volley. $940, $960, $980, $1,000. And then the increments are stepped up. $1,100, $1,200, $1,300, $1,400, $1,500, $1,600, $1,700. Then a pause, and the auctioneer repeats the $1,700 bid. "Down it goes. Fair warning." Before he drops his hammer, the auctioneer looks directly at the bespectacled man in a tartan plaid blazer. He looks up at the auctioneer and removes his eyeglasses, and in doing so, registers the final bid. The audience applauds, and the attendants replace the picture with the next lot.

There's an otherworldliness that sets an international auction apart from all other auctions. There are a few people in a room of, say 500, bidding thousands of dollars, with unflagging determination, for something no one really needs. And yet, when you are seated in the middle of the windowless room, the extravagance of the circumstance seems to vanish as the rhythm of the auctioneer's calls echoes through the public address system. "Against the room, down it goes. Five thousand to start." And then it begins again, those numbers, and all around you people are paying those numbers in dollars by lifting their paddles, index fingers, eyeglasses, pencils, or making various other signals. How do they know when to bid?

"It's a little like the first time I jumped into a rope being swung by two other little girls," explained a woman bidder. "After a while you just know when to do it." Seasoned bidders generally watch the auctioneer *very* closely. They watch his lips move and listen to the cadence of his voice. The speed of the rhythm determines how long the price plateaus will last, how large the price jumps will be, how soon the lot will be sold, and, in general, how fast the pace of a sale, in which over 400 lots are knocked down in a minute or less apiece, will be.

TOO RICH FOR YOUR BLOOD?

As glamorous as they are, fine art and antique auctions are not, as we shall see, off limits to the average auction goer. The big purchases get the publicity—but *more than half* the lots sold by the major houses go for less than $1,000.

Though everything falls into the luxury category, there are literally thousands of things—American oil paintings, Old Master prints, Chippendale-style furniture—that sell for less than $500, and they want you there. Like any other American business, auction houses want everyone to get involved, get the habit, buy, sell and swap in their salesroom. In fact, Sotheby's and Christie's have special salesrooms for less expensive and not-in-fashion things. At Sotheby's on York Avenue, there are two salesrooms: one for major sales and another for less costly sales. And at Christie's East on 67th Street and Third Avenue, there are sales every week of "good" furniture, decorations, and paintings; they also have sales four times a year of photographs, antique clothing, and other specialties that are accessible to general buyers.

Feeding the image: The international auction houses in America nevertheless strive to perpetuate the otherworldly image, which sets them apart from other auction houses. Special functions, like an evening of Russian folk dancers to coincide with a sale of Russian icons, are hosted. When a notable celebrity auctions his or her collection or estate, lavish cocktail parties are thrown for socialites as well as important collectors. It is all part of a well-honed publicity push to get the name of the auction house in the business, art, and society pages of dailies. The impression that most people get from the media of such auction houses is that they're glittering spots where the most important, the rarest, and the finest are sold to the wealthiest and worldliest.

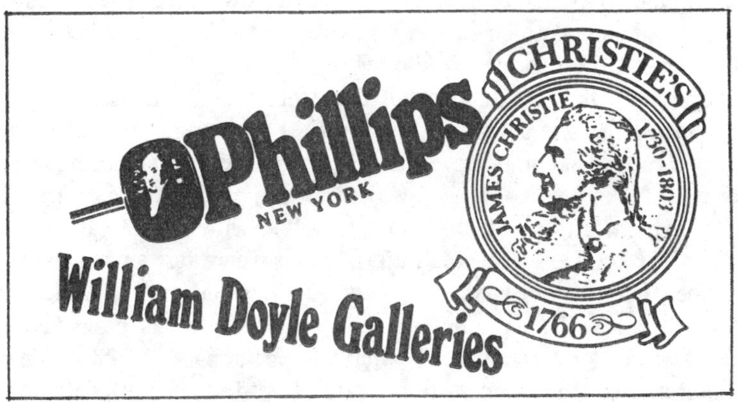

Setting the stage: The one thing that distinguishes fine art and antique auctions from other auctions is their studied and bureaucratically administered professionalism. At some houses, sales are coordinated up to a year in advance in over 20 major categories, from paperweights to Oceanic art to Old Master paintings. Experts who oversee the different specialties are required to keep abreast of scholarly as well as market developments in their respective fields.

The focal point of every sale is one or two very important masterpieces, generally from either a museum or an important private collection. At a sale of American paintings, for example, a portrait of John Singer Sargent might be singled out of the 400 or so lots and given special promotion and advertising. This is how auction houses such as Sotheby's and Christie's still maintain their aura of exclusivity. Like any other deluxe merchandising and marketing corporation, they *want* people to spend more than they intend to. And by all accounts, they seem to be succeeding. In 1979, Sotheby's reported $200 million in sales worldwide, which by comparison to Bergdorf

Goodman's $61 million and Bloomingdales' $150 million, puts them in league with top luxury retailers.

Yet, you don't have to be looking for a Sargent to take advantage of such a sale. Remember that there are 400 other lots, and many will go for prices that you may be quite willing to contemplate.

Attracting smaller buyers: Bringing luxury items to the rest of us in an open market, the top houses have introduced warehouse-style auctions of less-than-currently-hot luxury items, also known as collectibles. Victorian lace undergarments, mechanical banks, posters, black memorabilia, bottle tops, and other collecting specialties—in short, ephemera which formerly found a place in flea markets—have been recently auctioned by Sotheby's, Christie's, Phillips and their many competitors. Not to insult their regulars, the houses have set up special houses such as Christie's East to handle the collectibles crowd. These auctions are conducted more like the standard country auction. Sales are faster, catalog descriptions are briefer, and the pre-sale exhibitions are set up warehouse-style with things stacked one on top of another. It has reached the point where just about anything collected by anyone, and just about anything old and valuable, can be found at a fine art and antique auction. "It has happened so quickly we don't really know what's happening most of the time," admitted Paul Viney, an auctioneer at Phillips in New York City.

BACKGROUND OF THE INTERNATIONAL HOUSES

Fine art and antique auctions date back to 18th-century London. For generations, well-heeled Britons selected an auctioneer much in the way they selected a lawyer or stockbroker. Sales were conducted with utmost discretion. No one knew, for example, that the Duke of Gloucester *had* to sell his Chinese snuffbox collection to pay his mistress's annuity. The snuffboxes were cataloged "property of a gentleman," and the poor duke was spared from disgrace. The purchaser might have been an American industrialist, an Italian count, or, strange to say, an agent of the mistress. Since nearly all art and antique traffic, including property of the King of Poland, Marie Antionette and Queen Victoria, ended up at either Sotheby's, Christie's, or Phillips in London, this is where the action was.

The English way of doing things did a lot to improve the bad reputation auctioneering had in America. Until around 1970, most auctioneers on this side of the Atlantic were considered to be but a cut

above a bill collector. They were needed only in unfortunate circumstances and didn't really merit any respect. By contrast, the English
were decorous, graceful and knowledgeable—everything that Anglo-
philic Americans swoon over. When Sotheby's opened its New York
salesroom in 1967, a gala presale exhibition was staged and pre-
sented with the theatricality the Metropolitan Museum of Art, a few
blocks north, devotes to major openings. During the next decade,
Christie's, Phillips and William Doyle Gallery each opened New
York salesrooms, while a host of imitators in San Francisco, Miami,
Boston, Detroit and other major cities set up professional art auction
houses. And while the English-run houses adapted American marketing savvy, the American-run houses polished the brass and hired a
few British figureheads in a drive for tone. One new firm, Trosby's,
with offices in West Palm Beach, Miami, and Atlanta, called itself
"the Christie's of the south." And the Sotheby's merchandising approach—the house has branches in all five major continents, as well
as new branches in the oil-rich sunbelt from Palm Beach to Houston,
Los Angeles, Mexico City and Caracas—has earned Sotheby's not un-
welcome sobriquet: "Macy's to the carriage trade."

Now it is safe to assume that wherever quantities of old money
exist, a sizeable international auction house thrives. Summer-season
auctions at Richard A. Bourne in Hyannis Port on Cape Cod (Massachusetts) have turned into such spectacularly successful events that
the house now conducts auctions year-round. And on approximately
the same turf, Robert Skinner, Auctioneers in Bolton, Massachusetts,
southwest of Boston, has been able to carve out a niche, which now
includes buyers from all 50 states.

In the vast and populous midwest, however, there are only two internationally acknowledged auction houses. In the historic Ohio
River Valley, there is Garths Auction House, located in Delaware,
Ohio, which specializes in top American folk art. And in Detroit,
there is Du Mouchelle Art Galleries, a house that specializes in Victorian and Art Nouveau. On the West Coast, there is, at the moment,
only one well-established, world-acclaimed auction house, Butterfield
and Butterfield, which boasts a salesroom in San Francisco and
branches in Portland and Seattle. "Despite the current auction boom,
it would be foolish to establish an auction house far from the source
of good antiques," explained one auction official.

THE AUCTION CIRCUIT

With worldwide sales now approaching an estimated $500 million, the fine art and antique auction business has come of age. The media-popularized faces of just about anyone who's anyone in high fashion and high finance can often be seen bidding at one or several of the major houses. In fact, there are several cliques of international auction goers that move, like migratory birds, from London to Zurich to Geneva, and from New York to Los Angeles. In some cases, they can make the rounds without ever leaving a Sotheby's. Collectors and dealers of contemporary and Impressionist paintings might start out at a small sale in Zurich in April, then move to New York in May, London in June and Monte Carlo in July. In the fall, there is another circuit for collectors of Old Master paintings and drawings—New York in September, followed by London in October and Zurich in November. It is something of a whirlwind. Both buyers and sellers converge on the sale prior to the first day of exhibition. They stay in the same hotels, eat in the same restaurants, and sometimes develop and maintain long-term auction friendships. (In New York, the hotel is the Stanhope, the restaurant is Les Pleiades, and the real insiders' spot is a Greek-run coffee shop called Three Guys on Madison at 75th Street.) Now that Sotheby's hosts regular sales in Los Angeles and at the Drake Hotel in Chicago, those two cities will surely be included in the international circuit.

THE NEW YORK SCENE

By far the largest and most regular sales occur in New York City. Houses there tend to set the pace for the rest of the nation. And with good reason. New York has a long and honorable tradition of exporting and importing fine art and antiques. In addition, it is perhaps today's world center of the international money market. Sales at Sotheby's, Christie's, Phillips, Plaza, and William Doyle Gallery amounted to over $200 million last year in New York alone—more than half the total sales in America. Since there are five fine art and antique houses all sharing the same Upper-East Side turf, New York is probably the best vantage point for a look into the top-level art auctions. By snaking a path from Christie's at 59th and Park, uptown to the new Sotheby's at 72nd and York, Phillips at 72nd and York, Plaza at 79th and York, Sotheby's on Madison at 76th Street, and

William Doyle Gallery at 87th and Third, a newcomer can grasp the range of auction offerings elsewhere, both in the United States and internationally.

Each of the five houses offers a slightly different clientele, tone and selection of items. With two large salesrooms generating over half the sales in town, Sotheby's is clearly the leader. It is a slick oper-

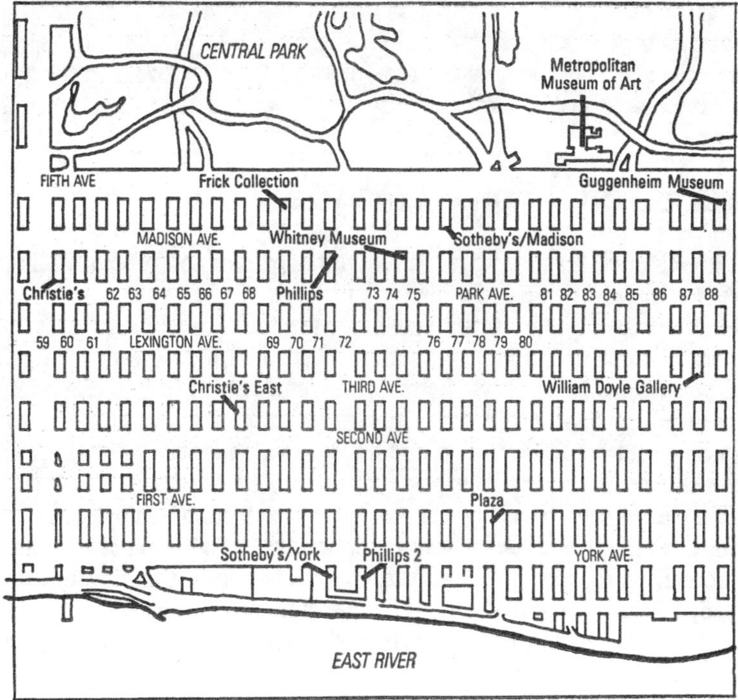

ation that closely resembles a chic department store. The commotion and size of Sotheby's is apt to seem a bit bewildering at first, although the management is well aware of the problem of scale, and in response, tries to make customer service representatives available to everyone. In contrast, Christie's is a small, clubbish operation that retains all the best and worst qualities of its English parentage. Both Sotheby's and Christie's can be quite charming, although there's an air, probably through no fault of their own, of brusqueness that can seem off-putting. "We're a bit tradition-bound," concedes Christie's president, David Bathurst. Christie's offers virtually everything Sotheby's does in the way of sale selection, but on a smaller scale. Christie's has done exceptionally well in sales of jewelry, Art Nouveau, and ethnography, which is its strong suit in London.

The smallest of the three English-run firms, Phillips, might be called seriously trendy, and attempts to cater to American quirkiness by featuring unanticipated collectibles like Automobilia and Aeronautica or political memorabilia. William Doyle Gallery is a family-run, eight-year-old, Yankee-style auction house which specializes in sales of decorative arts and furnishings and some paintings for the home. Plaza is a small but quite slick operation that is thoroughly Americanized. It dates back to 1913 and is the only house in town to accept major credit cards; it also probably has the fastest sale in town.

WHERE THE GOODS COME FROM

It is estimated that well over 400,000 lots of rare and precious things were sold worldwide at Sotheby's and Christie's last year, and where the lots will all come from next year, no one is really sure. Despite every attempt to modernize auctions, "it is still a day-to-day pursuit of consignments," says Sotheby's president, John Marion. Each and every house has a web of appraisal techniques to make sure that nothing that could be sold in the house goes unnoticed and winds up in a competitor's sale. There are museum liaisons who work directly with curators to encourage them to "deacquisition" things they no longer want. It is a useful way for museums, in these pinched times, to continue to open their collections by constantly thinning out unneeded items. In addition, private collectors are cultivated by the in-house experts in the hope that they will gain a steady source of consignments.

As has always been true of auctions, and will probably continue to be true, the primary source of items comes from death and bankruptcy. Every auctioneer heads for the obits first thing in the morning paper. In fact, I saw two recent obit headlines above an auctioneer's desk. One said "Steel Head Dies;" the other said "Rubber Head Dies." This is not to say they are morbid people—it's all in a day's work.

For smaller houses, gaining consignments to sell is a tough battle. William (Bill) Doyle of William Doyle Gallery in Manhattan divides his time between the gallery and out-of-town trips to major pockets of wealth. Upon hearing that a wealthy widow in upstate New York passed away, he might jump in his car, or, if it is sufficiently important, even charter a private plane to get there before the other guys do. During the winter season in Florida, he makes the rounds in Palm Beach and Miami "just in case anyone cannot meet his expenses." According to Doyle, however, it is not all that grubby. "I always say, 'Look, you only borrow these things. You can't take them with you.'"

Soliciting appraisals and consignments: The Doyle Gallery, along with every other gallery, offers free, in-house, informal appraisal, and for a moderate fee ($50 or so), you can get a formal appraisal. If an appraiser must come to your house, the auction house will charge an additional transportation fee.

Both Sotheby's and Christie's have a vast network of agents across the country in almost every major city. And they also hold fund raising appraisal days at what Sotheby's calls "Heirloom Discovery Days" in towns and villages in almost every bend in the road. Last year alone, Sotheby's held 35 Heirloom Discovery Days. Anyone that had anything to be appraised could pay a flat fee, say $25, which was donated to a local museum or historical society. It all adds up to a massive sweep to bring in anything of value that might be stashed in an attic or tucked in a drawer. And things do turn up. A woman in Topeka brought in a rare silk Heriz rug that her husband had used to cover his pool table. It brought $26,000. And a West Virginia man brought in a rare American quilt which brought $8,000. However, most auctioneers concede that only about 15 percent of all consignments turn up this way.

Bad day at Sotheby's: At approximately 6:30 a.m., the line was already three blocks long. All of the people in the line had something in their hands: some had big paintings of rugged landscapes, others had things small and silvery, one man had a wooden cigar-store Indian. It was a cool crisp October morning, and many of the city folk, who were accustomed to long lines and delays, had been there since the frosty first signs of dawn. By 8:00, the line was already five blocks long and growing. The patient crowd sipped coffee in plastic delicatessen cups. Kids walking up and down the line hawked the *Times* and *News*. At 9:00, the double doors in front of Sotheby's were opened. The date was October 1977, and according to one participant, "it was a madhouse."

Sotheby's claims it was the last time they will ever sponsor appraisal days in Manhattan: "It was just a half-page ad in the *Times*, but it seems like half of Manhattan turned out with things which were, in most cases, embarrassingly valueless." One woman sat down and cried when she was told the oilcloth painting she had held under her arm for six hours while waiting in line—"The Last Supper" by Leonardo da Vinci—was worth about 95 cents. She was sure it was the real thing; "it had been in the family for years," she said. On the other hand, there was a man whose turn came about a half-hour later. He pulled a small silver cigarette case from his pocket, which turned out to be a rare French Art Deco silver design worth $5,000. And a little later, a woman appeared with a small, awkwardly-framed still life which turned out to be a Picasso worth $50,000. She was a retired school teacher who told the experts she would use the money to buy something she had always wanted—a Rolls Royce.

Estates: The largest chunk of consignments come in from large estates. These days, the heirs rarely have room for the personal property they are left by their relatives, and since personal property is just what auction houses deal in, it makes a lot of sense to consign the personal effects of an estate. In the case of big estates, a house will generally bend its rules a bit to get the business. And with good reason. Instead of consigning just a few fine objects, an estate generally consigns several hundred. In the case of the estate of Mrs. Gilbert Miller, sold at Christie's in April 1980, there were over 1,000 lots of fine and precious things, as well as her television sets, shoes, hats and three travel alarms that did not work.

According to Hugh Hildesley, head of the estate and trust department at Sotheby's: "Big estates are our backbone. When one comes up, we have to prepare lengthy directives spelling out exactly how we will catalog, exhibit, and advertise the property. And we generally have to do it quickly." And there are bargaining leverages, such as rescinding part of the seller's fee, photography fee, or storage fees.

Outdoor sales: In the past, big estates were often sold on premises during fair-weather months. Rather than cart everything to the auction house, the estate was simply cataloged and sold out of doors in a large pavilion or tent. On-premises sales are generally something of a festival: concession stands are set up to sell food, big tents are set up on the grounds, and everyone, including the staff, has a good time. And the prices are generally higher, since many private buyers (like you) flock to the site to view the big old house and maybe take home a few souvenirs. At one sale I attended outside Philadelphia, there were cars parked up to a mile away from the main house and sale site. Everyone from Christie's in New York had moved down there for the week, and the house was open for public viewing while furniture and paintings were removed room by room.

CONSIGNING YOUR OWN GOODS

If you decide to sell something at auction and don't have a big estate to use in bargaining, send a snapshot of the consignment to several houses closest to you. Include a brief description—dimensions, condition, what you think it is—and where you bought it.

You should get responses within six to eight weeks. If it turns out to be valuable, you should get a formal appraisal, which you will have to pay money for. From among the responses, decide which house is best to sell your possessions. Check around and find out who holds the record price.

The house's expert or cataloger will assign a presale estimate, which is negotiable. If you decide to set a reserve (minimum price), you will have to pay a special fee if the item does not sell. You will, in any case, have to pay a special fee for photographs, and a 10-percent seller's fee taken from the price you get at auction. Finally, if the item does not sell and you want to include it in the next sale, you will have to pay a storage and handling fee.

In general, as one regular put it, "They get you coming and going." Auctioneers are agents acting on the seller's behalf, and for this they will make you pay. This is not to say that you cannot do well selling at auction. Your consignment will receive wider visibility and coverage than it would anywhere else. And the prices are generally competitive.

PREPARING FOR AN AUCTION

One thing that no one would deny about bidding at an international auction (or, for that matter, any auction) is that it is work. You have to know exactly what it is you are buying; you have to go before the sale and inspect it; you have to go to the sale, bid, and then arrange to have your purchase carted home. This is not to say that it isn't fun. Like spending an evening at the gambling table or a day at the races, auctions are fun because they are full of surprises. And there is a practical side to them: almost everything sold there is sold at rock-bottom prices.

If you are interested in attending an international fine art and antique auction, the first thing you should do is find out when and where they are held. Though most New York houses are closed for extended recesses between Christmas and January 15 and during August, they are open the rest of the year. I have discovered that the most exciting sales occur in the fall, during October and November, and in the spring, during April and May. To learn more about the auction schedules, you might want to get on their mailing lists. For a nominal subscription fee (under $5), you will receive a year of a monthly newsletter, which lists upcoming sales, special events and a brief feature article on one aspect behind the scenes. The newsletter will also alert you to dates of presale exhibitions (for inspection) and hours they are open. In addition, it will contain a special order form for sale catalogs.

HOW TO USE THE CATALOG

A catalog is usually referred to in correspondences by either a number or, in the case of Christie's, a woman's name (like hurricanes). At Sotheby's, a sale of Art Nouveau and Art Deco will be cataloged and assigned a number like 4653. At Christie's, it will be assigned a name, like Antoinette or Gigi. Catalogs can cost up to $25, but they are invaluable guides to every machination at an auction. To go to an international auction without a catalog is like going on a back-road car trip without a roadmap.

Everything that is offered at these auctions goes into a catalog. In some cases, a lengthy and elaborate description will be included with a picture of the item. The example here is from a Christie's auction of American paintings, drawings and sculpture of the 18th, 19th, and 20th centuries, held in New York on October 24, 1979.

AUGUSTUS SAINT-GAUDENS

● 128   "VICTORY-PEACE", A BRONZE ALLEGORICAL FEMALE HEAD
her hair swept-up in a chignon, a wreath crowning her head, inscribed *NIKH-EIPHNH* and *A.ST.GAVDENS.-ASPET.MCMIV*   and   stamped   *GORHAMCO FOUNDERS*   *7½in. (19cm.) high,*
on green marble base, medium brown patina

This is the second study for the head of the figure of Victory, part of the William Tecumseh Sherman monument located in New York City at the Grand Army Plaza, Fifth Avenue and 59th Street. Though St-Gaudens preferred this model, he felt that his earlier version was better suited to the monument. The profile of this later study was subsequently used for the new penny and ten dollar coin.

By reading this description carefully, the prospective bidder can learn quite a bit about the Augustus Saint-Gaudens bronze. It is a female head with hair swept-up under a wreath crown, colored brown on a green marble base, standing 7-1/2 inches high. It was made at the Gorham Company foundry in 1904 and inscribed by Saint-Gaudens. In addition, the cataloger included an anecdote (which is not usually included) telling the reader that Saint-Gaudens preferred this model over an earlier model, which was the prototype for a statue in Grand Army Plaza in New York City, and that the profile of the bronze was subsequently used for new penny and dollar coins.

In contrast to this is one (below) from the same sale, which gives a pithy description of an oil painting:

JOHN M. GAMBLE

● 176   CALIFORNIA LANDSCAPE
signed   12 × 18*in.* (30.5 × 46*cm.*)

In this instance, not only is there no picture of the painting, but from the description, one can only infer that it is a landscape in a state noted for various landscapes.

Catalogers and experts take great pains to make sure the catalog looks attractive and adequately represents the sale. Teams of researchers inspect each lot, check previous ownership, and construct melodious descriptions. Of course, the important lots receive the greatest attention. In fact, catalogs are considered to be the most important advertising put out by the house. They are slick, glossy compendiums of everything the auction house knows about the lots.

Conditions of sale: For the beginner, the front section of the catalog, which spells out the "conditions of sale" in modern legalese, is an important first step. After you have digested it, you won't have to bother with it again; it never changes, although it does differ from house to house. Basically, it is to protect the auction house from any claims of misrepresentation. Everything is sold "as is," and all catalog descriptions are simply "in our qualified opinion." This should be understood. Caveat emptor is good advice at any auction, but the slick catalogs and smooth presentation at international auctions may convince you that what is listed is guaranteed to be what you are buying. By carefully reading sections called "absence of other warranties," "conditions of sale," "limited warranty" and any other warnings to prospective buyers, you will learn what your responsibilities are. Most seasoned bidders use the catalog as a guide and follow the dictates of their own opinion.

FIVE IMPORTANT "CONDITIONS OF SALE"

1. The auction house is an agent for the consignor (seller) and as such acts in the consignor's best interest.
2. The auction house reserves the right to refuse to sell a lot if the price is too low, or in any number of other situations.
3. All buyers must pay a buyer's premium.
4. Authorship is guaranteed only under the conditions listed in the glossary (explained below).
5. Successful bidders must remove the property within a specified time limit.

An important thing to remember is that the auction house usually does not own the lots. They belong to consignors.

Attributions: In the glossary of each catalog you will find a different list of authorship codes. These vary from house to house and from sale to sale. They are basically used to aid the cataloger in describing things they really cannot verify for sure. For example, a catalog from a Christie's painting sale has seven different degrees of authorship identification, as follows:

1. **FRANCESCO GUARDI (The artist's first name or names and last names)**	In our opinion a work by the artist.
2. **Attributed to FRANCESCO GUARDI***	In our qualified opinion a work of the period of the artist which may be in whole or part the work of the artist.
3. **Circle of FRANCESCO GUARDI***	In our qualified opinion a work of the period of the artist and closely related to his style.
4. **Studio of; Workshop of FRANCESCO GUARDI***	In our qualified opinion a work possibly executed under the supervision of the artist.
5. **School of FRANCESCO GUARDI***	In our qualified opinion a work by a pupil or follower of the artist.
6. **Manner of FRANCESCO GUARDI***	In our qualified opinion a work in the style of the artist, possibly of a later period.
7. **After FRANCESCO GUARDI***	In our qualified opinion a copy of the work of the artist.

Given the flexible interpretation of degree 7, *you* could paint a Picasso-like painting tomorrow and bring it into Christie's and they might catalog it "After Pablo Picasso." In contrast to Christie's attributions of authorship are Sotheby's, listed as follows:

a. FREDERICK CHILDE HASSAM—The work is, in our best judgment, by the named artist. This is our highest category of authenticity in the present catalogue.

b. *RUBENS PEALE—While ascribed to the named artist, no unqualified statement as to authorship is made or intended as described in Paragraph 2 under the Terms of Guarantee.

c. ATTRIBUTED TO RUBENS PEALE—In our best judgment, on the basis of style, the work can be ascribed to the named artist, but less certainty is expressed as to authorship than in the preceding categories.

Whereas the Sotheby's attributions of authorship are less specific than those at Christie's, neither house will guarantee them, so they should both be treated only as general guidelines. Most seasoned bidders prefer to rely on their own eye and judgment using the attributions of authorship as a springboard for further research.

Provenance: Many things sold at auction have had a long and illustrious life with previous owners, some or all of whom will be listed in catalogs under the heading "Provenance." If the provenance includes notable collectors or major museums, a buyer might pay a premium for it. For example, at a Sotheby's American painting sale, the provenance for a painting entitled "August Afternoon, Appledore, Maine" by Frederick Childe Hassam, was listed as follows:

> *Provenance*
> Collection of Desmond Fitzgerald, Boston, (Sale: Anderson Art Galleries, New York, April 22, 1927, no. 179)
> Mr. Hersey Egginton, Long Island, New York
> The Milch Galleries, New York
> Stephen Dreyfoos
> Hirschl & Adler Galleries, New York

A strong provenance will always help the value of a painting unless there is considerable doubt as to the authenticity of the provenance, which, like everything else, is not guaranteed. Although it is not guaranteed, one thing that is easy to verify is the list of exhibitions in which the object or picture has been included. It is usually listed as in the following example, from a Sotheby's American paintings sale, for a Marsden Hartley painting, "Sea Window Summer #2":

> *Exhibitions*
> San Francisco, Golden Gate International Exposition, 1940-41
> Washington, DC, Phillips Memorial Gallery, 1942
> New York, Paul Rosenberg Gallery, 1942

Probably the single most helpful listing in the catalog is the literature. It will serve as a springboard for further research, which will begin the long road to connoisseurship. When it is applicable, you will find it listed, as in this example from Sotheby's for a Frederic Remington painting, "Splitting the Herd":

> *Literature*
> Harold McCracken, *Frederic Remington: Artist of the Old West* (Philadelphia: J.B. Lippincott Company, 1947) p. 125
> Lucius Beebe and Charles Clegg, *The American West* (New York: Bonanza Books, 1955), p. 83 illus.

Many seasoned bidders rely on scholarly literature as much as on their own opinion.

Estimates: In the back of every catalog you will find a listing headed "Estimates (U.S. $)" with a list of numbers that correspond to the lot numbers, and a price range such as 7,000-10,000 next to it. Although some enlightened auction houses have started listing the estimates in the body of the text, the top houses still, for the most part, retain the traditional practice. At first, it may seem a bit bothersome to have to flip back to the estimates, but after a while, you'll get used to it. In general, estimates serve two purposes. First, they will steer you away from items you truly cannot afford. At certain important sales, the estimates might be mostly in four and five figures. Secondly, estimates will help you to arrive at your own maximum prices. However, it is wise to keep in mind that, once again, the estimate is only the qualified opinion of a particular expert. There are countless sales where every estimate is surpassed. On the other hand, there are often times when the estimates are not even realized. Because estimates are computed by the expert based on previous "knockdown" prices for a similar or like object, and because at auction "any price is fair price," the estimates are often disregarded by seasoned bidders. "When you get to know a particular field well enough to bid comfortably, you will *know*, sort of intuitively, what should be paid for it," explained one veteran.

Reserve prices: To make sure that nothing gets sold for much less than it should, the auction house will allow the seller, within reason, to place a reserve price that the bids must meet. Amounts of reserves are, for obvious reasons, not given out, although the house must indicate in the lot description whether there is a reserve on that lot. In most houses, it is denoted by a small black box or an asterisk. Although the procedure varies considerably from house to house, a reserve usually does not exceed the low estimate and never exceeds the high. It is, in most cases, a percentage, say 85 percent of the low estimate.

Your own maximum price: As at all other auctions, the prices paid here are generally wholesale. You are competing directly against dealers, art galleries, museums and private buyers who will attempt to resell their acquisition for a profit. There are many sad stories about the cautious collector who would not outbid a dealer on, say, a Shaker cupboard only to discover, much to his disappointment, that the dealer doubled the price of the cupboard after the sale and easily received the resale price. Thus, the price you decide to pay should be determined after serious comparison with the market outside the auction house.

You will discover that careful preparation before the sale will diminish the uneasiness that, frankly, all beginners feel. If you know exactly what it is you are buying, and what the market is for that item, all that's left is knowing how to bid, which, in the words of one bidder, "is the icing on the cake."

THE PRESALE EXHIBITION

It is Saturday afternoon at Sotheby's on Madison Avenue. Outside the closed elevator doors in the lobby there is a crowd of people dressed in casual clothes—from jeans and cardigan sweaters to navy blazers and plaid trousers, and on one woman with stylishly frizzy hair, a kimono. There are about 10 or 12 cool Abstract Expressionist paintings hung randomly from the molding around the lobby wall. Buzzing around a circular information booth, which protrudes at a right angle from the left wall, is a bustle of young women buying catalogs. The crowd must negotiate itself around a scattered maze of French Rococo furniture from the reigns of three Louis'.

On the third floor, the elevator doors open onto a low-ceilinged hallway beyond which a larger room bustling with more people and things can be seen. Oriental rugs in sizes up to 30-feet long hang from the walls, cushion the floor and muffle the sound of prospective bidders at work. The kimono-clad woman removes a tape measure from her pocket and measures one of the rugs. She then writes something in her catalog. A young couple finger the pile of another rug. Beyond this room is a room with porcelain figurines behind soon-to-be-smudged glass display cases.

Don't be shy: The presale exhibition is a good chance for beginners to scout out the big houses, as well as an essential convenience for the serious buyer. The first step across the threshold of an international auction house is often the most difficult step. Many people think Sotheby's and Christie's are reserved for the rich; they fear they will be intimidated, humiliated, or worst of all, simply asked to leave. Others fear that steep admission charges will be levied. Still others are burdened by the misapprehension that auctions are only for dealers and other professionals. This is nonsense. The auction houses want your attendance. They want your business. In fact, the top houses employ customer service representatives to guide beginners, like you, through the labyrinth of chambers they use to exhibit, sell and store the lots. In addition, they will conduct formal group tours for more than five. One note of caution: customer service representatives are employed by auction houses to convince newcomers that their house is tops. You will probably get an ample dosage of in-house propaganda along with your tour.

With or without a guide, your first stop should be the presale exhibition. An exhibition is mounted several days before the sale, and its hours and date are announced in the front of the catalog.

Inspecting the "goods": The presale exhibition is where the really important decisions are made. It is here that you will actually see, touch and inspect the items listed in your catalog. And at some of the splashier houses, the furnishings and objects are artfully arranged into vignettes by an exhibition designer. In others, the items are simply arranged in order to correspond with the catalog. Whereas at still others, you might discover that you have to dig and poke around to find what you want. Whatever the setup, you should inspect your prospective purchases thoroughly.

Say you are hunting for a sturdy Chippendale-style dining-room table, and there are three in a catalog of English furniture and decoration. The first thing you might do is take the measurements of the three with a tape measure. Then, you might check the glued joints to see if they are still strong. Next, inspect the hardware to see if it has rusted. Seasoned bidders all agree that a table with a scratched surface or one weak leg might be something of a bargain. Take into account with your maximum price the cost of refinishing and other repairs. Don't be afraid to pick the table up, check underneath the top and otherwise inspect it thoroughly.

Do not hesitate to ask for advice and assistance from staff members. In many cases, I have discovered they will be able to add a tidbit about the item in question. For example, I once inquired about a painting. The guard told me it had been included in a sale three months before. As it turned out, the unwitting purchaser had discovered it was a fake, turned around and consigned it to the house again. Without knowing it to be a fake, the house merely cataloged it as it had before. In addition to the employees on the floor, you might query the expert or cataloger that identified the item or picture to begin with. Though such a personage may at first appear to be totally inaccessible, with a little persistence on your part he will come out of his office and talk with you. Basically, although they are extremely busy people, experts want to cultivate interested collectors and purchasers. They have gone to great lengths to make sure the exhibit and catalog represent their sale, and if there are any problems, they want to solve them.

Establishing credit: In every metropolitan auction house, there is a small institutional-green room lit by shadowless fluorescent lamps. This room is where all the credit information on up to 20,000 buyers is stored and processed. It is a bustling room: ten or more attractive women in their mid-twenties jostling each other in a 10-by-15-foot area stacked to the ceiling with paperwork. This is where you will end up when you decide to establish your creditworthiness. It is not a simple process, however. With the exception of Plaza in New York, no one accepts major credit cards. Auction houses are traditionally old-fashioned cash-and-carry operations. To apply for credit, you will first have to offer your bank references for inspection. The auction house will want to know how much money you have in the bank, not how long Sears has extended your credit. Since credit is one aspect of American business machinations the British seem to struggle to understand, you will probably have to wait at least 90 days, and will most likely be turned down at first. Not to worry. Like the old-fashioned corner grocer, the auction houses will accommodate regular buyers. Once you have established a strong cash buying record, you will soon find your credit line being established and even extended. Even so, you will generally have to pay within 30 days. Since so many costly things are sold at auction, credit is, of course, always extended to wealthy people who are buying $100,000 oil paintings and so on.

ATTENDING AN AUCTION

Go early: On the day of the auction, you should plan to arrive about a half hour before the sale time, which is generally 10:15 a.m. for morning sessions, 2:00 p.m. for afternoon sessions and 8:00 p.m. for evening sessions. You will need the extra time to register for a paddle, find a good seat, and settle in. You should always bring a substantial piece of identification with you, even if you have already established creditworthiness. A major credit card, a passport, or in some cases, just a driver's license will do. Although some established auctions, such as Sotheby's on Madison, do not require bidders to register before they have made a successful bid, it has become the practice at most of the newer houses. At Christie's East, for example, you must register and get a bright shiny plastic paddle, shaped like an oversized ping pong paddle, with a bidder's number embossed on one side. This number corresponds to the number on your registration card. It will speed things along during the auction. From that point on, you will be known as simply number 38, a system most Americans should feel comfortable with.

Where to sit: Though I always prefer to sit as close to the front as possible, there is no perfect place to sit at an auction. You will notice that some of the most successful bidders actually stand more or less in the wings. In fact, it is really the auctioneer who has the best seat in the house. All of the real action happens on the floor. A newcomer might find that the best position is in the very back of the room or, when possible, in the balcony. In addition, all of the front-section seats are reserved at important evening painting sales. Only those with strong bidding records or good prospects of purchasing a major work will be allowed to sit in the reserved seats, which are usually taken up to six months in advance. If you happen to find yourself at one of these sales, you will probably end up seated in a small room adjacent to the main salesroom and watching the sale over closed-circuit television. In theory, bidders in this room are given ample opportunity to place their bids through a spotter who will then relay them to the auctioneer. It may seem disconcerting to be out of the main action, however.

Waiting for your lot: Auctions, particularly the English-style ones, start on time. Since somewhere around 400 lots will be sold during the course of a sale, it is imperative that things be handled expeditiously. You can generally gauge how soon your lot will come up by allowing approximately one lot per minute, then subtracting five minutes or so to make sure you don't miss it. Hence, if your lot is number 104, and the sale begins at 10:00 a.m., somewhere before noon (probably around 11:50), you will have to be ready to bid. What to do before the lot comes up is a problem for most people. Many people just follow the sale by writing the knockdown prices in their catalogs. By doing this, you will get a good idea of how the sale is proceeding: the pace, rhythm and prices realized. Every sale is a unique occurrence, and even the most seasoned auction goers usually find there is enough going on to keep them from getting bored.

BIDDING

There is no need to sit stock-still. A scratch on the nose, forehead or arm will not usually be read as a bid. In fact, no one is going to force you to buy anything you truly do not want. Even if you wave your paddle frantically and then realize you've paid too much for the lot, you can simply tell the attendant or auctioneer you've made a mistake—the bid will be withdrawn and awarded to the next-to-last bidder. You won't endear yourself to the auctioneer this way, however. Too many interruptions slow down the proceedings, and in fact, sloppy bidders are asked to leave a sale.

The single most important thing to remember when it comes time for you to bid is how much you are willing to pay. To be safe, all you really need to do is simply hold up your paddle until the auctioneer calls out the price you have set as your limit. It is quite simple. But there is such a thing as auction fever. Everybody wants to be a winner. And it can be frustrating to sit through an entire sale day only to go home empty-handed. Yet, it is even worse to go home with something you really cannot afford. Of course, as I stated before, it is wise, when figuring your maximum price, to figure out what the retail market is.

Ignored bids: It's possible that you'll make a bid that is ignored by the auctioneer and his attendants. Since this has happened to countless bidders—first-timers and seasoned bidders—you should not feel victimized when it happens to you. It is a virtually unbending law that when the auctioneer's hammer falls on the last bid, that bidder is the new owner. If you feel you have been slighted, you can holler and protest, but in general, your complaint will fall on deaf ears. The auctioneer must move quickly from lot to lot, although auction houses certainly want to get the most money for each lot. Auctioneers find that a lot of people change their minds after the hammer falls and want to register a bid. It's generally felt that "fair warning" means just that.

Mail bids: Bidders are the main attraction in an auction. Everybody will be watching you as you raise your paddle, and spectators might even applaud a particularly brilliant coup. Many newcomers are hesitant about bidding for that very reason; they fear that everyone will think them to be foolish. For the shy, wary and otherwise homebound, there are alternatives. You may not be assured you will get what you want this way, but it is easy and convenient. In the back of an auction house's catalog, there is a mail-bid form. You simply tear it out, fill in your name, address, bank references and indicate the lot number, lot description and top limit of bid. Put it in the envelope and mark it "Attention—Bid Department." When your lot comes up, an attendant from the house's bid department will act in your place.

Mail bids are generally successful only when the lot is something of a sleeper. Say you bid $500 on a painting and the bidding on the floor stops at $250, then it is yours for the next highest bid—$260, if the bidding is in $10 increments—plus extra handling charges (tax, buyer's premium, and so on). But, if the bidding stops at $500 and someone on the floor has made the $500 bid, it then goes to the floor bidder. To make extra sure that they won't lose an item by just one bid, expert bidders generally write in their limit plus one increment— for example, "$500 & 1." Then, if someone on the floor bids $500, the house will make the next bid for you, raising the previous bid by whatever increment has been the norm during the bidding. The houses generally spell out very clearly that mail bids are placed as a *special service;* they disavow all responsibility for misplaced or forgotten bids. It is wise to phone the bid office on the day of the sale and make sure they have your mail bid in hand.

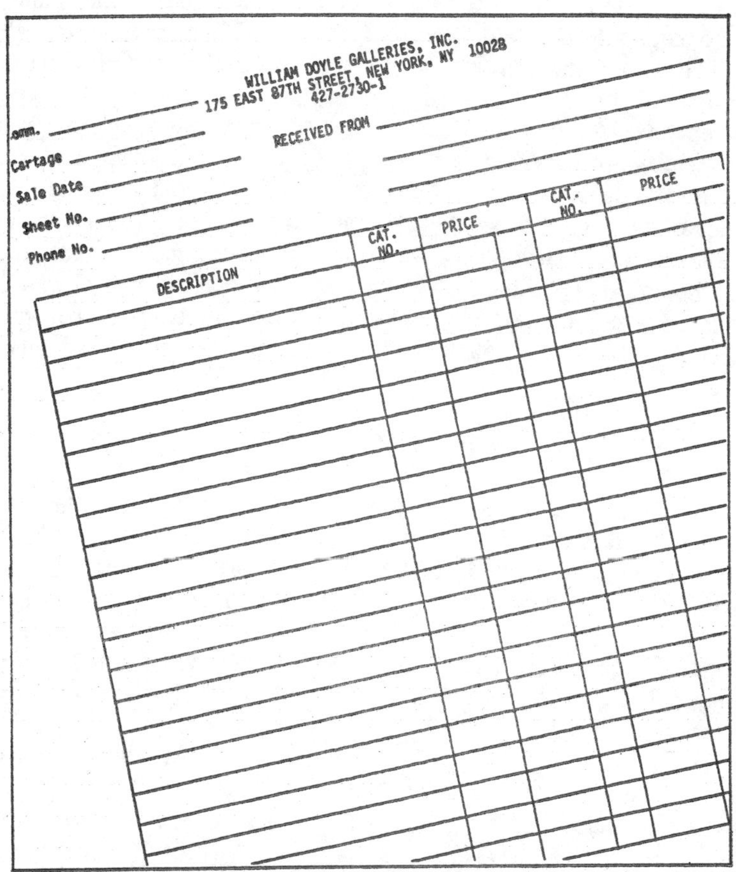

Phone bids: Another method of armchair bidding is bidding over the telephone. Because only a few phone lines can be hooked up to a sale, phone bidding is generally restricted to big-time bidders who, for one reason or another, are unable to attend. Thus, you'll probably never be a telephone bidder. But if you ever are, on the day of the sale or even several weeks before, you arrange with the expert who put together the sale to bid over the telephone. About 15 minutes before the lot comes up, the auction house will place a call to you. The attendant will give you a brief report on the sale, and then repeat everything the auctioneer is saying as your lot is hammered down. Since the attendant is generally seated right next to the auctioneer, you will be able to register your bids. In fact, some very important paintings have been hotly contested over the telephone. At a Christie's sale of a Van Gogh, "Le Jardin du Poete ,arles," that went to $5.2 million, two bidders, both of whom were out of the country, hooked up to the salesroom via satellite. This sale was especially otherworldly; the audience just sat dumbfounded as the price on the bid board climbed.

Gimmicks: Auction rooms are using more and more technology to present and move the goods. At sales of jewelry and other small objects, the lights may be dimmed so a slide of the small bracelet or pair of earrings can be projected on a screen. Closed-circuit television screens, as mentioned, extend the salesroom into different parts of the house. At Sotheby's, a computerized system speeds an acquisition through the salesroom in half the previous time. One expert predicts: "Future sales will become increasingly specialized and much faster."

PAYING FOR YOUR PURCHASES

Currency is never exchanged on the floor in American auctions of fine art and antiques, although that is the practice in certain European nations. Once at Christie's in New York, a Viennese bidder tried to pay the attendant $10,000 in crisp $100 bills. This caused quite a stir and even a few rude guffaws. "You know these rich Europeans," quipped a Christie's official. "He probably thought it was play money." The practice here is to leave the salesroom and proceed directly to the accounting office. If you pay in cash (as the Viennese man did) or certified check or have already established credit, you can take possession of your purchase immediately. If you have not established credit and choose to write a check, you will probably have to wait for the check to clear before you can pick up your item.

In addition to the knockdown price you agreed to pay on the floor, you will have to pay a 10 percent buyer's premium plus applicable sales tax (8 percent in New York City, 5 percent in Massachusetts, and so on). And if you cannot retrieve your purchase within, say, five days, you will have to pay a special storage charge.

To make sure your purchase gets home safely, you should bring your own packing materials and arrange for delivery beforehand. Unlike department stores, auction houses do not generally maintain large shipping departments. Most of them do offer referral services, and if they can accommodate it, they will put your new possession in a box or some sort of container. As one auctioneer put it: "Everything we sell is unique and one of a kind. How can we possibly package it?" If you bid by phone or mail and cannot come yourself to claim your purchases, the auction house's customer service department will arrange for a competent packager and delivery service.

Damaged goods: One complaint, which has soured a lot of beginners, is that a purchase turns out to be damaged. The auction house, as stated earlier, makes absolutely no guarantee of the condition or attribution of an item. Once you pay for it, in general, it's yours for keeps. Vases get chipped after the presale exhibition, wings come unglued on bird carvings, table tops get scratched and so on. Because, in general, there is no opportunity to inspect during the sale, there are attempts made to update the description of items which might have been damaged after the close of the presale exhibition. But, many times, the house is unaware of such damage. Bear in mind that the auction houses do not want this to happen, but given the load they must hammer down during the course of a week, it is not hard to understand that the circumstances are pregnant with possibilities. If you discover that the Lalique vase you paid $12,000 for has acquired a fresh chip since you carefully inspected it the day before the sale, the burden of proof rests on your shoulders. Many times, you will discover your only recourse is simply to prove that you are in the right.

BEHIND THE SCENES

The growth of the international auction houses has been so phenomenal during the 1970s that major changes in the organization and day to day operation of the houses is currently under way. The major problem that they all face is the volume of things which must pass through their salesrooms each and every day. Pieces *do* get broken. And each piece requires a ream of paperwork to trace its course through the house. Hence, the most conspicuous change will be made behind the scenes, where computers are being introduced to smoothly speed the flow of things through the houses. And space planners are being engaged to redesign both the exhibition and salesrooms so that the number of times an object is moved can be reduced. At the new Sotheby's on York Avenue in Manhattan, the exhibition area, salesroom and pick-up area are all adjacent to each other.

And major changes are being made in the key personnel at the top houses. Whereas official positions were once filled from within the ranks of the house, it is now the practice to hire corporate-trained executives from large corporations and banks such as Morgan Stanley, IBM and TIME, Inc. "Now that Sotheby's is a public corporation, we owe it to our stockholders to get the best possible officials," said John Marion. What the new auction executives will offer to the experts and auctioneers is an objective reappraisal of their operations and efficiency. In addition, bankers have been brought in to handle the investment-bound auction goers who have become a visible force in the important sales. But the auction houses insist they do not promise a return or a sound investment, as a stock-broker might. "We simply tell them that they can expect a 15 percent rate of appreciation based on figures from past years. We do caution them that art does not pay a dividend and cannot usually be used as collateral," said one official.

Although the corporateness of the top houses has become increasingly evident—in the way they coordinate the sales, speed things through and the overall sense of professionalism—it is still the skill of one man, the auctioneer, that makes or breaks a sale. At every house, the auctioneers *are* the most valued employees. Without a crew of efficient, well-trained auctioneers, any auction house is destined to fail. At Sotheby's, Christie's and Phillips, auctioneers are culled from the ranks of experts and put through a training period led by one of the chief officers. Like fledgling actors, they usually begin by practicing on each other. In a class of, say, 10, one of the students will stand up in front of the class and run through the calls. But the real test comes when they finally get up in front of a live, eager-to-bid audience.

Looking at an auction audience through the eyes of a seasoned auctioneer, it is easy to see why auctions have become an increasingly popular consumer activity. "There are 1500 faces all watching me, waiting to bid on their lot. And I can see from their expressions that each and every one of them really wants to bid. In fact, my job is to sometimes restrain their enthusiasm to make sales flow and also to make them even more eager to bid," explained one auctioneer. Another one confessed, "I love to push 'em. The crowd wants to believe that they are paying too little for something. Even if they aren't I make them believe they are. I cajole them into being ashamed that they are either paying too little or getting upset that someone else is getting away with a steal. And it works. I don't have to act like a carnival barker. I let them know with my intonation and gestures." And still another admits, "I can get a crowd going so furious and fast that it seems like they will bid anything. I once convinced a woman to bid on something she didn't even know about. And she loved it." But all auctioneers agree that the most important bidders are the newcomers, for they are the ones who usually generate the most enthusiasm. "The more people, the better the sale," is an often-echoed refrain. And although the auctioneer's responsibilities are seemingly vast, the one thing that most agreed was the worst thing they could do was "lose my voice."

COUNTRY AUCTIONS

Virtually anything anyone might have owned has been sold at a country auction, from a Sheraton highboy that stood in the front hallway for five generations to a one-year-old garden sprinkler. Grandmother's costume jewelry, packets of garden seeds, livestock, and the rare collection of merganser duck decoys someone's Uncle Elmer kept in the shed all go under the hammer, usually in an atmosphere of mild revelry that makes the auction a social occasion for local residents and upcountry folks from miles around.

In the minds of most people a country auction is an on-the-premises auction. But, these days, you are also likely to find a country auction held in a permanent location, such as a local barn or granary. Both types of country auctions differ from all other auctions in their informality and flexibility. They sell almost everything imaginable, and, in fact, sometimes a country auction is the only place to find a large assortment of everyday things.

ON-PREMISES AUCTIONS

An on-premises country auction is a day-long festival of free enterprise. The auctioneer and his crew arrive first, at the crack of dawn. Some haul heavy furniture room by room from the old house while others pitch a canopy or pavilion in the dew-soaked lawn or meadow by the house. Shortly thereafter, a group of local church ladies arrive with coffee, doughnuts, and sandwiches for both the workers and the bargain hunters who are already looking through the contents of the soon-to-be-empty house. Piquant odors of age—musty cloth and fabric, furniture wax and talcum powder—filter through the rooms as layers of past generations' belongings are peeled away. There are discoveries in almost every room.

There is usually no published list or catalog of the household contents, though the notice or newspaper advertisement of the auction will list a few of the highlights. Each prospective bidder must make his way through the vast inventory alone. And many bidders do this with patience and forbearance, armed with tape measure, magnifier, a directory of antique furniture styles and other paraphernalia, and always on the watch for the overlooked and undervalued.

By 8:00 the sun has already warmed the inside of the canvas tent. The crowd starts to occupy the folding wooden chairs lined up in neat rows. A sly bidder sits in a rocking chair in the hope that no one else will notice it before the sale. Still, most people appear to come for the social gathering. They crowd under the tent, rearranging the chairs to suit their group, reviving friendships from past seasons. As the canvas sides flap in the breeze and conversations turn to the weather and general gossip, it seems as though the auction itself is mere happenstance. That's certainly the case for the dozens of kids who will be underfoot all day—though even some of them will get into the bidding when a bicycle, an old telescope, a pair of skates, or just a box of attractive junk comes up.

Around 10:00 the auctioneer, in rolled-up shirt sleeves and bow tie, ascends the wooden platform at one end of the rectangular tent. "Good morning, ladies and gentlemen. Thank you for coming today. Everything sold as is for the most I can get you to pay. We're gonna knock it down, clear it out, and leave this lovely home broom-clean by the end of the day."

The salutation is followed by a little commotion on the side of the platform. A young associate holds up a fishing rod and the auctioneer describes it: "One fly-casting rod with a box of flies, hooks and extra line. Hear tell it caught a twenty-pounder up at the stream last spring." A few of the locals guffaw at this exaggeration while the auctioneer solicits the first bid.

And then the sport begins. "Do I have five dollars to start? Five dollars, five, five," the auctioneer echoes and then readjusts his lead bid: "Give me four, four, what about four?" A man in the front row stops talking and raises his hand. "I'll give ya four dollars for that ole rod," he calls out to the auctioneer. His neighbor retorts—"Ain't much better 'n an old hickory stick if you ask me." A few people laugh and the bidding gets under way. The auctioneer's singsong voice fills the hollow outside the tent with numbers. "Four-fifty, four-fifty, four-fifty . . . thank you, sir. Five dollars, five, come on over there. Five-fifty, five-fifty. All right! Six dollars, six, six, going once, twice, three times."

For the next hour or so, a parade of things that once constituted a household are marched across the block in no particular order. There is a clothes hamper that goes for 50 cents preceded by a black-and-white television set for $10, a Victorian carved-oak horse-hair-filled davenport for $500, a cherrywood mantel clock for $150, a box of miscellaneous kitchen tools for $3, and so on. And then the crowd quiets as a beautiful mahogany chest-on-chest is hoisted onto the podium by four burly men. The bidding starts at $200 and increases at $10 intervals quite rapidly until it reaches $500 and then at $100 increments until a bid of $2,700 is achieved. The entire audience sits stock-still. The only sound is that of a few flies buzzing around the concession. The auctioneer continues, "Twenty-seven hundred, twenty-seven, aw, come on, let's make it three thousand. Shame on you all. Are you gonna let him get away with armed robbery?" he cajoles. "All right. Down it goes at twenty-seven hundred dollars . . . once . . . twice . . . everybody happy with that? All right. Three times. Sold!" he bellows. The next lot is an oil painting of a seascape by an amateur painter. It brings $15. And the sale continues, sometimes with a break for lunch, until the shadows on the lawn are long and everything that has found a bidder is gone.

Sadly, the on-premises country auction is getting rarer. Although its popularity has never been greater, the number of sales which can be held during each fair-weather season is waning, for several reasons. According to most auctioneers I talked with, heirs of large extended-family homes now tend to cling to valuable possessions and liquidate only less-valuable things at a general auction. In addition, as more and more large extended-family households are broken down there are simply fewer remaining to be sold. As one Virginia auctioneer put it, "If we sell a big household estate, then we've gotta figure we can't sell it again for at least fifty years. That's how long it takes to build a good estate."

BARN AUCTIONS

It is the general and specialized country auction staged in a barn, grange hall, or other large building that is overshadowing the on-premises auction. In fact, there is hardly a single auctioneer around who still conducts *only* on-premises auctions. Most also hold indoor auctions year-round of general household things and also some specialized sales of collectibles such as dolls, stamps, and so on.

However, barn auctions are still country, and they sell country things. Like country music, country things are big business. Antique tools, folk carvings, quilts, scrimshaw, and other ostensibly country things are the order of the day at a country auction. In addition, antique appliances, wood-burning stoves and other, country style things are sold there. Some even sell livestock and farm equipment. One midwestern auctioneer reports that he had 17 cows inside the barn next to television sets and ranges. He sold all 17 of them to a city couple who had just purchased a working farm nearby.

WHERE DO THESE THINGS COME FROM?

When William Godfrey, one of Vermont's oldest "backyard" auctioneers, is not conducting auctions, he is busy running a large funeral business. About his dual professions, Godfrey maintained philosophically (*Country Journal*, September 1978): "People tell me, 'Make sure you do my funeral when I die,' and all that stuff. And then it works the other way. They die and I go and settle their estate. One I had the other day, he left it in his will. Nobody was to have it but me, and all his stuff was to be turned into money and I should do the auction."

That, quite simply, is where all country auctioneers, big and small, get most of their consignments. And it is particularly true of the single-family household sold on premises. In some cases, the proverbial last spinster sister has passed away without a single surviving relative. In others, the heirs have decided to end disagreements by liquidating personal property at auction. And, of course, there are cases in which the probate specifies that the personal property be turned into cash.

In the case of general and specialized sales, there are a variety of sources aside from death. People who are simplifying their lives by selling their homes and moving into condominium apartments will often consign some of their unwanted furnishings. And the high prices brought at auction have also lured transient families into selling the things which will not fit in their home. In addition, private collectors and museums have discovered that some country auctions can bring prices as high as any other type of auction.

SELLING AT A COUNTRY AUCTION

It should be clear from the start that an auction in the country does not necessarily mean low prices. There is, after all, a lot of wisdom to the ways of the country auctioneer. By jumbling costly things with mundane everyday things, the country auctioneer can get higher prices for things most would not even sell. For example, what is an old garden hose with worn washers and pin punctures really worth? At country auctions such an item, and humbler ones, can usually bring a few dollars. And when you are selling a household full of everyday things, the small sales mount up. "These days people are truly surprised when they find out how much all those things they thought were worthless are really worth. I recently sold a houseful expected to bring around thirteen thousand dollars. Though it was just an average household—seven rooms of furniture and things, none of which was older than fifty years or what you might call antique—it brought thirty-two thousand," remarked a Michigan auctioneer.

FINDING AN AUCTIONEER

In theory, you should select an auctioneer in much the same way as you select any other professional. You might want to rely on a prominent establishment in your area or, in the event that there is no one established firm, you can consult the listing of state associations in your phone directory. Country auctions all have certain set fees which can vary from a day rate as low as $150 to anywhere from 12 to 25 percent of the gross intake. In the case of on-premises auctions, the auctioneer will usually pass on the cost of erecting the tent and seating.

The most important thing to remember about an auctioneer is that you are entrusting him with a large sum of money—first, in the form of your possessions, and second, in the form of the cash he gets for them. The tales of nefarious and avaricious country auctioneers are founded in some fact. You should always at least make sure the auctioneer is bonded and licensed.

Not all auctioneers are licensed simply because not all states require such certification. There are many antiquated local and state auction laws which beset the country auction field. In Baton Rouge, Louisiana, for example, all forms of auctioneering are illegal. In the rest of the state, there are very stiff laws governing auctions; only a Louisiana resident who has posted a $5,000 bond and passed both state and local exams can conduct an auction. By comparison, Mississippi, Alabama, and Connecticut, among other states, have no licensing laws or set bond.

But, to the advantage of the auction buyer and seller, most states are reviewing and updating their auction laws and statutes. In South Carolina, for example, a three-year-old auction law (the first since Colonial days) specifies that a would-be auctioneer either apprentice himself to a licensed auctioneer for two years or complete a program at an accredited auction school. In either case, the aspirant must also sit for an exam and post a $5,000 bond. To make sure a licensed auctioneer conducts every sale in the state, the licensing board scrutinizes every local newspaper for auction advertisements. And for the simple reason that the states want to collect tax revenue from auctions, the situation in South Carolina is becoming fairly universal.

WHAT'S FOR SALE?

A country auction is where you will find a mind-boggling variety of ordinary things, and also a few extraordinary ones. You can walk away with a broken washtub for 50 cents or a fine Dunlop painted chest for $21,000.

This is not to say only high prices are paid for antiques at a country auction. Depending upon who attends the sale, it is still the place for an occasional coup. I recently heard from an inveterate auction goer in Bucks County, Pennsylvania, who was enthusiastic about the bargains she had netted at local auctions. The most outrageous one was a genuine Louis XVI chair she purchased for $50 at a Bucks County auction and two months later sold at Sotheby's in New York for $11,000. Because the chair had been included in a house sale of good but rather ordinary late-20th-century reproduction furniture, it had been missed by the big-time bidders.

Aside from once-in-a-lifetime finds, there is always plenty of serviceable if ordinary furniture, and there are automobiles, television sets, dishwashers, bicycles, typewriters, and so on. I can't list everything I've seen or even bought at country auctions, but I can break the variety down into several major categories.

AMERICANA

In spite of the nascent specialized auction corporations branching out across America, the informal country auction is still a prime source of good old-fashioned Americana. By this I mean things made roughly between 1750 and 1900. It includes plain pine cupboards, Chinese export porcelain, Windsor bow-back chairs, cigar-store Indian carvings, Currier and Ives prints. And it is featured especially in New England, where a rich vein of such things still exists.

Unfortunately, the prices for Americana have soared since around 1970. Now that collectors and investors are an important and visible force in the market, prices for fine, rare and unusual items of Americana have moved into the five-figure range, even at country auctions. For example, a set of six Chippendale dining-room chairs which once sold for a rather steep $1,000 now goes for up to $40,000. It really has become something of a problem for bidders like you and me; a problem I've devoted enough attention to to come up with a few practical solutions, as follows.

★ I always go with an open mind. I might have in mind a set of Chinese porcelain. But if there are some unusual tinware items or Victorian glass plates I suspect will not arouse too much attention, I bid on those.

★ I get to know local and city dealers in attendance. This serves two purposes. First, I can watch what they inspect before the sale. Second, it is true that they will not bid openly against someone they suspect to be a potential client.

★ I look for furniture that has been in some way *altered*. Big-time dealers will usually pass over furniture which has been altered in form or design or in some cases just painted.

★ I steer away from currently "hot" collectibles. These include dolls, tin toys, scrimshaw, and a host of other specialties. The people who bid on such things can only be described as fanatics.

REGIONAL AMERICANA

In every section of America there are things in which local residents take pride. It is called Texana in Texas, Michigania in Michigan, Arcadian or Cajun in Louisiana, and so on. It includes letters, historical documents, locally made furniture, and anything else with special regional significance. And some of these items will bring real money at auctions. For example, an early Louisiana French Provincial cypress chair has brought as much as $10,000 at auction. A rough-hewn dark oak bench and table from the Alamo days of Texas can bring up to $25,000. But there is a catch. In order to bring such high prices, the item must be sold at an auction in the region from which it sprang. No one, for example, would bid so much for a Cajun Louisiana chair at a Connecticut auction. It is a purely regional quirk, which country auctioneers, dealers, and collectors are keenly aware of.

HOUSEWARES

At almost every country auction there are dozens of housewares which are hammered down for small change. I have purchased a dish drainer, potato peeler, strainer, and a lot of other homely but handy necessities for a couple of silver coins each. In addition there are stainless-steel carving knife sets that sell for a couple of dollars; and there are copper-bottom pots and pans which go for considerably less than their replacement value. In fact, almost categorically, things which are neither antiques nor collectibles sell for less than half today's retail price. This is where the auction goer can find bargains.

TOOLS

Tools are found at almost every country auction. These include carpentry hand tools, garden tools, engineering and surveying tools, and so on. Country homes are generally stocked with a variety of tools you can pick up for less than replacement cost. I recently purchased a small metal toolbox complete with a basic set of carpentry tools for only $12. And at another sale I bought a set of garden tools—rakes, hoes, shovels, and even a pitchfork—for a good price.

Collectible tools: Some tools have also become collector's items. Old blacksmith irons and forges, anvils, awls, molding planes, and various old-fashioned hand harvesting tools have found a place in collectors' cabinets. Unfortunately, the prices for these somewhat exotic tools tend to be higher than I choose to pay for "industrial" decoration.

APPLIANCES AND MACHINERY

Since many on-premises country auctions are staged on "working" farms, you will also find agricultural machines and equipment. I have seen a John Deere tractor with disk harrow sold for $625, a price I was told represented "a steal." In addition, there is also equipment and machinery more useful in the average household. There are hot-water heaters, kitchen ranges and refrigerators, small gasoline electric generators, wood-burning cast-iron stoves, and so on. A friend recently purchased a cast-iron wood-burning stove for $75.

LIVESTOCK

A sale conducted on a farm might also include livestock tied up outside the tent—cows, horses, pigs, chickens, geese, and even perhaps the family hunting dogs. Although livestock "lots" may not intrigue you, they do add to the carnival atmosphere of an on-premises auction. And if you do want to replace your lawnmower with a pair of goats, get a few ducks or geese for the pond you just dug, or even buy a pony, you can do well at an auction.

MISCELLANY

The most exciting things to be found at a country auction fall into the category of miscellany. At almost every sale there are things you don't expect to find and will become attached to. These are the surprises—small things such as a cigarette case and lighter or some bits of semiprecious gems someone's great-uncle brought back from a trip to Montana fifty years ago. Or there might be old costume jewelry made for a Victorian grandmother or even a bizarre piece of hair jewelry, a locket containing a snippet of ancient hair. The array of things in this category is limitless. And in most cases, since it might be of little interest to anyone but you, the prices can be amazingly low. In fact, it is safe to say that almost everyone walks away with a souvenir at a country auction.

ANTIQUE AUCTION

HAVING SOLD MOST OF MY REAL ESTATE, WISHING TO SEMI-RETIRE, I WILL SELL AT PUBLIC AUCTION AT CHARLESTON HOLIDAY INN IN CHARLESTON, ILL. MY COLLECTION AND ACCUMULATION FROM MY 3-STORY HOME, ON

SUNDAY, APRIL 27

1980, COMMENCING AT 10:00 A.M.

FURNITURE—OVER 80 PIECES CLEAN, LOVELY FURNITURE

Beautiful old oak, curved glass, china cabinet, clawfeet; 8' Victorian walnut dresser, 3 pieces of white marble, teardrop pulls; oak Murphy bed, with brass pulls; large wooden ice box, pressed designs in door, brass hardware; walnut matching Victorian parlor rocker and ladies' chair, heavily carved; 7' buried walnut fullsize bed; old fashion high wheel baby carriage; 7½' oak Story & Clark pump organ, excellent condition, and organ stool; golden oak spring platform rocker; 5-leg square harvest table; 2-pc. mirror back Victorian parlor set; oak washstand, with towel bar; restored walnut buried bureau; oak library table; oak toilet tree; walnut platform rocker; walnut fold-up dentist's chair, 100 years old; 6' oak sideboard, with mirror; kitchen cabinet; glass ball claw foot table; unique music cabinet, with curved glass; oak curio-china cabinet combination; fainting couch; 2-pc. love seat and chair; French cabinet; oak stand tables; walnut floor what-not; marble pillar table; full size brass and oak beds; 78" walnut gun cabinet; 6 matching cane back and bottom chairs; child's mahogany rocker and chair; solid walnut spindle couch, with velvet cushions; spindle desk chair; mahogany sewing rocker; potbelly stove; child's oak rocker; 6' credenza, made of nut wood dipped in black, gallery top; 5½' Marquette upright clock and radio; ornamental and pair of oriental floor lamps, one with glass bended shade; wicker items, sewing, magazine cabinets, chaise lounge; fern stands; ornate iron bed, with flower designs; wicker baby buggy; wrought iron 5' yard bench; ornate wood-coal air tight Moore's heater, dated 1878; child's 5-pc. ice cream set.

COMPETITION

The tent was packed with ready bidders. Yet, by the fourth lot of Victorian furniture, knocked down to the same bidder, the eagerness soured. Three men, leaning against one of the barn posts in the back of the room dressed in red flannel shirts and blue jeans, were going for something of a grand slam. They took a round, ornately carved oak table with a pedestal base for $800, then a Victorian dresser with a marble top for $1,500. The crowd glared at the trio. A large carved-oak rocking chair was hoisted onto the block. The bidding started, and as usual, the trio were pitted against everyone else. The bidding reached $1,800, then $1,900, and then at $2,000 the men dropped out of the contest and let the chair go to someone else. By all appearances the winning bidder had been just goading the men on. But his pride got the better part of him and he refused to renege on the bid.

After that, all 18 lots of oak furniture went to the trio for low prices. Since most in attendance had come specifically to bid on the oak furniture, there was much disappointment.

This was not a typical country auction. Oak furniture—very hot right now—was there in quantity and had attracted a major buyer. But even at ordinary country auctions, if you're after the trendy items, you may face competition from large buying syndicates and cartels.

It goes like this: West Coast entrepreneurs hire "haulers" to transport antiques from the northeast to the coast. There is nothing illegal about it. What they do is buy truckloads of Victorian oak antiques and fashionable Art Nouveau decorations to transport from, say, New England to southern California or from the Ohio River Valley to Dallas, Texas. Because they are bringing a supply of things to a market with no or limited supply, they can charge almost any price and hence can bid almost any price. It is a classic case of free enterprise.

This is not to say that every auction in the country is jinxed by long-distance truckers buying up everything and taking it to Phoenix or L.A. But it is a complaint that echoes loudly from some of the old-timers. One Vermonter who maintains that buying at auction has been a way of life in her small community for over 200 years laments she doesn't buy at auction anymore because "outsiders" are driving up the prices. And a man in Massachusetts maintains the number of auctioneers in that state has increased tenfold in the past five years to keep up with the demand from "outsiders."

On the other hand, some of the auctioneers claim business has never been so good. In fact, they maintain they sell things they would have donated to a foundling home or just thrown away five years ago. "Take this oak Victorian furniture. Nobody would've bought it back when I started. Too fussy," said Vermonter William Godfrey. "Or take those little bottles—you've probably never seen one—that pepper sauce came in. They used to have them for cold meats, every restaurant did. They were twisted like a rope, those bottles were, and green-colored. You could buy them, pepper sauce and all, for fifteen cents. I've sold those darn little bottles for seventeen dollars apiece, empty."

Despite all changes, a country auction is still perhaps the easiest auction arena to enter with a few dollars in your pocket. Of course, there will be competition from dealers and big-time collectors. This is where they get their stock. And there will be times when another auction shopper wants what you want just as badly as you do. In every instance it is important that you maintain a firm grasp on your financial situation and follow the instructions spelled out in the chapter on general merchandise. To go to auctions without expecting some sort of competition would be foolhardy.

BIDDING

Perhaps the most idiosyncratic bidding signals are found at a country auction. Everything from a simple raised hand to a hoot, a holler or a more discreet tipped hat brim has been used to signal a country auctioneer. As is true at any auction, the motive behind bidding signals is to get the auctioneer's attention. But at a country auction you might have to "voice" your opening bid. Once the auctioneer acknowledges your first bid, he will return to you for a second, third, and fourth, and in some instances will hound you for a closing bid. The persistent coaxing of a country auctioneer is to be expected; it's all part of the game.

Getting to know the auctioneer before the sale begins is the recommended way to make sure your bid is acknowledged. Both the informal nature of a country auction and the characteristic gregariousness of the auctioneer will make it easy for you to mingle with the personnel before the sale. In doing so you will be able to learn insiders' gossip and get to know what the general order of the sale will be, and, of course, when the sale begins your face will be a familiar one.

There is another good reason to get to know the auctioneer before the sale begins. Since there is usually no particular order in which things are sold, the auctioneer generally tries to accommodate the schedules of the bidders. This way what you want to bid on will appear on the block when you want it to. At a' sale I usually attend every spring in New Hampshire, the auctioneer always sells my lots before the end of the morning session. Though I have never been able to figure out how he can operate in such a casual manner, it seems to work at his and many other auctions like his across the country.

PREPARING FOR A COUNTRY AUCTION

Arrive early is the most significant advice for a country auction goer. You will have to inspect all lots sold at an on-premises sale on the auction day. And since you will have to decide what you want to bid on and how much you will bid quickly, you should go to the sale prepared to inspect everything expeditiously and thoroughly. The viewing time will be for two hours or so the morning of the sale.

If you learn to use directories of antique terms and styles and major artists, you can accomplish a fair amount of on-the-spot research and identification. A simple magnifier will aid you in checking artists' signatures, watermarks on prints, and hallmarks on silver. To find out what kind of wood is underneath the paint, carry a small pocket knife to scratch away layers of paint in a small inconspicuous place on furniture. To ascertain whether a chest or table will fit through your front door, carry a tape measure. Of course, the most important tool is your eyes, which will become increasingly sophisticated as time goes on.

PAYMENT AT AUCTIONS

When it comes time to pay for your purchases, you will discover that the informality which characterizes the country auction extends even to this most practical aspect. Though credit cards are usually not acceptable, almost every other means of exchange has been accepted. One New England auctioneer will gladly "barter" with you after you have made your winning bid. Say you purchased a 1967 Chevrolet

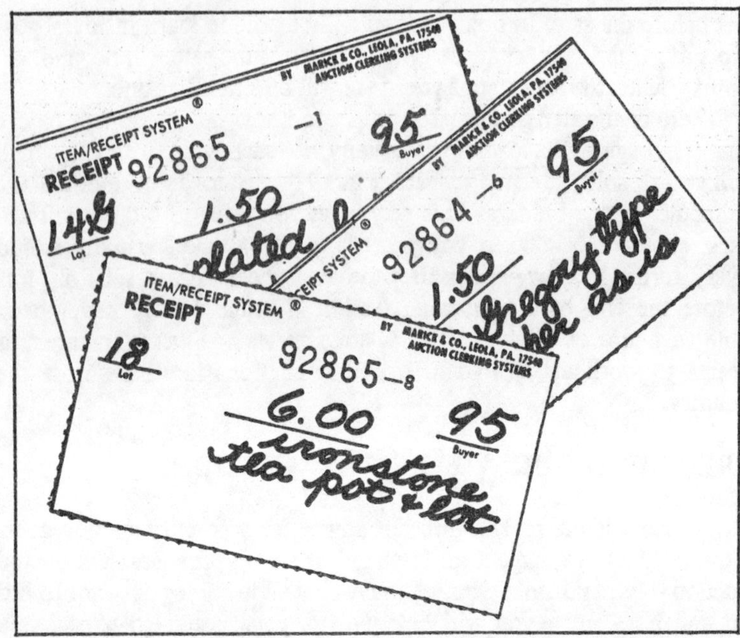

sedan; you can then pay for it by exchanging your 1965 Chevrolet and an antique table. In addition, many New England auctioneers I've dealt with will accept a personal check from almost anyone solely on the basis of their appearance. As one Down Easter put it, "Haven't had a rubber check in my life. After fifty years why should I stop takin' checks?" All told, however, the best and safest way to prepare to pay at a country auction is with traveler's checks or cash.

FINDING AUCTIONS

Finding out about on-premises country auctions is often half the battle, and announcements are occasionally posted up to six months in advance in newspapers and antique traders. But, in most cases, the sale will be posted only about a month beforehand. The location of a country auction can affect its outcome. If the sale is held in a remote, inaccessible part of the backwoods and is poorly publicized, it might be the best sale you've ever attended. On the other hand, a sale held in a resort area in the "season" is generally a poor place for bargains.

To locate on-premises auctions, I usually check the listings and advertisements in any number of antique periodicals. Several top auctioneers also mail announcements. The three periodicals I rely on are *The Maine Antique Digest, The Newtown Bee,* and *Antiques Monthly.* In addition there are literally thousands of newsletters, traders, and other periodicals that service regional and specialized markets. General country auction sales held in barns and so on are usually conducted biweekly or monthly throughout the year.

THE BIGGEST AUCTION HOUSE IN THE WORLD

By any standard it has to be the largest auction house in the world. The array of items it sells is mind-boggling—everything from rare coins, cameras, and electric typewriters to Cadillacs and trailer trucks—and it has branches all over the United States, from New York City to Honolulu. Its clientele is equally broad, including all kinds of specialists—junk dealers, land developers, precious-metal refiners, and so on—as well as weekend bargain hunters. It is a multiservice conglomerate as well, and describes itself as the world's largest commodities broker. Finally, this organization is totally subsidized by the U.S. government. In fact it *is* the U.S. government, specifically the agency known as the General Services Administration, or GSA. Since you are paying to keep this enormous enterprise going, through your taxes, you might as well take advantage of it and learn how to shop its dozens of catalogs for bargains.

The kinds of real property sold by the GSA are almost as varied as the surplus personal property it handles. Anything from a helipad to a building in the Wall Street area of Manhattan is likely to show up in a GSA sale. A few years ago the GSA sold off what was a controversial eight-story building during the Vietnam War. It was the Whitehall Induction Center in lower Manhattan made famous (or notorious) in Arlo Guthrie's *Alice's Restaurant*. It was bought by a developer as a site for apartments and a health club. Buying property through the GSA is not as simple as going through a real estate agent, but it is never without variety.

THE FUNCTION OF THE GSA

The GSA was established by the Federal Property and Administrative Services Act of 1949 to act as the U.S. government's office manager. The GSA manages and keeps track of the billions of dollars' worth of material and property that government—exclusive of the military—buys, uses, and gets rid of. Just about everything, from staples and paper clips to cars and boats, that is used by the government is purchased under the watchful eyes of the GSA. The agency also has other duties, such as leasing, operating, maintaining, and even constructing government buildings and overseeing the National Archives and other important government filing systems.

Either buying or selling: The GSA activities that concern the auction goer are carried on by the branch known as the Federal Supply Service. This part of the GSA is the purchasing agent for the government.

It decides which pencils to use, what paper, what office furniture, what kinds of cars, what kinds of garbage cans, what surgical tools for VA hospitals. It determines the brand, size, style, and color of just about everything government employees ever have to requisition. Every year this branch of the GSA spends an average of $3 billion to keep the government supplied with what it needs. Many of the items it buys are disposable—they get worn out, used up, and thrown away. But there are many other items that, once the government no longer wants them, still have great utility and value. Rather than just throw away a fleet of used cars or a warehouse full of used office furniture or tape recorders or X-ray machines a VA hospital no longer needs, the GSA sells them for the best price it can get. Which means it takes its merchandise to the auction block and makes it available to an interested prospective buyer: you.

WHEN IS IT SURPLUS?

The government doesn't like to waste its resources and property, and it has a standing policy of reutilization. Simply put, this means it tries to get the most out of all of its property by constantly rerouting items from where they are no longer needed to where they can be useful. If one branch of the government finds it no longer needs some property, whether it's a building or just a desk, that item is declared excess and gets handed over to the GSA disposal experts. The GSA then looks around for another government branch that could use that excess property. If there is none that can use it, then that item is declared surplus and is offered for public sale. It's at this point that you will hear about it.

Real estate, which is discussed in detail later in this chapter, is offered not only to agencies of the federal government but to state and local governments as well, before it is declared surplus.

SHOPPING THE GSA FOR PERSONAL PROPERTY

You name it, and most likely the GSA has sold it at one time or another in the recent past. The agency is a clearinghouse for material from just about every nonmilitary government agency, from the FBI to the Social Security Administration. In this catalog you will see surplus bone-surgery sets from a Veteran's Administration Hospital; boats from the Coast Guard; cars and motorcycles seized by the Drug Enforcement Administration; crumbs of precious metal from the Government Assay Office; even horses from the U.S. Fish and Wildlife Service. A GSA official in New York City, of all places, once sold a 12-year-old Morgan horse that was being put out to pasture by a local branch of the Fish and Wildlife Service. They had used the animal for riding patrol on one of the beaches of Long Island. A woman who had seen and admired the animal for years heard of the sale, made an offer, and got it for $50. "I was more concerned about getting it a good home and keeping it from being turned into dog food than getting a good price," admits the GSA official who sold it.

Usually unusual: Because of the variety of items it handles, there is no such thing as a typical GSA personal property sale. As just one example, here's a partial list of the kinds of items you would be likely to run across in one sales announcement marked "Office Equipment & Misc.": a Magic Chef Stove from the Wildlife Service; a Polaroid SX-70 from the Bureau of Alcohol, Tobacco, & Firearms; a lot of seven children's cribs; two dental chairs and dental lights; an electric forklift with a 3,000-pound capacity; a piledriver hammer; an envelope sealer from the Social Security Administration; various used electric and manual Royal, Remington, Smith-Corona, and Olympia typewriters from various government agencies; a 20-year-old three-wheeled Cushman motor scooter; a boat trailer for a flat-bottomed boat; a photographic sink from the FBI; a paper shredder

SALE OF GOVERNMENT PROPERTY—ITEM BID PAGE—SEALED BID
RETURN WITH BID
IFB NUMBER 2DPS-80-45   PAGE 5.

ITEM NO.	ARTICLES FOR SALE	QUANTITY (No. of Units)	UNIT OF MEASURE	PRICE BID PER UNIT	TOTAL PRICE BID DOLLARS	CTS	ITEM NO.
14.	BOWRIDER Mfr. Browning Aerocraft, St. Charles, Ml, 1979, Fiberglass Cathedral Hull, O/B, 17'1"x7'1", Model Mustang II-OB, w/convertable top, w/30 Gal Cap. fuel tank. Hull No. BAM24580M79H-5 Acq. Cost: $3,888.00 (Boat D2-52)	1	Each				14.
15.	RUNABOUT Mfr. Cee Bee, Lynwood, Ca., 1978, Fiberglass Modified-V, Model 183, O/B, 18'4"x6'7". Hull No. CBMF9314M78A Acq. Cost: $4,328.00 (Boat D2-53)	1	Each				1

from the Internal Revenue Service; an electric hole puncher from a U.S. Public Health hospital; a portable hospital operating table; and a wooden wheelchair. A bizarre mix of 83 lots in all to bid on.

MYTHS

GSA sales are a great opportunity—but they are not giveaways. Tips on how to take best advantage of these sales are given throughout this chapter, but before going any deeper into the subject, let's explore a few myths.

Myth #1: Getting something for nothing: Contrary to what you might believe, the government likes to make money on what it sells as much as you do. Although it doesn't consider selling surplus goods a high-profit enterprise, the GSA is looking for a fair market price on everything it offers. For that reason, don't be too surprised if your $20 bid on a camera that might be worth $120 isn't snapped up immediately. The GSA also has the option of pulling an item from a sale if it doesn't get the price it feels the item deserves (called the upset price).

In one recent example of this, the GSA was given the job of selling off close to 3 million silver dollars that had been minted in the late 1800s and were lost or forgotten in a government building until the early 1970s. The GSA offered them on a one-to-a-customer basis at a fixed price in a public sale. They sold the first 2 million at two different sales without a hitch and were about to offer that last million for sale when the price of silver started going through the ceiling. When this happened, the GSA cancelled the sale, raised the price of the old dollars to reflect the silver price rise, and reoffered them. In ten days every one was sold, making the government about $51 million. The buyers got a good deal—but the GSA wasn't going to just give money away.

Myth #2: Special insider's lists: Very often you'll see advertisements for information on government surplus sales. You send in a few dollars and are promised all kinds of inside dope on getting real bargains. In fact what happens, if anything happens at all, is that the mail-order firm simply forwards your name to the central GSA mail list office in Boulder, Colorado. The GSA goes through its usual process of putting you on the specific mailing lists in the categories that you have checked off, and you get the exact same government sales notices that you would get for free if you wrote to the GSA yourself. This is probably one of the most venerable of all the mail-order cons. In this case the only one who gets something for nothing is the mail-order house that passed on your name to the government.

Myth #3: The $50 jeep: One of the great legends surrounding government auctions is that at some unnamed warehouse in the United States are stockpiled thousands of war-surplus jeeps in mint condition which have never been driven. Some versions of the legend have it that these virginal jeeps are packed in grease and haven't even been exposed to air since V-J Day. And, the story continues, these jeeps are constantly being auctioned off by the carload by the government. If you know when and where to go, you can get yourself an unused jeep for about the price of a radial tire.

Not true, say government auctioneers. That's not to say that jeeps don't get sold off. But they don't go for $50 and they are far from new. GSA auctioneer Russell McClain says he has sold jeeps in the past for a few hundred dollars, but they were hardly in drive-off-the-lot condition. In fact, he remembers one that went for about $575 and had a totally rusted-out body, a worn-out transmission, and a blown engine.

Such a wreck is, of course, a bargain if you have a use for it. If you happen to be a jeep collector and are looking for pieces, the GSA and, as explained elsewhere, the Department of Defense are sources of vintage jeeps that you can use for parts.

Whatever you're buying, jeeps or jack hammers, GSA officials caution that you use your common sense as a shrewd shopper when you inspect its goods. Appraise what you have in front of you realistically and be prepared to offer a reasonable price. Government sales are not sweepstakes, and your attitude should be "Look what I bought" not "Look what I won."

TYPES OF GSA SALES

Government officials avoid using the term "auction" when they talk about selling government property to the public. They prefer instead the more general term "public sale," simply because this broader term covers all the methods—of which auctioning is just one—they use to sell off property. There are four types of sales; three of them are significant opportunities for the general public and will be discussed in detail later in this chapter.

Open-bidding auctions: For these you register for the sale and are assigned a registration number, which for the duration of the auction is your identity. That is how the auctioneer recognizes you and your bid. This number may be printed on a large paddle, on a piece of paper, or on any portable little sign you can hold up when you want to make a bid. As in all auctions, the highest acceptable bid gets whatever is being offered.

Sealed-bid sales: At a sealed-bid sale you can name only one bid. You answer no bids and no one else can answer yours. You make your bid by writing it out on a special form and mailing it in to the appropriate GSA office. If your bid is the highest one submitted, you own the property you bid on. Depending on the sale, the sealed bids may be either *formal* or *informal.* Formal sealed-bid sales are often used for disposing of very expensive items, such as a large batch of silver-rich exposed X-ray film which might sell for millions of dollars. The government usually requires a large deposit, usually 20 percent of the bid, with a bid of this type. More likely you will run into the informal sealed-bid sale, in which the GSA has a hodgepodge of individual items to sell. Usually no deposit is required when you send in an informal sealed bid.

Spot-bid sales: In a spot-bid sale you sit in a room with other bidders and fill out cards with your bids for whatever items happen to be up for sale. The cards are then collected and whoever had the highest

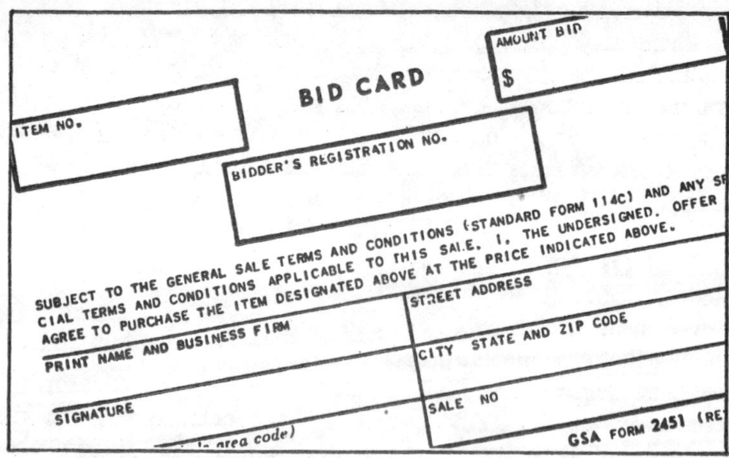

acceptable bid is awarded the item. GSA officials will use whichever technique they think will generate the most money for a particular lot of property. By experience, for example, they have found that sealed-bid sales work best for selling batches of similar items such as boats or vehicles, while spot bids may work better for a mixed collection of goods.

Negotiated sales: Of the four methods used by the GSA, this is the least likely to demand your attention, since it usually involves a large-scale purchase. The sale is negotiated between the GSA and a small number of buyers, or sometimes a single buyer. For example, a salvager may negotiate with the GSA to purchase a pile of government scrap. Or negotiations may involve a mutually acceptable business deal between the GSA and a large buyer, which could be a company or even a branch of local government. For example, if a large manufacturer has its research facilities attached to a military installation and the government decides to sell off the installation, the manufacturer might negotiate a deal with the GSA for the property. Or a state government might negotiate with the GSA to take over a military installation that has been permanently closed down by the federal government.

FINDING OUT ABOUT GSA SALES

Every year the GSA takes in between $60 and $65 million from sales of surplus government real estate and an additional $39 million from sales of surplus personal property. To keep this multimillion-dollar enterprise going, it has to have an efficient way of getting the word of its sales out to as many people as possible. The main method it uses is customized mailing lists. So your first step is to sign up for the GSA's computerized mailing lists. There are two offices to write to, one for personal property and the other for real estate.

MAILING LISTS FOR PERSONAL PROPERTY

If you're interested in sales of personal property, which includes everything but real estate, write to: *General Services Administration, Federal Supply Service, Personal Property Division,* at the GSA regional office for your location. (You'll find a national breakdown of regional addresses at the end of this chapter and detailed in the Auction Pages.) While you're at it, also request a copy of the government pamphlet "Buying Government Surplus Personal Property." This is a handy little primer on the rules and procedures of buying from government agencies.

Filing applications: What you will eventually receive in the mail is what is officially called a "Surplus Personal Property Mailing List

Application," a form that looks like a large white postcard. Simply fill in your name and address, check off the geographical area or areas in which you are interested—usually one or more of the states in your GSA region—and finally check off the category or categories of personal property you want to hear about.

In all there are 55 categories. Unless you're a large-scale salvager or reprocessor, the first 45 are the ones you'll be interested in. They're gathered under the heading of "Usable Personal Property Supplies and Equipment." Arranged in alphabetical order, some of the categories run: Agricultural Machinery & Supplies; Aircraft; Aircraft Engines and Parts; Automotive: Jeeps & 4-Wheel Drive Vehicles; Automotive: Motorcycles & Scooters; Automotive: Parts, Tires, Tubes, etc.; Automotive Vehicles, Sedans, Station Wagons, Buses, Trucks, Truck Tractors, and Truck Trailers; Bearings, All Sizes & Types; Boats and Marine Equipment; Books, Maps & Other Publications; Clothing, Textile & Leather Goods; Construction and Building Materials; Data Processing Equipment; Electronics & Communications Equipment; Fire-Fighting, Rescue & Safety Equipment; Furniture: Office & Household, Including Furnishings & Appliances; Hardware, Hand and Measuring Tools; Heavy Equipment, Highway Excavation, Mining & Building; Livestock; Medical, Dental and Laboratory Equipment; Musical Instrument, Athletic & Recreational Equipment; Optical & Surveying Instruments; Photographic Supplies & Equipment; Railway Equipment; Structures, Prefabricated (Quonset Huts); Timber; Watches, Clocks & Jewelry; Woodworking Equipment; Mobile Homes & House Trailers—just to give you a sampling. Each category has a specific code number and corresponding box on the card where you can mark off the groupings that interest you.

The remaining ten categories are grouped together under the heading "Scrap and Waste." They include items such as "Food Waste (garbage, grease, fat)" and "Waste Oil." These "waste" items are in fact necessary materials for certain industries and could even be of interest to you—for example, if you need several hundred gallons of oil to dress a private road.

Once you have marked off the groups which interest you the most, put a stamp on the card and mail it to the GSA mailing list center in Denver, Colorado. (The address is printed on the card.) Computers there will record your name and region as well as the kinds of public sales you say you want to hear about. The next time a public sale of any of these items is scheduled in your region, the regional GSA officials will call the Denver office and order a list of mailing labels for "Office Machines, Printing & Duplicating Equipment & Supplies," for example. If you checked off that section on your application form, you will be included on that computerized list. The labels are run off and stuck onto fliers which notify you of the upcoming sale: what is being sold, how it is being sold (open auction, spot bid,

sealed bid), where it is available for inspection and when you can inspect it, and full details of the rules of the sale.

There is no charge for getting these notices. You have no obligation to buy anything or even go to any of the sales. You can keep getting the notices as long as you like. The government, understandably enough, would like to continue mailing only to those people who have an active interest in the GSA sales. For that reason you will receive a notice once a year asking you if you want to continue to receive notices. This is how the government "purges" its lists. As one GSA official put it: "What we don't want are sightseers. We want people on the list who are interested in the specific types of property we're offering."

PUBLICITY FOR GSA SALES

In addition to the mailing list, the GSA may try to drum up additional interest in its sales in real estate, for example, by advertising in local papers, by trying to stir up a story angle so the sale gets covered by local TV and radio stations, and also by putting notices of the sales in the *Commerce Business Daily*. Every field office of the Department of Commerce will have copies of this, as will most local departments of commerce. If you want to spend the money you can subscribe to it (at the steep rate of $105 a year) by writing to: *Superintendent of Documents, Government Printing Office, Washington, DC 20402.*

REALITIES OF GSA SALES

As is, where is: On each and every form the GSA sends you appears the phrase "as is, where is"—which could be the government motto for these public sales. It means exactly what you think it means: you have to accept whatever condition the property you've bid on is in, and you have to pick it up where it is being stored. For some sealed-bid sales the items listed may be stored at the various offices of the agencies that are getting rid of them. If you want to see what the typewriters the FBI is getting rid of are like, you may have to go there and see for yourself. Or if you want to find out what kind of condition the tape recorder at the IRS office in another city is in, you have to go to that office. In each instance the address of the office is given as is the name and home number of the person acting as the custodian.

See for yourself: Because of the "as is, where is" policy, the GSA highly recommends that you inspect the goods in person. For sealed-bid sales there are usually four days set aside during which you can do this before bids are finally accepted on the fifth day. If there's a typewriter you are interested in, tap on a few keys to see if it's functioning. If it's a vehicle, you can check out the engine and even start it up—but you can't take it for a test drive. The custodians sometimes can give you useful information about the background of whatever the item is: where it came from, how old it is, where the government got it, maybe even what the item cost originally.

If you don't go check out an item because you can't get away, you can still find out something about it by calling the custodian and talking to him or her about the background and condition of whatever it is. This is a poor substitute for going to the place and looking it over yourself, however.

Truth in government: GSA officials do guarantee their descriptions of the individual lots. That is, they try to indicate the general condition of something in a few words. For example, an electric forklift with 3,000-pound capacity may have the notation: "Without battery (controls rusted)." Granted, this is not much of a description, but there is room for only the most basic information. As one GSA official puts it, "If we say we've got a '72 Valiant and it's got all its wheels and so forth, that is what we guarantee. If it's got a busted wheel or a block that is cracked or anything major and we know about it, we reveal that as well. After all, we want people to come back to our sales."

The GSA does its best to safeguard items until the buyers take possession. Thus you won't find that a boat you bid on on Tuesday has changed for the worse—a windshield missing, a new hole in the hull—when you come to pick it up the following Tuesday. That boat should be in the same condition when you pick it up as the day you saw it. The "as is, where is" statement obligates the government as well as you.

Upset prices: For all its public sales, GSA officials look over a typewriter, desk, or whatever and assign it an upset price. That is, using a little educated guesswork, they arrive at what they think is a fair price for an item and look to get that when they sell it. "We do our own appraisals," explains Mr. Walter Grancher, head of the Personal Property division at Region 2 headquarters in New York City. "And we know furniture, vehicles, and so on. We also take into consideration how the items have been used, and where we're selling—whether it's in the boondocks or near a large city. Then we set an upset price. It's for guideline purposes. It's not necessarily a firm price, one we won't budge from."

There are times when the GSA will help you arrive at your own upset price right in its sales announcements by telling an item's acquisition cost—that is, how much the government paid for it originally. For example, in one announcement of a sale of "Electronic, Industrial & Misc." items, you are told that an IBM Model 41 typewriter cost the government $629 new and an Underwood Touch Master manual typewriter came with an original price tag of $122. In another sale, one of boats, the GSA lists the original costs of a Grumman aluminum-hulled fishing boat as $842, and of a deck boat as $9,621.72. Knowing this and taking into account the condition of these items and the prices asked for similar used items by second-hand dealers and in classified ads, you might decide that the IBM typewriter would be a good buy at $300, the Underwood at $40, the aluminum boat at $150, and the deck boat at $4,000.

Although GSA appraisers usually gauge their upset prices fairly accurately, they will check into an item if its upset price bears no resemblance to the bids being offered for it. Suppose the GSA has set an upset price of about $1,000 for an item but the bids hover somewhere between $10,000 and $15,000. The government may have the item reappraised before awarding it to the highest bidder. It may even pull it from the sale and offer it again at a new higher upset price.

The GSA will do this for the benefit of the bidder as well. "Say we offer an item for that same $1,000, and 199 out of 200 people put in bids around that sum. But one bidder offers $10,000. Obviously there is a possibility he's made an error. We'll call him and ask him to verify that bid," says one GSA expert. "Maybe he wanted to bid only $1,000 and got the decimal point wrong. But he has to come up with some proof that was his intention." Although it will get all the money it can for an item, the GSA will try to do it as fairly as possible as well.

OPEN-BID AUCTIONS OF PERSONAL PROPERTY

The open-bidding procedure for selling off a batch of goods takes a total of five days. The first four days are for viewing or inspecting the goods, and the fifth day is for the auction itself. Assume for the moment you had checked off the office-machines category of personal property. You will get a notice in the mail about the sale and when and where you can inspect it.

Look it over: Go to the inspection site and register. There you'll get a list of the merchandise for sale as well as a brief description of each item. Decide what you are interested in bidding on and how much you want to spend. Talk to the custodian and find out every-

thing you can about the item—how old it is, who used it, what it cost originally, and anything else that might help you decide on a price.
Reach up and be counted: At an open-bid sale, unlike the sealed-bid and spot-bid sales, you must be physically present to bid. Show up at the place of auction at the time designated, and sign your name in the register. You will be assigned a number and given some sort of small sign or paddle to hold up to tell the auctioneer that you want to bid. Different regions use different equipment. Some have white wooden bidding paddles with the black number painted on, while others simply rely on a large piece of paper or cardboard with the number boldly printed on it. In any case, they are all used the same way: when you want to bid, hold your number high.

The "crying" or calling of the auction goes as it usually does with any auction. The auctioneer tries to keep the momentum of bidding going for as long as possible, and when he sees he's gotten the highest possible price for an item, he announces the winning, or knockdown, bid, states the number of the bidder who offered it, and to confirm it asks that bidder to hold up his or her number. The auctioneer does not call out the bidder's number each time he acknowledges a bid—that would slow down his patter—but he does make a point of announcing out loud the number of the winning bidder and the amount of the bid.

Cash or check and carry: When you're the winning bidder, you go to a clerk's office right by the auction room, pay for the item with either cash, certified check, or personal check, and receive in exchange your receipt, called a notice of award. As a general rule, full payment is required the day of the sale and you have up to five working days to pick up the item you bought. Leave it any longer than that and the government will charge you storage fees.

Ground rules: That is the general format of an auction. Specific ones will vary according to the amount of property being sold and the turnout of the bidding crowd. Regulations require there to be at least two GSA officials present at the auction, but there may be three or four times this number present to do the auctioning and supervise the procedure. The crowd may be only a dozen people or so if the auction is at an out-of-the-way location, or it may be a hundred or more if the auction is near a big city.

To keep the record straight, auctions are usually tape-recorded. If there is disagreement about who made the final bid, the tape is played back. Whatever is recorded on there is the number of the person who pays. If you don't want to bid, you are warned to keep your paddle (or its equivalent) down, but if you do, hold it high so it can be seen.

SEALED-BID SALES OF PERSONAL PROPERTY

For sealed-bid sales, the GSA solicits your bid, if you're on the appropriate mailing list, by sending you a flyer. The first page of the flyer, listing all the items, is the bid page. It has spaces on it where you can put down the number of the item you want and the amount of money you are bidding for it. The form also tells you when you may inspect the property and when and where the sealed bids will be

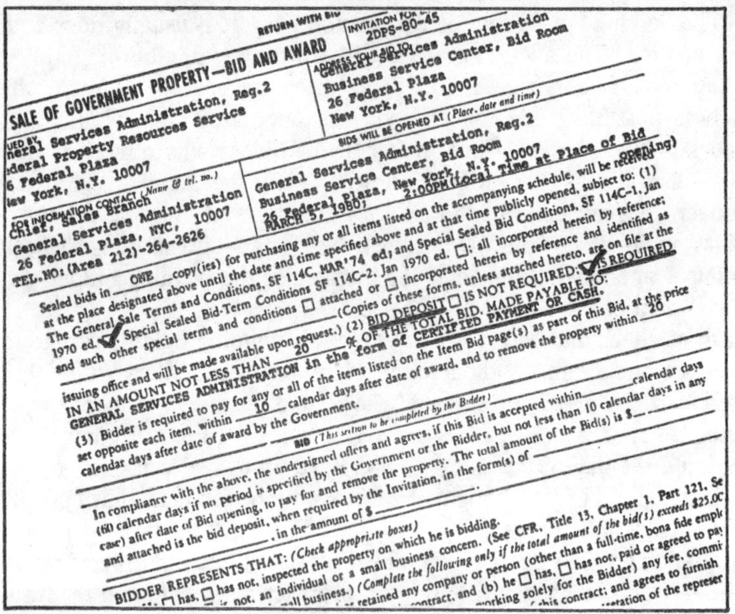

SALE OF GOVERNMENT PROPERTY—BID AND AWARD

RETURN WITH BID

INVITATION FOR BID 2DPS-80-45

ISSUED BY
General Services Administration, Reg.2
Federal Property Resources Service
26 Federal Plaza
New York, N.Y. 10007

ADDRESS YOUR BID TO:
General Services Administration
Business Service Center, Bid Room
26 Federal Plaza
New York, N.Y. 10007

FOR INFORMATION CONTACT (Name & tel. no.)
Chief, Sales Branch
General Services Administration
26 Federal Plaza, NYC, 10007
TEL. NO: (Area 212)-264-2626

BIDS WILL BE OPENED AT (Place, date and time)
General Services Administration, Reg.2
Business Service Center, Bid Room
26 Federal Plaza, New York, N.Y. 10007
MARCH 5, 1980; 2:00PM (Local Time at Place of Bid opening)

Sealed bids in _____ ONE _____ copy(ies) for purchasing any or all items listed on the accompanying schedule, will be received at the place designated above until the date and time specified above and at that time publicly opened, subject to: (1) The General Sale Terms and Conditions, SF 114C, MAR'74 ed, and Special Sealed Bid Conditions, SF 114C-1, Jan 1970 ed. ✓, Special Sealed Bid-Term Conditions SF 114C-2, Jan 1970 ed. ☐; all incorporated herein by reference; and such other special terms and conditions ☐ attached or ☐ incorporated herein by reference and identified as _____ (Copies of these forms, unless attached hereto, are on file at the issuing office and will be made available upon request.) (2) BID DEPOSIT ☐ IS NOT REQUIRED; ✓ IS REQUIRED IN AN AMOUNT NOT LESS THAN _____ 20 _____ % OF THE TOTAL BID. MADE PAYABLE TO: GENERAL SERVICES ADMINISTRATION in the form of CERTIFIED PAYMENT OR CASH.
(3) Bidder is required to pay for any or all of the items listed on the Item Bid page(s) as part of this Bid, at the price set opposite each item, within _____ 10 _____ calendar days after date of award, and to remove the property within _____ 20 _____ calendar days after date of award by the Government.

BID (This section to be completed by the Bidder)
In compliance with the above, the undersigned offers and agrees, if this Bid is accepted within _____ calendar days (60) calendar days if no period is specified by the Government or the Bidder, but not less than 10 calendar days in any case) after date of Bid opening, to pay for and remove the property. The total amount of the Bid(s) is $ _____ and attached is the bid deposit, when required by the Invitation, in the form(s) of _____ , in the amount of $ _____ .

BIDDER REPRESENTS THAT: (Check appropriate boxes)
..._ ☐ has, ☐ has not, inspected the property on which he is bidding.
..._ ☐ is not, an individual or a small business concern. (See CFR, Title 13, Chapter 1, Part 121. Se ...small business.) (Complete the following only if the total amount of the bid(s) exceeds $25,00 ...retained any company or person (other than a full-time, bona fide empl ...contract, and (b) he ☐ has, ☐ has not, paid or agreed to pay ...working solely for the Bidder) any fee, commi ...this contract; and agrees to furnish ...oration of the represen

opened, and it has a place for you to fill in your name and address. In addition there is a sale number and bid opening date recorded on the form that you have to mark on the outside of the envelope enclosing your bid (or bids).

Via the mails: You don't have to send any money. Just fill out the form and mail it to the bid room at your regional GSA headquarters. There the bid envelopes are stored in a safe until the day of the opening. GSA officials then go through the mailed-in bids for each item, pick out the one that is the highest, and notify you by mail that the piledriver hammer you've always wanted, for example, is yours. You have up to ten days to pay for the property and up to 20 days to collect it after you've received a form from the GSA releasing the property to you. It's that simple—almost.

SPOT-BID SALES OF PERSONAL PROPERTY

The spot-bid sale is often the preferred way of disposing of vast amounts of highly desirable property very quickly. The GSA often uses this method in selling vehicles and office furniture, two very popular items. Just as for open-bid auctions and sealed-bid sales, four days are allowed for inspecting the items, and the actual sale is held on the fifth day. When you go in and inspect a batch of government surplus desks, for example, and see something you like, you fill out a bid card with your bid and name and address and drop it in a box. At the end of the five days all the cards are gathered up and read. They are collected into piles, one pile for each item, with the card holding the highest bid on top.

Second thoughts: But the bidding is not over. On the fifth day GSA officials also solicit one last batch of bids from anyone who cares to appear at the sales site at the time noted on their Invitation for Bids form, or IFB as it is called. People gather in a room and a GSA official starts the bidding by asking for bids on item number 1. (You can usually spot the more experienced bidders, since they already have their names and addresses filled out on a whole batch of cards.) Anyone who wants to bid simply writes the bid on his card and raises his hand so a runner for the auctioneer can go and pick it up. No one knows what the high bid is from the bid box. Everyone has to decide on his own what to offer.

Once the cards are collected, all the bidding is stopped and the high bid from the floor is compared with the high bid from the box. Whichever is the higher, of course, is awarded the item. However, one GSA official adds that the government has the prerogative of accepting or rejecting bids, and that sometimes there are other considerations and the high bid *doesn't* win.

Cash or check and carry: If you are at the spot-bid sale and your bid is accepted, you can take immediate possession of what you bid on if you can pay in cash, certified check, or even personal check. But no credit cards. If you do not have the money with you, you have five days to pay for and collect your item.

If you didn't bother to go to the sale on the fifth day, but your box bid was the one that topped all the others, you will be notified by mail that yours was the winning bid. Then you have ten days to pay up and collect your property.

Trying until you get it right: The spot-bid sale, like the sealed-bid sale, gives you the opportunity to make an offer for an item without having to show up at bid-opening time. The big difference between the two is that spot bidding continues on the day the bids are opened. For that reason the spot-bid sale gives you access to some other items you might have missed. "You can't raise your bid from the floor," explains GSA official Walter Grancher, "but you do get to see how the bids are running. Let's say you bid on a vehicle and didn't get it. You still have a second chance to bid on another. You can raise your bids until you get what you want."

BUYING VEHICLES

Motor vehicles, from ordinary passenger cars to trucks and various kinds of specialized equipment, are one of the most popular categories to GSA shoppers. Typically many of the vehicles come out of some government motor pool once their useful vehicle life, determined by a variety of complex mileage/repair-cost formulas, is over. Some end up as scrap; others are in drivable condition and with some repairs and careful maintenance can go on serving you for years.

In other words: A typical description of a scrap vehicle might read "Extensive damage to left side and under carriage, in scrap condition"—in other words, basically a totaled car with the left side stove in and the bottom ripped out, the result, in the government's understatement, of "Accident Damage." Such a car is nevertheless an economical source of parts. Just a step up from that might be a repairable vehicle that needs some heavy work, such as "Sedan, 1976, Plymouth Gran Fury, 4 Dr., A/T, A/C (brakes and front end repairs required)." In other words, if you get the car at a good price and are willing to invest a few hundred dollars more in repair bills, you might have a good deal.

Good guys and bad guys: Most of these vehicles are fleet vehicles and have been given routine maintenance, but not the personal care private owners would give them. Possibly better cared-for are cars belonging to individuals who crossed the path of some government agency. For example, every year the Drug Enforcement Administration seizes hundreds of cars, some of which end up on a GSA sales lot. By law that agency is allowed to seize any item—a boat, a car, even a bicycle or hot dog stand—that has been used in committing a crime. That item can then be forfeited to the U.S. government, which then can dispose of it as it sees fit. Usually the exotic cars or vans of drug dealers are not sold; they get recycled through the Drug Enforcement Administration for use by undercover agents. It's the more conservative four- and six-cylinder cars that usually end up being sold off by the GSA. However, at one GSA spot-bid sale held in the northeast, among the conservative Plymouths and American Motors cars there were an occasional Jaguar coupe, Cadillac, big Buick, Oldsmobile, etc., courtesy of the Drug Enforcement Administration.

BUYING OFFICE EQUIPMENT

Another very popular GSA category is office equipment and office supplies. With the amount of paperwork generated by government agencies it's not surprising that they are always retiring typewriters, for example, after years of typing up government forms and reports. Even sought-after machines like IBM Selectric typewriters are always appearing at these sales. New, these machines will cost $800 or more depending on the model and the outlet. In one region a GSA official says IBM Selectrics sell for between $300 and $400 depending on the condition of the machines and how the bids are running that day. Many of the machines need reconditioning of some kind, but at those prices you can spend a good amount of money on refurbishing an old IBM and still consider it a bargain. For people not so brand-conscious, there is also a wide selection of other makes and types of typewriters to choose from at many of these larger sales.

Office furniture—desks, chairs, filing cabinets—is also very popular. Don't expect to walk away with an antique oak desk from a government sale, however. What you'll see will be very heavily used steel furniture. It is sturdy and practical but may not be in tip-top shape. The GSA is characteristically frank about the condition of such goods. "When furniture reaches me," says one GSA personal property expert, "it has seen better days. Don't forget they've tried to use all this stuff within the government. They've tried to donate it. Then it's turned over to me."

As we have seen, the GSA sells an endless variety of items. Nevertheless, you may not get a chance to buy a particular kind of item if there is a government policy against selling it for the time being. Recently, for example, a directive was passed down to halt the sales of many kinds of office furniture, essentially eliminating that whole market. Anyone who wants to buy either will have to wait until the restrictions are lifted—as they may have been by the time you're reading this—or buy what he needs new. For reasons like this, getting a good buy from the government may occasionally require patience.

TIPS ON SHOPPING THE GSA

If you're willing to spend the time, be patient in looking around, and be realistic about pricing what you see, you'll do well at a government sale. The first step is to get on the government's mailing list *only for the items that interest you.* Don't be greedy in choosing your property categories or your mailbox will be stuffed almost every day with invitations to bid on items you'll never look at. Make a point of going to inspect items and attending some auctions at spot-bid sales if only for the practice.

Pick your season: There is a seasonal feature to the government sales. As a matter of policy the government does hold sales the year round, but there are slow times when selling is sparse. Generally the GSA tends to avoid sales, or at least big sales, soon after Christmas, when many of the big buyers are on vacation and when many people aren't in a buying mood simply because the holiday season has strained their finances. Also, at this time of year in many parts of the country, road conditions make traveling to inspection and sales sites more difficult than usual.

For these reasons most GSA regions tend to concentrate their sales in spring and summer months. Generally you'll find that items offered at these seasons will be more varied and of better quality. Of course, you will also find the competition a little more intense.

Some of the regions hold their public sales on a regular schedule. For example, the National Capital Region (since it includes the bureaucratic heart of the nation, Washington, D.C.) has to handle vast quantities of government surplus goods and has set sales schedules. Vehicles are offered once a month on the second Wednesday of the month, and office furniture and equipment are offered twice a month every other Thursday. This GSA region does this because it has a dependably large volume of items constantly flowing through its system. Other regions will run on a looser schedule, making their sales offerings as inventories in one or another group of items build up.

There is a seasonal rhythm from region to region. The simplest way to find out about how the GSA sales run in your part of the country is save the notices you get in the mail and note how often they arrive. As a general rule you will probably find that the sales recur every five or six weeks, often enough so that you shouldn't feel pressure to buy at the first sale you attend. If you don't find what you want at one sale, you can be reasonably sure of getting another chance.

Pick your region: Certain GSA regions are more apt than others to have certain items. For example, the northeastern regional-headquarters cities, New York and Boston in particular, have high concentrations of office workers and thus, as you might expect, a large surplus of used office furniture and equipment. Vehicles in those regions tend to be predominantly cars, whereas in parts of the midwest and west, you will find more four-wheel-drive vehicles used by agencies such as the Soil Conservation Service of the Department of Agriculture. As you become familiar with the notices for sales in your area, you should be able to get some sense of what the specialty items tend to be.

ADVICE FROM THE GSA

To a person, GSA officials involved in personal property sales say they need and want individual private buyers at their sales. Interviews with several of them produced the following advice.

★ Always inspect the property before submitting your bid. It can only help you arrive at a sound bid and spare you disappointment when you go to claim your property.

★ Talk to the custodian present and learn from him as much about the item as you can: its original cost, age, and facts about its condition, to name a few things.

★ Use this information to arrive at a sound, rational bid. A government sale is no bingo game, a matter of luck. The shrewd bidder who manages to offer the highest *reasonable* price is the one who gets the bargain.

★ Don't bid any more on an item than the item is worth to you. This is especially important in an open-bidding situation, since the crowd's excitement can be contagious and may spur you on to offer a price you'll later regret. Set a bid ceiling. Stick to it.

★ You can increase the odds of getting what you want by paying attention to the sales held away from big cities and regional headquarters. Fewer bidders attend these, and very often the knockdown prices tend to run a little lower.

SHOPPING THE GSA FOR REAL ESTATE

Ever wonder what they do with old Coast Guard stations, or who was given the job of selling former President Nixon's helicopter pad at his old Key Biscayne house? They end up in the hands of the GSA as well, specifically its Real Property division. In addition to disposing of property unneeded by the government, the GSA can also act as the government's real estate agent by looking for buyers for its excess property. (Just in case you were wondering, there were 38 offers for the old Nixon helipad, ranging from $250 to the winning bid of $87,500. That got the new owner a small piece of history and a little over an acre of dry land and ocean bottom combined.)

Well before real property is offered for public sale, it goes through a process of being offered within the government first, just as personal property does. Before this offering is done, however, GSA experts do a careful title search to confirm that the government in fact owns the land. The title search completed, the agency then screens federal agencies asking if any have a need for what has been declared excess land. Should a federal agency want that land, it has to buy it from the other agency for roughly 50 percent of its fair market value. On occasion property might be transferred from one agency to the other without money changing hands, but that is the exception, not the rule. If there are no takers on the federal level, the property is then declared surplus. It is still several steps away from the open market, however.

The next GSA step is to send a letter to state and local governments asking whether they can use the land. These governments may buy the land or get it for free depending on the planned use. If a local government will use the land for a college or hospital or park, very often the local government will receive the title for free. First the application has to be approved by the appropriate government agency. Land allocated for a college, for example, or anything that would qualify as an education institution, must be used for that purpose for at least 30 years. Parks sometimes must be used in perpetuity for that purpose. If in the end no federal agency or state or local government wants the land, it is put up for public sale.

MAILING LISTS FOR REAL ESTATE

There is another address to write to for information about real property, better known as real estate. You can get on the GSA sale mailing list for that by writing: *Director of Real Property, General Services Administration,* in your regional headquarters. (The addresses are the same as for personal property and are listed at the end of this chapter.) It is also a good idea to request a copy of the GSA pamphlet "Disposal of Surplus Real Property" for background on how the government disposes of its surplus land.

Filing applications: Within four to six weeks you will receive a copy of the "Real Property Mailing List Application Card." Put your name and address on it and check which of the four types of property interest you the most. The four types are: agriculture, timber, grazing, and mineral-related real estate; commercial and industrial real estate; buildings for off-site use; and residential and waterfront resort property. In addition you are also asked to check off the value range of the property you want to know about. You have three choices: under $50,000; $50,000 to $100,000; and over $100,000. Lastly, you are asked to specify in which states of your region you would like to hear about sales. If you wish, you can also be notified of real estate sales in any of the 50 states and U.S. possessions, but only for property valued at $100,000 or more.

Send the completed card to the centralized mailing list office, also in Denver. There it will be coded, just as was described for the personal property form, and you will be mailed notices of all the sales you specified. Like the personal property list, the real estate list goes through a once-yearly purging. You have to respond to the government's annual query about whether or not you want to remain on the list.

HOW REAL ESTATE IS SOLD

As with the surplus personal property, the GSA can choose to sell through auctions, sealed bids, or negotiation. In addition, the agency may hire brokers to help it dispose of vast tracts of property that can or might be developed as industrial lands. The sealed-bid sale is the type most commonly used for disposing of government real property.

You will get to find out about properties for sale by getting your name on the GSA mailing list, as explained earlier in the chapter. In addition, to set up interest, the GSA often places advertisements in local papers. What you receive when you respond to an ad or are on the mailing list is a neat package of information called an Invitation for Bids (IFB).

Making bids on real estate: The Invitation for Bids includes the vital statistics of a property: name, location, physical description, sometimes with photos. You will also see the conditions of sale, including whether there is a government mortgage available on the property, and will have bid forms to fill out.

Once you complete these forms in duplicate, you send them to the GSA office along with a certified or cashier's check made out to the GSA for 10 percent of your bid. You then seal the envelope with a sticker provided on which you mark the bid invitation number, the date and time the bid should be opened, and the property bid for. On the envelope itself you have to put your name and address, the invitation number, the date and hour of the bid opening, and in the lower left-hand corner the phrase "Bid for Real Property." This goes to the GSA, which holds the bids until the specified date and time and then opens them. If your bid is accepted you are notified. If it's not, they send your deposit back within a week.

In most cases you are told on the Invitation to Bid form what the minimum acceptable bid, or upset price, is for that property. For your bid to be considered a "responsive bid"—that is, one worth considering—you must offer at least the upset price.

This upset price is based on the government's evaluation of what a piece of property is worth in the current real estate market. You cannot find out what the government's top estimate is, but you can take in your own assessor to look over the property and come up with your own assessment. In fact, the government recommends that at the very least you personally visit the property before you formally submit a bid. You can't get out of a sale by claiming ignorance about one or another aspect of the land—that it was right next door to a practice artillery range or that it is on a deserted stretch of an island.

Don't expect desirable real estate to be a giveaway. One cluster of three small houses on a one-acre parcel of land formerly owned by the Coast Guard recently sold for $150,000. It also drew some optimistic bids such as the man who offered $1,001 or the woman who thought she had a chance with a $200 bid.

Most real estate offerings are announced up to three months in advance, so you should have plenty of time to inspect the property before submitting a bid. The Invitation for Bid form also gives you the name and telephone number of someone who can show you the property at a mutually agreeable time.

Payment: Most real property sales are cash sales. That is, if your bid is accepted, you have to pay the full amount, less your 10 percent deposit with a cashier's or a certified check within 60 days. If you don't, the government can not only keep your deposit, it can sue you for the rest of the money.

Occasionally the government will offer a mortgage on property. The terms follow a set formula over the duration of a decade. The rate of interest you pay for this short-term mortgage is pegged to whatever the current rate for ten-year government bonds happens to be plus 1.5 percent to give the government a reasonable rate of return on the loan. Since the bond rate usually reflects the current rate of inflation, what you end up getting is a mortgage rate very similar to what banks are currently offering their borrowers. The rate is computed from the day your bid is accepted.

GSA MAILING LISTS

If you wish to be included on the GSA auction mailing lists, address your requests for applications to the following regional offices. Remember to specify which auction list application (Personal or Real Property) you wish to receive. For inclusion on the Personal Property mailing list, address: *General Services Administration, Director of Personal Property Division* (insert local address from following list).

Requests for inclusion on the Real Property Auction mailing list should be addressed to: *General Services Administration, Director of Real Property Division* (insert local address from following list).

Region One: Connecticut, Maine, Massachusetts, New Hampshire, Rhode Island, and Vermont

John W. McCormack Post Office and Courthouse Boston, MA 02109

Region Two: New York, New Jersey, Puerto Rico, Virgin Islands

26 Federal Plaza New York, NY 10007

Region Three: District of Columbia, Delaware, Maryland, Pennsylvania, Virginia, and West Virginia

7th and D St., SW Washington, DC 20407

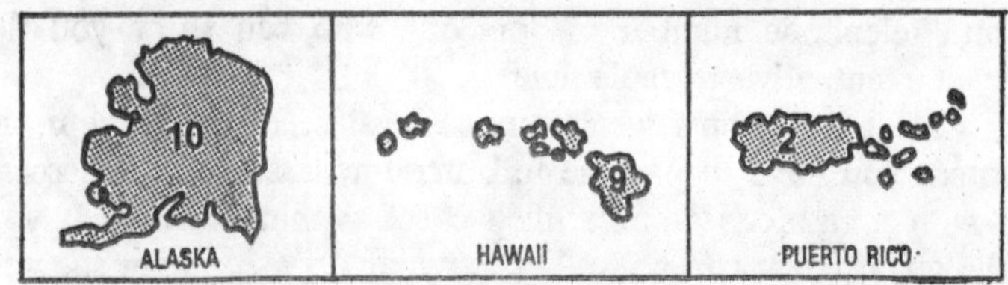

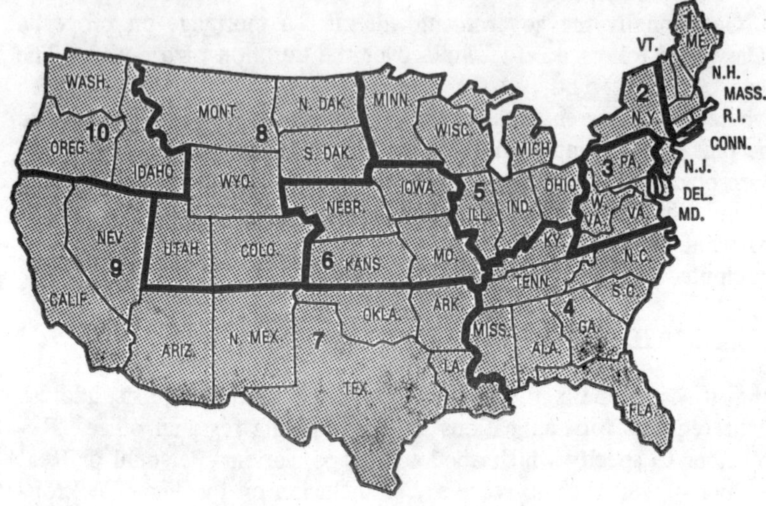

Region Four: Alabama, Florida, Georgia, Kentucky, Mississippi, North Carolina, South Carolina, and Tennessee

1776 Peachtree St. NW Atlanta, GA 30309

Region Five: Illinois, Indiana, Michigan, Minnesota, Ohio, and Wisconsin

230 South Dearborn St. Chicago, IL 60604

Region Six: Iowa, Kansas, Missouri, and Nebraska

1500 East Bannister Rd. Kansas City, MO 64131

Region Seven: Arkansas, Louisiana, New Mexico, Oklahoma, and Texas

819 Taylor St. Fort Worth, TX 76102

Region Eight: Colorado, Montana, North Dakota, South Dakota, Utah, and Wyoming

Denver Federal Center Building 41 Denver, CO 80225

Region Nine: American Samoa, Arizona, California, Guam, Hawaii, Nevada, the Trust Territory of the Pacific Islands

525 Market St. San Francisco, CA 94105

Region Ten: Alaska, Idaho, Oregon, and Washington

GSA Chapter Auburn, WA 98002

SHOPPING AT THE BIG PX

Parked in the garage of Captain Robert Truax, U.S. Navy (retired), is his current obsession: a one-astronaut, 30-foot-long rocket capable of carrying a human 50 miles through space. The ingenuity and skill it took to build the rocket came from Truax's years of personal experience first flying, and later, designing spacecraft for the U.S. government. The bits and pieces he used in putting the rocket together came from the DPDS.

Parked in the stable of Bill and Terry Schwedes is their daughter's horse, Neon Moon, USMC (retired). An 11-year-old palomino, who had a long career as a parade ground horse, Neon Moon now gets all his care and feeding from his 10-year-old mistress, Sheila Schwedes, who, in turn, got this horse of her dreams where Truax got his rocket parts: the DPDS.

So what, you might wonder, is the DPDS? It's the Defense Property Disposal Service, the Department of Defense's clearing house for military surplus goods. The DPDS is part of the Defense Logistics Agency, which is one of the administrative offspring of the Secretary of Defense's office. Next to the General Services Administration (GSA), the DPDS is the largest single source of surplus government goods. All military surplus goods sold to the public are sold by the DPDS—everything from combat boots to used boxcars. There is only one type of property it doesn't sell, and that's real estate, which the GSA handles. So if you want to buy a government building, a piece of government land or an old missile silo, contact the GSA. If you're looking for a good buy on a military surplus plane, boat, car or typewriter, contact the DPDS.

In addition to the obvious military sources—the Army, Navy, Coast Guard and Air Force—the DPDS also gets the items it sells from the National Aeronautics and Space Administration (NASA), the Federal Aviation Administration and even the Natick Development Center in Natick, Massachusetts, which runs various research and development programs for the Defense Department, such as testing material to see if it is up to contract standards.

HOW MILITARY PROPERTY REACHES THE PUBLIC

Before any Department of Defense property gets to a public sale you might attend, the Defense Department goes through a series of steps in which it offers the material in a set bureaucratic ritual to a variety of organizations. First, the material is screened by the original owning agency—say, the Army. If the Army can't use or no longer needs an airplane, or a boxcar or whatever, it is then declared excess—no longer needed by its original owners. Item managers at one of the Defense Property Disposal Offices, or DPDOs, of which there are over 200 located in the United States and around the world, then screen this excess piece of property to see what kind of shape it's in. **Insiders:** If it has possibilities, it then may be offered to some other branch of the Department of Defense, such as the Marines. If the Marines don't want it, and no other Defense Department division does either, then the item may be offered for sale or paper transfer to one of our allied countries. When this happens, the State Department gets into the act and decides what country is awarded or offered the item.

Assuming none of our allies is in the market for a used boxcar or twin-engine aircraft, then the item gets offered to the various civilian agencies within the government. If a civilian agency can establish a need for the item, the agency is given it. When there are no takers in the government, that item is then declared surplus—no longer wanted or needed by the government.

Your turn: There is still another stage before an item is offered to the public. Like the real estate handled by the GSA, DPDO surplus items may be offered to some nonfederal agency or organization—a state or city government, a college or perhaps an organization like the Boy Scouts of America. If no takers are found, the item then is released for public sale.

You are eligible to bid on Department of Defense surplus if you are 18 years old or older and are not a member of any of the armed forces (which includes the Coast Guard), a civilian Defense Department employee in any business sense connected with the DPDSs, or an immediate family member in the household of anyone with such disqualifying affiliations.

Classifying: When an item is declared surplus, it is assigned one of the more than 400 class numbers (four-digit description codes) and is put in either the "scrap and waste" category or the "usable item" category. There are 60 kinds of items in the usable items category, from adhesives and aircraft to tools and woodworking machinery and equipment. In this amazingly long shopping list, you can find holsters, single-engine aircraft, tugboats, aircraft carriers, trucks, buses, firefighting equipment, home furniture, military clothing, live animals and office equipment. It is hard to think of anything that doesn't appear on this long and elaborate roster.

TYPES OF DPDS SALES

The DPDS system for selling its surplus goods is very much like the GSA system. The sales you are most likely to get involved with are sealed-bid sales, open-bid sales and spot-bid sales.

Bid systems: For sealed-bid sales, you pick out what you want to bid on, write the bid on a form and send it in to a DPDS office. For spot-bid sales, you also write your bid on a form and either send it in to a DPDS office or go there in person and submit the bid. For open-bid sales—at which, of course, you must appear in person—you're given a registration number and a numbered paddle to match. When you see something you'd like to bid on at the auction, you just hold up the numbered paddle where the auctioneer can see it. There is a fourth selling method, negotiated sales, usually reserved for large deals be-

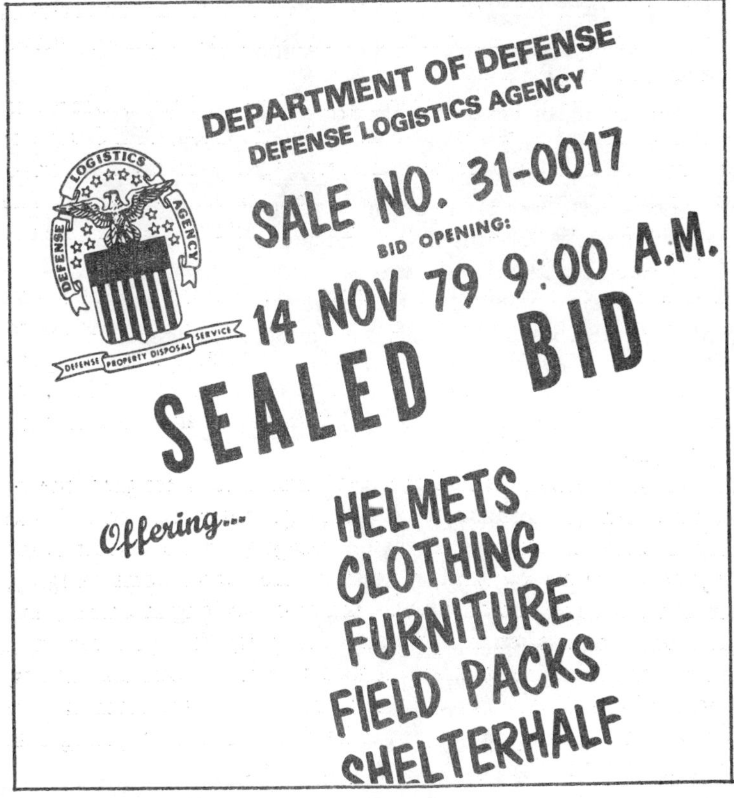

tween the federal government and state or municipal government. All of these methods are explained in greater detail in the chapter on the General Services Administration.

One aspect of DPDS sales that's different from the GSA is that the Defense Department categorizes sales on two levels: national and local.

NATIONAL DPDS SALES

The DPDS divides the country, for administrative purposes, into three regions, each with its own headquarters. On a set schedule, each region takes turns selling usable items loosely grouped in three commodity groupings: *vehicular, aircraft components and electrical components,* and a *miscellaneous* category that includes just about everything else. As we'll explain later, the three regions take turns selling items from these three groups with sales that are made public to the entire United States.

These national sales include a huge section of the country—an area covered by one of the three enormous regions—and they usually involve the selling of large quantities of goods: 4,200 pairs of pants, 420 rain ponchos, 422 desks, 218 steel helmets, a bidding lot of 15 briefcases and 26 suitcases, or large pieces of equipment such as tugboats, airplanes, and even landing craft and amphibious vehicles. The equipment is advertised in a catalog put out by one regional headquarters, but the items themselves may be located anywhere in the country or even anywhere the Department has a presence in the world. The DPDS maintains offices in Europe, throughout the Pacific and in the Far East as well.

FINDING OUT ABOUT NATIONAL SALES

If you want to find out about national DPDS sales, the first thing you have to do is get on the mailing list for the sales notifications. It's a two-step process. First, simply write: *DoD Surplus Sales, P.O. Box 1370, Battle Creek, MI 49016.* Ask for a copy of the Department of Defense Surplus Property Bidders Application. You'll get the form and a copy of a pamphlet entitled "Classes of Surplus Personal Property Sold by the Department of Defense," which is a mini-directory explaining what group of goods each of the four-digit class numbers on the application forms signifies. For more information, in general, about Department of Defense sales, you should also write to: *De-*

fense Property Disposal Service, Federal Center, Battle Creek, MI 49016. Ask for a copy of the "How to Buy Surplus Personal Property from the Department of Defense." It's full of good background information on all kinds of sales.

Once you've returned a completed application form, the information on it—your name and address, as well as items whose class numbers you've circled—is fed into a central mailing list computer. When the DPDS schedules a national sale of any of the classes of items you've circled—say office furniture or still cameras—the computer pulls your name from its memory bank, and an Invitation for Bid (IFB) is automatically sent off to you.

The information: The next step is up to you. Read through the IFB, which is also a catalog of the items for sale with a brief description of each. These descriptions will tell you what the item is, what its original cost to the government was, the total weight (this makes it possible for you to figure out shipping costs), whether the item was unused or used and its current condition. The Defense Department uses a three-level, three-word rating system—good, fair and poor—to rate the condition. The IFB will also tell you where the item is, whom you can call for more information about the item, when it may be inspected, the time and date of the bid opening (or, if it's an auction, when the selling starts) and what the conditions of the sale are: if you have to make a bid deposit, how you pay, what restrictions there might be on using the item and stipulations on removing it once you've purchased it.

Staying on the mailing list: Because of the cost of the mailings, the Defense Department reviews its mailing list carefully and insists that prospective buyers mark off specific categories of goods on the application form. If you circled every category or simply said you wanted to see all the IFBs, you'd be getting an average of 20 to 30 catalogs a week. For that reason, you must be selective. You also must stay actively interested in the sales; there is a periodic "purge" of the mailing lists, and if after getting two IFBs you make no response, your name will be pulled from the list.

You make a response either by sending in a bid or, if you've seen nothing of interest in those two sales, sending in a simple "Change Form" which is included on the back of each Invitation to Bid. This is simply a notice to the DPDS that you are interested in continuing to receive the catalogs. You'll know your name is about to be purged from the mailing list if the code "@ 2 @" appears on the address label. When you see this, fill out the Change Form and send it in.

Publicity for national sales: There are other ways to find out about the national DPDS sales besides the mailing list. Often they are mentioned in the Department of Commerce's *Commerce Business Daily*. This is available directly from the Department of Commerce for a hefty subscription price of $105 per year, or it's viewable for free at your local chamber of commerce office. Generally speaking, the best single source of information about the national sales is still the IFB mailing list.

GOODS OFFERED AT NATIONAL DPDS SALES

Before you start writing them off, however, you should know a few more facts about the national sales. What is most distinctive about them is their scale. These are the sales by which the Defense Department cleans out its surplus of bulk items, things either large in size, such as a bulldozer or a battleship, or large in quantity, such as hundreds of pairs of combat boots. Items and quantities this big mean equally big prices, and bidders able to offer the kind of money— hundreds of thousands or even millions of dollars—it takes to buy these goods.

Although the private, solo buyer can find things to buy at these sales, he will find in reading the catalog that whatever the selling method used—sealed-bid, spot-bid, or auction—the scale of the items offered is geared toward the big-quantity buyer: salvage companies, army surplus buyers, heavy-equipment companies, construction companies and parts dealers, for example.

Three categories–Three regions: Each of the three regional headquarters—located in Memphis, Tennessee; Columbus, Ohio; and Ogden, Utah—has a national sale each month of the year. However, in a given month, each regional headquarters is selling surplus goods from only one of the three categories mentioned earlier: vehicular, aircraft components and electrical components or miscellaneous. For example, in December 1979, the Memphis DPDR (Defense Department Disposal Region) was handling all national sales in the vehicular category, the Ogden DPDR was taking care of aircraft components and electrical components, and the Columbus DPDR was selling all miscellaneous goods. The following month, the Columbus DPDR took over the vehicles, Memphis had the aircraft components and electrical components, and Ogden handled the miscellaneous group.

As explained at the end of this chapter, there are overseas offices and a special office at Portsmouth, Rhode Island, that handles surplus vessels; the Ogden office handles all surplus aircraft.

Sales conditions: These national sales may be either sealed-bid, spot-bid, or auction sales. You have to appear at the auctions in person and come up with at least 20 percent of what you put in for a winning bid that same day. The property won't be released to you until you have paid off the remaining 80 percent. You don't have to put in a personal appearance at a sealed-bid sale, but you usually have to send in 20 percent of your bid along with the completed bid form. You may or may not have to put in a deposit at a spot-bid sale. The Invitation for Bid you get will tell you that information.

Publication of selling prices: In the wake of every sealed-bid offering or auction, the DPDS puts out a list of successful bidders listing all the items, listing the successful bidders for each item, including names and addresses, and most importantly for you, listing the selling price as well. The list is automatically available to every person who has submitted a bid on that sale. Such lists are extremely valuable because they will give you some sense of how much money is paid out for the types of items that interest you. Save these lists. They will come in handy for a price-comparison guide when you get ready to do some serious bidding, especially at sealed-bid sales.

They're big: In the end, the simplest thing to remember about national sales is that they are big—big in quantities, and big in the amounts of money paid out to the government. One motor vehicle auction held by the Ogden, Utah, regional headquarters had close to 400 items up for sale. You could get anything from a gas tanker truck (capacity 1,200 gallons) to fill with high-test and park in your backyard, to ten-ton garbage trucks, to quarter-ton pickup trucks. Originally valued at $10,653, the tanker, listed in fair condition, went for $4,750. Another buyer got a quarter-ton 1971 pickup truck,

```
90.    TRUCK, UTILITY:  ¼ ton, 1971, USe:
       CJ5, Serial J2F83-09579, 4 x 4, 6 cylinder
       gasoline engine, wheel size 15", 12 volt electrical
       system.  USMC 255652.
       Outside - Vehicle Lot - Used - Fair Condition
       Total Cost:  $3044
       Est. Total Wt.  2500 lbs.                    1 EACH
                                            PAGE NO.  9
```

originally valued at $3,044 and listed in fair condition, for $1,750. These were not bad buys but were not typical of the auction in that they were bought singly. Also at the same auction was a buyer who handed over about $150,000 for, among other things, 15 semi-trailers and a variety of trucks, bulldozer blades, tractors and one bus. That is the level of bidding you will often find at a national sale.

LOCAL DPDS SALES

DPDS officials generally agree that the national sales are primarily designed for big-money buyers who have a use for a private fleet of military surplus vehicles or a warehouse full of used uniforms. The average bargain hunter is much more apt to find items of interest to him at the local sales.

The local sale, which may be a sealed-bid, spot-bid, or open-bid sale, is held at a local Defense Department Disposal Office (DPDO). This is where you will consistently find the single item—the lone desk, typewriter or van—rather than huge quantities. The competition is not nearly as high-powered as at national sales, and you'll be able to pick a nearby location to shop around.

FINDING OUT ABOUT LOCAL SALES

Local sales are not as systematized as national sales. Generally, there is no set schedule for them—excess property is sold as it accumulates —and there is no sophisticated mailing list with prospective bidders ready to go for every sale.

The DPDO does, however, maintain local sale mailing lists of a general sort and will send you notices of local sales in your area. Most often these notifications will be in the form of a one-page press release with a description like: "Among the 424 items to be offered will be pickup trucks, office machines, clothing, refrigerators, furniture, ammo cans, hand trucks, drums, steel containers and desks." The notification will also tell you when you can view the items and where you can find a complete list to read over for the auction or spot-bid sale.

The mailings: To find out about local sales, simply write to the Defense Property Disposal Region headquarters that has your part of the country within its jurisdiction. (You'll find a list of the headquarters' addresses and the states they include at the end of this chapter and in the Auction Pages.) Tell the regional headquarters you would like to be notified of the local sales in its region. In a few weeks, your name will be included on its lists. You won't get on the lists by writing DPDS headquarters in Battle Creek. That office handles only national sales. If you're near the borderline between two regions, you should write to the headquarters in each region to get on both lists. Staying on these mailing lists is usually a little easier than staying on the national lists. Regions only occasionally purge their local lists, and you don't have to keep notifying them to keep your name active.

REQUEST FOR DEPARTMENT OF DEFENSE SURPLUS PROPERTY BIDDERS APPLICATION		
APPLICATION FOR: Type or Print Mailing Address		
U.S. REGIONS ☐	PACIFIC REGION ☐	EUROPE REGION ☐
Name of Firm or Individual:		
ATTN:		
P. O. Box or Street Address:		
City and State:		Zip Code:

GOODS OFFERED AT LOCAL DPDS SALES •

DPDS sales, like GSA sales, are a real opportunity for the bargain hunter—but again like GSA sales, they are not giveaways, and there are some foolish but durable myths about them.

Jeeps: The single, greatest myth, as is mentioned in the GSA chapter as well, is the cheap jeep. Not only are decent, drivable jeeps few and far between (one DPDS official admitted that he would never buy a surplus jeep for transportation), many of them were declared downright dangerous vehicles a number of years ago. The Department of Transportation forbade the government to sell the series 151 Korean

War vintage jeep for anything but scrap. The reason: they were involved in more than 7,000 road accidents between 1967 and 1970. They were too top heavy and tipped over a lot. Of course, if you want a scrap jeep, the DPDS is a fine source.

War toys: And the other stories such as buying your own tank or battleship? Unless you're an ally of the U.S. government, or someone of the stature of John Wayne (he had his own destroyer), you cannot buy potentially lethal military surplus, unless it is demilitarized—bureaucratese for cutting the tank, battleship or jet fighter into scrap metal.

How about owning a howitzer? "Not possible," says the Defense Department. You can get items that are loosely categorized such as accessories for weapons—rifle butts, ammo boxes and cans—but, you can't get the weapons themselves. If the Marines don't need a batch of rifles, and no other qualified recipient can be found for them through the ritual of reutilization, then the rifles will be broken up and sold for scrap metal. There was a time when the DPDS did sell surplus rifles. During the early 1960s, it sold off-bolt action, single-shot Remington rifles, which are now collector's items. But it won't do that anymore.

What you can buy: That still leaves a tremendous variety of goods for the marketplace. By one official's estimate, the DPDS has anywhere from 1,500 to 1,700 sales in an average year, and it sells off goods originally valued at around $1.5 billion. Somewhere in this mountain of surplus goods is something for you. Given that kind of turnover, there should be something you could find at a DPDS sealed-bid, spot-bid or auction sale.

Although you might not be able to get the aircraft carrier of your dreams, you can buy a tugboat or two, if you have the money. One shrewd bidder managed to buy two tugboats and two steel-hulled landing craft, all for a little less than $119,000. Or you could pick up a 10-year-old river patrol boat originally worth $15,000, for a little over $6,000 as one buyer did in another sealed-bid sale. Of course, it wasn't in the best of shape. It was listed in poor condition and was missing, among other things, its engines, transmission, clutch, bilge pump and navigation equipment. Yet, to the right buyer, it's still a bargain, especially when—at current prices—a new one might cost two or three times the original $15,000.

Though you can't buy war toys, you can buy intact planes, for example, that have nonmilitary equivalents available in the civilian world. At one recent DPDS surplus aircraft sale, you couldn't find any Phantom Jets, but if you had the money, you could send in a sealed bid on a 10-passenger, twin-engine Albatross amphibious plane; or a mammoth C-119, better known as the "Flying Boxcar," which is able to carry up to 12 tons of whatever you want to put inside; or you could try for a smaller plane, such as a 20-year-old Beechcraft Seminole which can carry a crew of two and two passengers. The real conversation pieces of the lot were the Boeing KC-97 Strato-freighters—long-range, high-altitude flying tankers used to refuel other aircraft in mid-flight. (As part of the sales conditions, you would have to remove the refueling tanks and the fuel boom before you took the plane away.)

Among the items that tend to be good buys, according to Paul Tulaino, who heads up the DPDO in Philadelphia, are trucks (from 3/4-ton to 5-ton), construction equipment, such as bulldozers and graders and much of the electronic gear that go on sale. Some of it is a little out of date but perfectly functional. Although the condition of them varies, vans and elongated station wagons, called carryalls, are also tremendously popular items at government sales as well. You should be aware that a public sale is the end of the line for a Defense

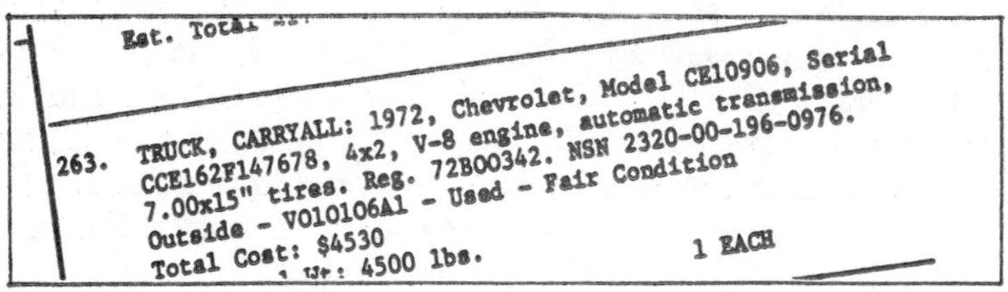

Est. Total ...

263. TRUCK, CARRYALL: 1972, Chevrolet, Model CE10906, Serial CCE162F147678, 4x2, V-8 engine, automatic transmission, 7.00x15" tires. Reg. 72B00342. NSN 2320-00-196-0976. Outside - VO10106A1 - Used - Fair Condition
Total Cost: $4530   1 EACH
         Wt: 4500 lbs.

Department vehicle. Typically, the vehicles are *very* used and often 10 to 15 years old by the time you get a chance to bid on them.

At a typical sale held at the DPDS office in Philadelphia, bidders saw the following get sold: one steel desk for $27; a batch of electric typewriters selling individually from $40 to $50; electric calculators for $30; an International Harvester bus (year-1967) for $220; one drafting board with a see-through top for $37; and one index card filing cabinet for $35. Appliances like stoves and refrigerators when they surface at the sale typically will go for between $10 and $50. If you don't find what you want at one sale, be patient. It may appear at the next.

At one of her first auctions, DPDS employee Pat Gray, the first woman to become an auctioneer for the DPDS, had to auction off

5,000 pounds of rubber-coated wire that had been considered totally valueless as scrap. A farmer in South Carolina, where the auction was held, bought the wire and used it to make a corral for his horses. Another item that proved to be a big seller was missile covers, which people were using to make culverts. In one DPDS auction, a buyer even bought the launch pad where John Glenn took off in Mercury 3 for his famous around-the-world orbital flight.

Bargains may surface where you least expect them. A 10-year-old girl found this out when she saw a newspaper ad for a local auction at a Marine base near her home in California. One of the featured items was a 11-year-old palomino horse that had been part of the Marine's mounted color guard.

Afflicted with a split hoof, the horse, known as Neon Moon, could not be ridden—that, in combination with his age, made him auctionable material. The young girl, Sheila Schwedes, showed the newspaper photo of the horse to her parents, who decided the animal might be worth looking over. They already had four horses and felt they had room for another.

The day of the auction, they drove to the base to look at the horse. There, in the middle of everything from surplus military lockers to some shipping cases ready to go up on the auction block, stood Neon Moon. The Schwedes family bid for the horse at a low price of $280. A check into the horse's background showed that it was registered with both the Quarter Horse Association and Palomino Association, and in all likelihood was actually worth between $500 and $800.

The value wasn't really what mattered to the Schwedes. Getting it for their daughter was what counted. With a special corrective shoe, the horse's hoof healed, and after a few months, young Sheila was able to ride the retired Marine horse. The auctioneer was pleased with the sale too. "It was better than sending him to the glue factory," he said.

Portrait of a DPDS shopper: The DPDS shopping list is too varied to permit a prediction of what will interest you. What you shop for will be guided by your interest. But I can at least tell the story of Robert Truax, who used the DPDS to further a project—an obsession, some would say—that would otherwise have been impossible for him. As was mentioned in the beginning of the chapter, Truax has, what is even for these sophisticated times, a far-out dream: to send the first privately launched astronaut 50 miles straight up into space, to the outer edge of our atmosphere. If anyone is likely to do it, Truax is. He organized and directed U.S. Navy rocket research in World War II and was heavily involved in the Navy's space program in pre-

SEE INSIDE FRONT ...
FOR FURTHER INFORMATION AND/...

3. Co

****
ITEMS 1 THRU 4 ARE LOCATED AT 753RD RADAR SQ., SAUTE STE
MARIE, MICHIGAN
****

1. TRANSMITTER SET: AN FRT 49, Consisting of:

2 Ea. - Transmitting set, electronic guidance signals, ITT, AN FRT 49, with transmitting group AO 2630/FRT 49 and radio frequency amplifier AM 2840/FRT 49. NSN 5895-00-805-6526.

2 Ea. - Cooler, liquid electron tube dummy load, Sheldon Engineering, HD 400/FRT 49, Serials 19, 20. NSN 5895-00-789-2335.

2 Ea. - Power Supply, PP2538/FRT 49, Serials 19, 20, ITT. NSN 5895-00-804-9447.

2 Ea. - Control, transmitter, mfr. unknown, C3185/FRT 49, Serials 19, 20. NSN 5895-00-771-4528.

1 Ea. - Tube, Eimac, Serial 1065. NSN 5960-00-628-7539.

Parts missing including antenna and cables.
Inside - Used - Poor Condition   1 LOT
Total cost $2410
Est. total wt. 25,000 lbs.
Following Articles apply:
AI: Military Munitions List Items
     radioactive Material
          Products   (PCBs), See

NASA days; he also helped direct the Air Force's space program. After he retired from the military in the 1960s, he continued to work on designing rockets, this time for aerospace corporations. He again retired from that work but continued to work on his rockets as a private designer. His last noted accomplishment, in addition to having come up with the idea of the Polaris submarine-launched missile as well as having been one of the seminal minds behind the Mercury space program, was the rocket-powered skycycle that sent Evel Knievel zooming partway across the Snake River Canyon in 1974. Now he's ready for the most dramatic solo flight since Lindbergh flew to Paris: he wants to send a civilian into space in one of his own handmade rockets.

He's already working on a model called the Volksrocket, a sleek, 24-foot-long, one-passenger bullet which will send its passenger shooting spaceward under the power of four liquid-fueled Atlas rocket engines. Truax already has someone who has invested $100,000 as partial payment toward the round-trip fare on the rocket. A tortilla entrepreneur, he is an amateur pilot and skydiver who would like to be the first privately launched astronaut. Close behind is another contributor and contender for that title, the stage manager of the Beach Boys.

The ride will be short—only ten minutes—and will consist of sketching an invisible parabola in the sky over the Pacific about 50 miles high. A drogue parachute will open during the descent at about 100,000 feet, and the main parachute will take hold at about 20,000 feet. Like the more renowned Space Shuttle, Truax's Volksrocket will be a reusable craft—just fuel it up and fire it off again. Unlike the Shuttle, it will be made of recycled rocket parts.

And where does a private rocket builder go for parts? "Everything on that vehicle is surplus that came either directly or indirectly from Defense Property Disposal Services," Truax says. Some parts he bought from the DPDS himself, and others he got from salvagers who had bought the parts from the DPDS. "Most of this stuff goes back into the civilian economy," he explains. "That's why you can buy some of these items at a fraction of the cost—nobody else wants them."

As examples of what he got and what he paid, he gave one reporter a tour of some of his homemade rocket pieces. He has an extremely sophisticated oscillograph he uses to monitor pressures in different areas of the rocket. The kind he uses was originally used in B-52s to constantly make sure all was well inside the H-bombs the planes carried. Brand new, they cost $14,000. His was $75. Another rather sophisticated piece is the inertial platform unit, an extremely delicate creation of aerospace engineering used to measure such things as roll, pitch, altitude and longitude. It took $25 million, Truax likes to point out, to develop them for the famous X-15 rocket plane. He got three of them for $35 apiece.

The total price tag for his rocket is around $100,000. "I bought some stuff I never used," he said. How much would it have cost to build the rocket from brand-new parts? There's really no way of knowing, but Truax thinks he's saved a minimum of $100,000.

Truax says he bought most of his parts in national sealed-bid sales, often bidding for the parts sight-unseen. As previously explained, in every Invitation for Bid that is sent to you on a national sale, you are told where an item is, so you can go and look at it; you are also told the name and phone number of the disposal officer in charge of that item. "I either rely on the description in the government book," says Truax, "or I get on the phone and talk to the disposal officers. They're usually very helpful. They've gone out to the warehouse for me to check on an item and answer my questions about it."

TIPS ON SHOPPING THE DPDS

Buying surplus goods from the Defense Department is a fairly simple affair for the private buyer, but here are some bits of advice culled from DPDS officials that can help make it as easy as possible.

Shop the local sales: To get what you want, spend more of your time and energy shopping the local sales. The lots tend to be smaller—single items—whereas lots of national sales can involve large quantities and very expensive goods.

Pay attention: Always inspect or, at the very least, call a DPDS custodian about an item you are interested in. Remember all of what the DPDS sells has usually been rejected by many other agencies and organizations before it is offered to you for sale. For your own protection and peace of mind, get as realistic an appraisal as possible of what you might buy. The DPDS does guarantee the descriptions in its Invitations for Bids. In other words, everything it says is on that truck or that boat or that airplane will be on it when you buy it. However, often the descriptions are not very detailed, since they are brief.

Sign and seal: Two of the most common mistakes people make on sealed-bid sales are forgetting to sign the bid form and not enclosing a bid deposit. If you forget to do either, you may as well not send in the bid, since it won't be officially recognized. Always double check before you send it off.

Set limits: One of the most common mistakes people make at auctions is to bid themselves into debt by going higher than they had planned. If this happens to you, and you simply walk off and leave your item behind, you will be sent a notice of default after the time has lapsed for pickup (usually five working days); you will then be given an additional 15 days to pay the balance, with a penalty thrown in. If you still don't respond, you will lose your bid deposit, which is usually 20 percent. To avoid this whole mess, simply follow the rules every good auction goer follows. Set yourself a limit and don't be swept beyond that in the enthusiasm and excitement of the auction. If you're really serious about your bid, make sure you have cash enough for a 20 percent deposit to make your bid good.

Read: Always read over the Invitation for Bids for your particular sale. Conditions of sales may vary. They will always be spelled out in the back of the IFB: the size of the deposit, if any is required; how the material has to be disposed of; when the property has to be removed; how much help the government will give you with removing it; what specific items (lines to moor boats, skids on which the equipment is sitting, etc.) are *not* included in the sale.

Take it home: Lastly, know how you're going to remove what you've bought. The government does not deliver, and although it will help you to load items in your car or truck, for example, it does not provide any kind of elaborate service to get that truck or boat off its property. Once you've bought something, how you get it home is basically your problem.

DPDS REGIONAL HEADQUARTERS

For administrative purposes, the Defense Property Disposal Service divides the United States into three parts, each with its own headquarters. These are the offices to write to for information about local sales. The Ogden, Utah, office includes most of the western states. The Memphis office takes in practically all of the south and part of the west, and the Columbus, Ohio, office covers the midwest and northeast. In addition, there is a special office in Portsmouth, Rhode Island, that deals exclusively in surplus vessels from rowboats to aircraft carriers. They may be docked anywhere in the world, but they will be sold through the Portsmouth office. In addition to being a regional headquarters, the Ogden office is also the exclusive DPDS outlet for surplus aircraft from all over the world.

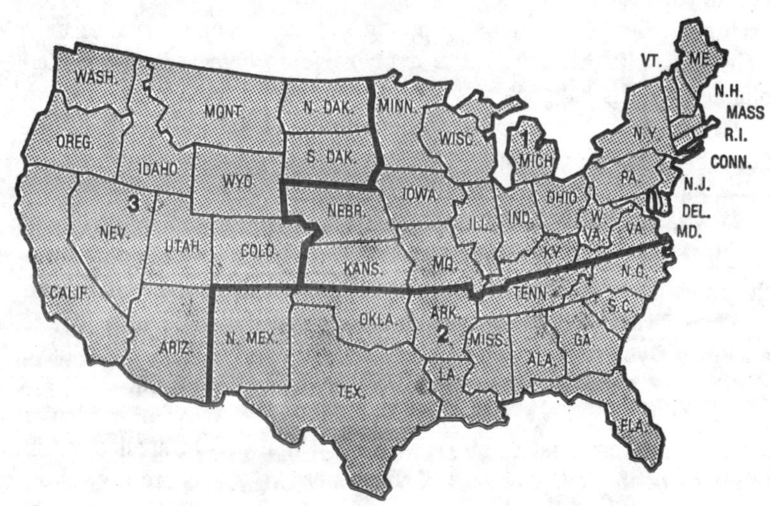

Region One: *DPDR-Columbus, Attn: DPDR-CMB*
3900 E. Broad St., Columbus, OH 43215

Region Two: *DPDR-Memphis, Attn: DPDR-MMB*
2163 Airways Blvd., Memphis, TN 38114

Region Three: *DPDR-Ogden, Attn: DPDR-OMB*
500 W. 12th St., Ogden, UT 84401

DPDR-Pacific, Attn: DPDR-PM Box 211 Pearl City, HI 96782

DPDR-Europe, APO, New York 09633

DPDR-Ship Sales Office, P.O. Box 100, Portsmouth, RI 02871

CUSTOMS, THE POST OFFICE AND THE IRS

Although they were not set up to be in the auction business, the U.S. Customs Service, the U.S. Post Office, and the Internal Revenue Service often find themselves in the role of institutional auctioneers. Goods seized for nonpayment of import duties, packages that end up in the dead-letter office, or property seized and sold by the IRS to pay back taxes frequently end up on the government auction block. If you attend these auctions, you will find an array of sometimes exotic, sometimes bizarre, but always interesting goods for sale.

THE CUSTOMS AUCTION

Every year at locations all over the country, from New York to San Francisco, Chicago to Tampa, the U.S. Customs Service, guardian of our country's borders, auctions off millions of dollars' worth of merchandise which it gets through enforcing our customs laws and regulations. Since its job is primarily to enforce laws and not warehouse illegal or unclaimed goods, it is constantly cleaning house, selling off what can be sold and destroying what can't (goods like perishables and drugs). If you get to any of the 43 district offices of the U.S. Customs Service scattered all over the country (see the listing in the Auction Pages), you have a chance to buy what is sold at one of this government agency's auctions.

What turns up at a Customs auction includes much that is weird or wonderful. Where else could you get a $227,000 tugboat for $29,000; an assortment of gold-plated sterling-silver cigarette lighters, gold pocket watches, and some antique jewelry for $4,400; one Seiko watch for $70; a half-dozen cassette and reel-to-reel tape recorders for $50; a Black and Decker half-inch drill for $20; 20 pairs of men's and children's shoes and sandals for $20; 97 cartons of men's cotton shirts for $16,000; 800 dozen stuffed rabbits for $5,600; 515,000 ballpoint pens for $5,850; 600 plastic acupuncture dummies for $675; 745 cans of quince paste for $1,100; or a 35mm two-reel movie entitled *Death Journey* for $40? And where else could you get the opportunity to bid on other assorted items such as 234 slabs of marble, 20,000 cotton swabs, a bale of unroasted coffee beans, or 875 pounds of human hair?

The typical item at a Customs auction almost defies description, but the goods can be roughly categorized. One group is made up of items beyond the financial reach and the interest of the average private bidder. This is the big-bid item like the steel-hulled trawler that went for $70,000 at one auction or the mammoth lots of stuffed bunny rabbits or of men's shirts.

More within reach are the small-batch items, such as the cartons of appraisers' samples that often appear at the Customs auctions, or a box of 30 ballpoint pens for a couple of dollars. The third group, also of interest, includes odd and usually interesting lots of individual items that surface at these auctions; items such as an 18K gold pin and a cultured pearl necklace, a neatly boxed 300X microscope, or a lone music box. They are all waiting to be discovered and bought.

LOT NO.	G.O. NO.	DESCRIPTION	QUANTITY	FOREIGN VALUE	DOMESTIC VALUE
82	6467	Ladies Wearing Apparel, Suede	1 ctn	60.00	180.00
83	6388	Intergrated Circuits	1 ctn	850.00	2400.00
84	6400	Hibachi	1 ctn	15.00	45.00
86	6513	Three test kits for Antinuclear Antibodies	1 ctn	90.00	90.00
87	6499	Hydropneumatic Accumulator	1 case	50.00	100.00
88	6477	Toy Samples—Children's Vehicle	1 case	12.00	25.00
89	0640	Paper Bags	1 ctn	5.00	8.00
90	0812	Ingition System	1 ctn		300.00
91	0767	Auto Radios	2 pieces	40.00	120.00
92	0090	Electric Motor & Parts	1 ctn	360.00	360.00
93	0109	Cotton Cloth	1 ctn	80.00	110.00

HOW CUSTOMS GETS ITS GOODS

Although the kind of merchandise the Customs Service puts up for auction varies widely, the reasons for their getting possession of it do not. U.S. Customs gets what it eventually auctions for two reasons: because the merchandise is considered *abandoned,* or because of *seizure.*

Abandoned merchandise: Generally speaking, abandoned merchandise is anything an owner lets the Customs Service keep rather than pay the import duty. This includes a whole variety of items, from large shipments of imported toys, clothing, or other merchandise for which the person being sent the items refuses to pay the import duty to a loose collection of bottles of wine or liquor which exceed the individual import quota, or even luggage mysteriously left behind by some people. "We get lots of luggage," explains John Driscoll, the officer in charge of sales and seizure for the New York City area. "It's just left behind on docks or ships. We try to find the owners, but generally don't have much luck." Very often the suitcases don't even contain any contraband, just the usual mix of personal effects.

Also lumped in with this general category is a slightly miscellaneous group which includes *appraisers' samples* and the *NCV* (for "no commercial value") group of items. When the Customs Service imposes a duty on a large shipment of goods, its appraisers sometimes take a sample or two from the load to examine in order to estimate the import duty. Often, the importer who provided the appraisers with the sample doesn't ask for the item or items back. In time, that sample is thrown in with a box of other odd samples and is put up for auction. Very often there is a minimum bid asked for the box based on the estimated value of the new sample items inside. What that box contains, according to one U.S. Customs official, could be anything from a fur cape to pairs of shoes to individual bottles of liquor or wine. And it usually sells as a bargain.

The *NCV,* no commercial value, category is the closest thing to junk the Customs Service auctions off. This is a totally random selection of odd items—one shoe, a large swatch of fabric, some odd pieces of silverware—dumped into a large bin and offered for whatever it brings, usually just a few dollars.

Seized goods: Anything involved in breaking the law can be taken and held by the Customs officials and so falls into the category of seized merchandise. This includes clearly illegal items—guns and drugs, for example, which will never get sold—or items implicated in an illegal act. It can be goods that a person failed to declare or whose value was deliberately undervalued. It can be vehicles or other conveyances involved in smuggling operations. Every year the U.S. Customs Service, in cooperation with the Drug Enforcement Administration and the U.S. Coast Guard, seizes hundreds of cars, boats, and airplanes used to transport drugs and other contraband.

Sometimes strange shipments end up in the seized-goods category. California Customs officials found themselves with a shipment of exotic birds on their hands because the shipper had violated certain import laws. The Service, through the San Diego Zoo, cared for the birds during the year it took to thrash out the legalities of seizure and prepare them for sale. Once everything was settled, 65 lots of fire-tufted barbets, hair-crested drongos, greater yellownape woodpeckers,

39.	1 ea Eclectus Parrot	$1,000.00
40.	1 ea White-crested Umbrella Cockatoo *Cacatua alba*	$800.00
41.	1 ea Philippine Red Vented Cockatoo *Cacatua Haematuropygia*	$400.00
42.	1 ea Philippine Red Vented Cockatoo	$400.00

Philippine red-vented cockatoos, and other live samples of exotic bird life were put up for auction.

HOW TO FIND OUT ABOUT CUSTOMS AUCTIONS

No U.S. Customs office has a set auction schedule as such. The frequency of the auctions depends on how much traffic a district handles. The Los Angeles district has auctions four times a year on the average, while the busier New York port has as many as ten a year.

Auctions are publicized differently in different areas. Officials in New York maintain a mailing list of people who have called the office expressing interest in attending an auction. Once an auction is scheduled, they print up a catalog and send it off to these people. The catalog comes complete with information on what items are for sale, where they can be viewed, what minimum bid, if any, there is on each lot of items, and a brief description of each lot as well.

Other districts, San Francisco and Tampa, for example, advertise in the local papers (the Sunday edition) three weekends in a row before the auctions. You can also find out by calling the district office, but there is no general mailing list.

HOW CUSTOMS AUCTIONS ARE RUN

Since what is being sold is not shown during the actual auction, you need a separate opportunity to view the merchandise. Usually two days are set inside before the actual auction for public viewing at a warehouse, a marina (for boats to be auctioned), or a motor pool (for vehicles) at specific hours. When there are large quantities of warehouse goods, some samples will be put out for you to inspect. Catalogs (if there are any) are usually available then.

Bidding: The auction is usually held on the day after the inspection period. How this is done varies from place to place. Some offices use a deposit-paddle method. You register for the auction by putting down a deposit, usually $20 or $25, and receive a numbered paddle. When you want to bid, you raise your paddle. If you don't bid or none of your bids is a top bid, your deposit is refunded. Otherwise it can be applied toward your purchases.

Other districts require no deposit. You simply bid as you would at any auction by making some kind of signal to the auctioneer. Whatever the local procedure, it will be immediately apparent the day you go to the auction.

Prices and payments vary. Some districts set no minimum bids on items except on liquor, and only then to equal the government tax on that quantity of that type of wine or liquor. Others set minimum bids on an item based in part on the assessed domestic value of a specific item or group of items. If there are minimum bids, they are announced in the catalogs and/or by the auctioneer.

Paying: How you pay also varies. Some districts require payment in full the day of the auction. Others will accept a partial payment, 20 or 50 percent of your bid, with the rest payable when you pick up your lot, usually within the next day or two. Confirm this in advance by a call to the local office.

Cash, a cashier's check, or a certified check for your whole bid or the accepted percentage of your bid are always acceptable. Some districts will take a personal check with proper identification for items sold below a certain amount—$500, for example. The money from the sales of big lots especially will be used to reimburse the shipper who transported the goods and got stuck with the bill. What is left over goes into the general government funds.

COMPETITION AT CUSTOMS AUCTIONS

What kind of bidding competition will you face at a Customs auction? Neil Lageman, director of the Tampa, Florida district, says there are four general types of people who come to his sales. First, there are the business people interested in buying the large lots of merchandise: the 22 cases of glassware, the 75 cartons of ladies' blouses, the 52 cartons of men's shirts. Typically their bids run into the thousands and tens of thousands of dollars.

Second are the flea-market people, who may bid on a dozen pairs of shoes or a carton of assorted figurines, mostly small lots of the same item, in the hopes of selling the goods for a slight profit at the next flea market. Third are the bargain hunters—just people who may have spotted something they could use and show up to bid on it. It might be a socket-wrench set they get for $12 or a microscope they manage to nail down for $28.

Fourth are the original owners of what is now up for auction. Every so often someone may deliberately choose not to pay the import duty on some goods and gamble instead that he can get the same shipment for less money at a U.S. Customs auction a year later. There is a story that a shrewd and successful businessman at least once used a tactic like this to import some expensive handmade French gloves.

He specified that his order be broken down into two shipments, one all right-hand gloves, and the other all left-hand gloves. In addition, he requested that they be sent through two different ports of entry. When they arrived in the United States, he did not pay the import duty on them, allowing them to become abandoned merchandise. After a decent interval, they were offered up for auction. As he thought, no one was interested in paying much for a large shipment of one-handed gloves, and he was able to get half the shipment for very little money. Similarly, the other half went as cheaply for him at the auction held in another customs district. In the end, the man and his gloves were reunited for a fraction of what the government would have liked to have seen him pay.

POSTAL SERVICE AUCTIONS

You can get more than just a book of stamps and some postcards from your local post office. In addition to the delivery service that made it famous, the United States Postal Service gets involved in sales as well as deliveries. If you are looking for a government surplus vehicle or some used office furnishings or equipment, or just enjoy the potluck challenge of a random auction, keep the Postal Service in mind. It offers you all three.

BRINGING DEAD PARCELS BACK TO LIFE

Throughout the year key post offices (see the Auction Pages for a complete listing) auction off a variety of goods which did not complete the postal trip from sender to receiver. These end up in the grim-sounding category of dead-letter parcels.

Usually the death of a parcel comes in one of three ways. First, it may be *unclaimed*. The addressee is no longer at a specific address and the sender doesn't want his package back. Second, a parcel gets to the receiver but is refused by him and, once returned to its point of origin, refused by the sender as well. Third, a parcel is undeliverable if the post office cannot figure out who either the sender or the addressee is. This happens if the wrapping or the labels get ripped off a parcel.

In addition to dead parcels, the postal service also finds on its hands damaged goods that had been insured. If an insured item is damaged in transit, the person who insured the parcel asks to be paid, the Postal Service keeps the item once it has paid the claim.

Before it claims possession of dead parcels, however, the Postal Service follows a certain ritual. With undeliverable first- or second-class items it opens the parcel to figure out who the sender or addressee might be. If that does no good, or if the parcel is unclaimed or refused, it may hold it for up to six months before declaring the parcel dead. For third- or fourth-class parcels, the time span is much shorter: 30 days. Once a parcel is dead or, in the case of damaged goods, the insurance on it has been paid, it becomes eligible for the auction block.

HOW TO FIND OUT ABOUT POSTAL SERVICE AUCTIONS

Some Dead Parcel Units make more of an effort than others to publicize their auctions, but they all use a mailing list to let people know about the time and place. Sales are held between four and six times a year depending on the volume of mail handled by the Bulk Mail Centers which the Dead Parcel Branch office serves. How you get on the list will vary. Sometimes all it takes is a phone call to the Dead Parcel Branch of the Claims, Inquiry and Undeliverable Mail Section of a local branch, as in the post office in Bell, California, which services the Los Angeles area. Elsewhere you may fill out a form in their auction catalog, as in New York City, which makes you eligible for one mailed notice of the next auction. A phone call to the Dead Parcel Branch nearest you will, at the very least, get you the date, time, and place of the next auction, and information concerning getting on the mailing list.

Post offices also put up flyers in other post offices in their areas announcing the time and place of an upcoming auction, and some, like the one in Chicago, take out ads in local papers.

In addition, branches have mailing lists designed for people with specific interests. The General Post Office in Philadelphia, for example, periodically sells books and has a special mailing list of people interested in them.

```
20.  Mens Rings, Watches, etc.          _______      56.  Air pots and small chests etc. _______
                                                           2 Shelves
21.  Ladies Mixed Jewelry, etc.         _______      57.  Mixed Speakers, 2 Shelves     _______
22.  Ladies Mixed Jewelry, etc.         _______      58.  Sansui speakers, 2 Shelves    _______
23.  Ladies Mixed Jewelry, etc.         _______      59.  Kenwood speakers, 2 Shelves   _______
24.  Glassware, etc.   2 Shelves        _______      60.  Ladies nite gowns, mixed sizes _______
25.  Glassware, etc.   2 Shelves        _______      61.  Small brass bound chest       _______
26.  Mens Watches                       _______      62.  Mixed Ladies clothing         _______
27.  Mixed Ladies & Mens Watchbands     _______      63.  Hi fi Speakers                _______
28.  Tea Set & Glassware, 2 Shelves     _______      64.  Mixed Mens clothing           _______
29.  Adoration plate, cups & glasses    _______      65.  Folding chairs, stools etc.   _______
        etc - 2 Shelves.                             66.  Pioneer turntable & speaker   _______
30.  Dishes, etc.  2 Shelves            _______      67.  Small chest & Mattress Pad    _______
31.  Adoration plates, glassware etc.   _______           (King size)
        2 Shelves
```

WHAT IS ON THE BLOCK AT POSTAL SERVICE AUCTIONS

The Postal Service will find itself with a jumble of items on its hands, but, to clear out the supply of items it's accumulated, it groups similar items—records, books, women's clothing—together in single lots. This draws higher bids (it likes to start bidding at around $10) and helps move the items very quickly. At a Postal Service auction you'll notice how quickly the merchandise moves—no small talk, no chatter. In the three, four, or five hours it takes to run an auction, hundreds of unseen items will come and go at the rate of about one every 30 seconds.

The merchandise: What are you likely to see at a postal auction? If it can be sent through the mail, it can end up here. Generally you will find several lots of records, books, clothing, stereo equipment, and some jewelry. Specifically, these were some items at a recent auction: 200 Pom Pom yarn kits (sold for $34); a bin of assorted records ($340); 458 silver dimes ($380); 23 Morgan silver dollars dated 1878 to 1885 ($420); five inexpensive digital watches ($26); one man's 46-long leather jacket ($40); 24 Calvin Klein shirts ($44); one Kenwood amplifier ($110); four sets of stainless-steel tableware ($80); a Sansui AM/FM receiver ($190); four Kosta crystal candle holders ($80); six Waterford crystal glasses ($160); one original Miró print ($3,000).

Although you may not find a Miró print or Waterford crystal at every auction, you will find items similar to the other lots on this list.

```
            WOULD YOU LIKE TO BE ON OUR MAILING LIST?

    If you wish to be notified of our next sale, please fill out the form
    below, and give it to one of our employees, or mail it to the Postmaster,
    Mail Classification, Main Post Office, Room 125, Memphis, Tennessee 38101.



                        PLEASE PRINT
                        ____________


    NAME: _______________________________________________

  . ADDRESS: ____________________________________________

    CITY: _________________ STATE: __________ ZIP CODE: ________
```

Competition: Where you have large quantities of items you will also find bulk buyers who are themselves dealers in one kind of merchandise or another, or who are working directly for a store. These dealers are stiff competition and sometimes drive prices up. They don't dominate the auction. Individual buyers like yourself are usually in the majority. Estimates from post offices around the country show that between 60 and 70 percent of the bidding audience is comprised of private buyers.

VIEWING AND BUYING

A typical mail auction notice will be a white postcard stating the date, time, and place (usually a room in the General Post Office Building) of the auction and the time you can view the items. Goods don't appear at the actual auction itself. All the auctioning is done from a list of items in the catalog, so you have to inspect what is available beforehand.

```
              UNITED STATES POSTAL SERVICE
       CLAIMS, INQUIRY AND UNDELIVERABLE MAIL SECTION
                 NEW YORK, NEW YORK 10001

   The Postmaster, New York, New York announces an Auction
   Sale of unclaimed merchandise of various descriptions on
   Tuesday,                   in Room 909 at 341 Ninth Avenue
   Morgan Mail Faci...  , New York, New York 10001.

   The auction will begin at 9:00 A.M. and continue until
   all lots are sold.

   Articles may be inspected in the basement of the General
   Post Office, 33rd Street and 8th Avenue, New York, New
   York 10001 on Monday,                        from 9:00 A.M.
   to 3:00 P.M. ONLY.
             THE PUBLIC IS INVITED TO ATTEND
   ALL MERCHANDISE MUST BE REMOVED WITHIN 48 HOURS OF THE
                     DATE OF AUCTION
   PATRONS ARE REQUIRED TO FURNISH THEIR OWN CONTAINERS FOR
             THE REMOVAL OF MERCHANDISE
```

Usually a separate day is set aside for people to view the items scheduled for sale. At other times the viewing is the day of the auction, with inspection possible from 8:00 to 10:00 in the morning, for example, and the auction from 10:00 to 3:00 p.m.

The basic rules and regulations covering Postal Service auctions are uniform throughout the country, but the procedures of the auctions themselves are not. In Chicago, for example, bidders pay a $25 registration fee and get a numbered paddle which they use as their bidding tool and identification. In Memphis, bidders pay no registration fee and have no paddles. When they want to bid, they simply hold their auction catalogs high in the air.

One aspect that is uniform is how you pay. The only forms of payment the Postal Service will accept are cash, certified check, cashier's check, and postal money order. No personal checks allowed. You must also pay as soon as possible after your winning bid has been accepted—at least before the end of the auction, and sometimes within an hour of your bid's being accepted.

AUCTIONS OF SURPLUS POSTAL SERVICE EQUIPMENT

Periodically the Postal Service auctions off surplus office equipment through one of its 28 Procurement Services Offices scattered around the country. (See the Auction Pages for their locations.) It disposes of a variety of unneeded items—desks, chairs, typewriters, adding machines, calculators, vacuum cleaners, even an occasional conveyor belt.

These auctions tend to be sporadic. They're held only when enough items accumulate to justify an auction. As an example, the Philadelphia post office has these auctions about two or three times a year on the average. The post office serving the Los Angeles area has them twice a year.

To find out about these auctions, there is a mailing list you can get on just by calling the Procurement Services Office. Offices also take out newspaper ads and try to get the auction covered as a story by local radio and television stations. Occasionally auctions of surplus equipment are also held at the same time as Dead Parcel Branch auctions to take advantage of the existing crowds.

Procedures are similar to regular dead-parcel auctions. You bid with a paddle but may not be asked to pay a deposit. In these auctions the individual has more of an advantage than at the dead-parcel sales. The reason is there is an even smaller percentage of bulk buyers here. Postal officials estimate 90 percent of the bidding crowd will be private individuals like yourself. Although there are minimum bids set, the postal service is more interested in selling the equipment than getting the minimum. At an average auction as much as 90 percent of what is up for bid will be sold. Prices are not ironclad and fluctuate with the turnout of the crowd. One postal employee, as one example, says he has seen electric typewriters go for as little as $50 and as much as $200. Your best ally in these auctions, as in all auctions, is patience. If you don't get what you want, go back and try again.

VEHICLES FROM THE POSTAL SERVICE

As you will see in the other sections of this book, one of the most durable myths around is the one about the cheap surplus jeep. There is really only one place you can get a safe, drivable jeep. And it is not the Department of Defense or the General Services Administration. It's the Postal Service.

Before you read on you should know that the Postal Service ordinarily offers its surplus vehicles for sale at fixed prices. But auctions and other bid sales do happen. If a post office loses the lease to its garage space, it may be forced to move its excess vehicles as quickly as possible, usually by a spot-bid sale. In Chicago, the Post Office uses a paddle auction method to sell its vehicles. It posts a minimum bid on each vehicle and requires the winning bidder to put at least a 10 percent down payment on his vehicle to hold it for him. The buyer then has seven days after the auction to pay in full for his vehicle and pick it up.

Fixed-price sales: Since you may become an afficionado of Postal Service sales and auctions, however, you might be interested in knowing a little about this new (since 1977) selling role of the U.S. Postal Service.

The service has a specific formula for computing the useful lifespan of its vehicles. The formula takes into consideration such variables as how many miles a vehicle has been driven, how often it's had to be repaired, and what kind of condition it's in now. When the formula indicates a vehicle has reached the end of its useful lifespan for Postal Service purposes, it is put up for sale.

Vehicles that fall in this category are the small delivery jeeps, the one-ton trucks (the vanlike vehicles you see picking up mail from boxes), and cars and trucks of other sizes as well, such as quarter-ton and pickup trucks.

Before offering the vehicle for sale, Postal Service mechanics do a complete overhaul, giving the vehicle a tuneup, a new paint job with government issue paint, sometimes even a new set of tires. They make any repairs or adjustments needed to render the vehicle safe to drive.

Once this is done, the Postal Service determines a fair market price for a similar vehicle in similar condition. Then the vehicle is offered for sale.

Finding out about vehicle sales: Unlike the auctions of dead parcels, auctions of vehicles are not the province of specific post offices. If you are interested in finding out about these sales, the simplest thing to do is call your local post office and ask the number of the nearest Postal Service Vehicle Maintenance Facility. This is where the vehicles will be refurbished for sale, and that is where you would go to

inspect them. Some post offices do maintain a mailing list and will notify you when there are vehicles for sale.

Guarantees: The Postal Service makes no guarantees for its vehicles. You will be taking as much of a chance as you would in buying a used vehicle from any reputable dealer. This does not mean the Postal Service is irresponsible. If your jeep should break down a mile from the facility or has a serious mechanical condition that should have been discovered and corrected in routine maintenance, the Postal Service will do the necessary repairs for free or even refund the money paid.

Prices: Most of the people who go to vehicle sales are private buyers like yourself, and the vehicles they favor the most are the one-ton truck (the large vanlike vehicle) and the jeep. According to Vehicle Maintenance Facilities surveyed all over the country, jeeps sell for anywhere between $500 and $2,000, with the average price hovering around $1,300. The one-ton trucks, which people use for everything from small moving vans to rolling hot-dog stands, bring in anywhere from $1,100 to $2,000. Cars fluctuate widely depending on the size and condition; they've been priced anywhere from $900 to $2,000.

Attending a vehicle sale: When you go to the facility, you will find the vehicle there with asking price attached. At the very least you can get to see the vehicle in action by having a Postal Service employee drive it for you. In some instances you may be allowed to take a short test drive within the boundaries of the facility itself. There is also a repair record for the vehicle available for you to look over.

Although there is a fixed price, it is not rigid. The Postal Service may negotiate, especially if sales have been slow and it wants to clear its lots.

Whatever the final price, you must pay in full with either cash, cashier's check, or certified check by the time you pick it up, which is within the week.

INTERNAL REVENUE SERVICE AUCTIONS

One of the always interesting, albeit sporadic, auction holders is the agency we all remember on April 15, the Internal Revenue Service. In principle, the job of the IRS is a simple one: collect the taxes owed the U.S. government. In fact, it gets a little complicated if someone cannot or will not pay.

In the bitter end, the IRS may seize and sell off at auction the property of someone who doesn't meet his tax payments. That is when you get your chance to bid on the goods. They are anything the IRS feels would bring in enough money to reimburse the government for the money owed. In recent years the IRS has auctioned off yachts, the summer home of at least one famous writer, the patent rights of a medical instrument company, and the cameras in a camera store belonging to a delinquent taxpayer. Before it gets to that point, the IRS follows a prescribed legal ritual of giving the tax debtor a second (or sometimes a third and fourth) chance.

HOW THE IRS GETS THE GOODS

The IRS is primarily organized to collect money, not hold auctions. For that reason it is willing to work out a series of arrangements with someone delinquent in his employment or income taxes short of grabbing and selling off property.

Once it's determined how much an individual owes, the IRS may work out a time-payment plan to let the taxpayer give back his money in installments. Or it may let the taxpayer (or in this instance the nontaxpayer) sell some property himself to raise the money to pay off the taxes. It is only after such arrangements have failed that the IRS will go through the complicated legal maneuvering it takes to seize a person's property.

Even after it does seize something, the IRS does not automatically prepare it for an auction. Sometimes the act of seizure is done to give the taxpayer an indication of how serious the IRS is about collecting its money; the IRS in effect uses the seized item as a kind of legal hostage for the payment.

As a last resort the IRS will get ready to sell, either at an auction or sealed-bid sale, what it has seized. Like any creditor, the agency prefers to follow the simplest path. It prefers to seize whatever can be taken and sold most easily. Given the choice of seizing your car, for example, or your patent rights on an invention, the IRS would go after the car because there are fewer legal headaches involved.

IRS agents follow two general guidelines in selecting what to seize. One is the forced-sale value of an item—what price something could reasonably expect to bring at an auction or public sale. This is not the same as the item's fair market value—that is, what it is worth. The forced-sale value is usually less.

The other feature of a piece of property they consider carefully is the owner's equity in it. They first go after something owned completely by the taxpayer, not shared in ownership with someone else. They want something in which the taxpayer actually has financial interest. To seize a boat that is totally financed, for example, would be an exercise in futility, since it is more a property of the finance company or bank than of the person using it. For this reason, the IRS will research the financial background of a piece of property, especially real property—land or buildings—to find out just how much the taxpayer really owns and how much of it may be subject to liens from other creditors. If there are other creditors, the IRS wants to make sure to establish that it is the creditor with first claim on the property. That established, the IRS then moves in and seizes.

In nearly nine out of ten cases, the seizure alone is enough to prompt the taxpayer to come up with the money for back taxes. In that tenth case, the government sets a minimum bid on the property— the least amount of money it expects from the sale—and offers the property for auction or sealed-bid sale.

Setting sails: What would they sell? In the San Francisco area, IRS agents seized a car and a boat belonging to one Hakeem Abdul Rasheed, self-proclaimed founder of the Church of Hakeem. The car was no ordinary car but a Rolls-Royce, and the boat was a 102-foot yacht valued at around $900,000.

The IRS auctioned off the boat, named either the *Gallant Lady 6* or the *Rasheed Academy Yacht,* depending on the source, to a wealthy Texan for a bargain $500,000. Considering that the yacht was worth nearly twice that amount, and that the IRS had to pay out approximately $83,000 to store and maintain it, the amount of money it gained was just a fraction of what the yacht was worth on the open market. And that is why the IRS prefers to persuade the taxpayer to pay directly rather than to try to recoup its money by an auction sale.

Diamond Betsy's Booty: Another, more glamorous auction was held a short time ago in Nashville to dispose of the goods of a Ms. Betty Inman, also known as Diamond Betsy. She came to the attention of the IRS after she had been stopped and searched in the San Juan, Puerto Rico, airport and found to be carrying 471 pounds of cocaine worth about $14 million and, what was of particular interest to the IRS, $65,000 in undeclared currency and $50,000 worth of unregistered jewelry.

After taking a look at Diamond Betsy's records, the IRS decided to make an adjustment in the amount of income tax she owed. When its arithmetic was complete, it decided she owed approximately $1.2 million in back taxes. To collect, it seized two lavishly furnished penthouse apartments the woman owned in Nashville and Wichita Falls, Texas. After setting aside the minimum necessities in furnishings and clothes prescribed by law, it auctioned off the rest.

The auction was heavily publicized and held at the State Fair Grounds, drawing a large crowd. Among the items put up for auction were 29 sets of luggage, 198 pairs of size 7-1/2 shoes, literally thousands of rock-and-roll cassettes broken down into salable lots of 20 to 30 tapes, 25 oriental rugs, one brass bed, 1,300 books, and the largest collection of Waterford crystal in the southeast. Some of Betsy's items, and prices they drew, include: a pile of brass candlesticks for $225; a carved oriental bed inlaid with ivory (worth $20,000) for $5,000; one oriental rug for $5,000; a Waterford crystal bowl for $400; a 7-1/2 carat diamond ring for $39,000; and six cans of tennis balls for $17.50.

HOW TO FIND OUT ABOUT IRS AUCTIONS

By law the IRS must advertise its auctions. At the very least it is required to advertise in one local paper of wide circulation and post notices of the auction in at least two public places. Typically the notices go up in the county courthouse and in the lobby of the post office nearest the auction site.

In addition the IRS sends out notices of upcoming auctions to anyone who wants to get on its district mailing list. Administratively the country is broken down into 58 IRS districts (you'll find a listing of them in the Auction Pages). Getting on one of these mailing lists is easy. Simply write: *Internal Revenue Service, Attention: Chief of Collection Division.* (See Auction Pages for your district.)

You can ask to be put on specific kinds of lists. Districts run lists for three kinds of goods: personal property, real property, and automobiles. If you wish, you can get on all three or just one or two.

Miscellaneous   **Miscellaneous**

DEPARTMENT OF THE TREASURY-INTERNAL REVENUE SERVICE
Notice of PUBLIC AUCTION SALE

Under authority contained in section 6331 of the Internal Revenue Code, the property described below has been seized for nonpayment of internal revenue taxes due from Sabbina Falco 146-24 Bayside Avenue, Flushing, N.Y. 11354. The property will be sold at public auction in accordance with the provisions of section 6335 of the Internal Revenue code, and related regulations. Date of Sale: March 26, 1980. Time of Sale: 10:00 AM. Place of Sale: 136-59 37 Avenue, Flushing, N.Y. Title Offered: Only the right, title and interest of Sabbina Falco in and to the property will be offered for sale. If requested the Internal

SPECIAL FEATURES OF IRS AUCTIONS

There are special features that set the IRS auctions or sealed-bid sales apart from the other kinds of government sales. First of all, the IRS will decide on an open-bid or sealed-bid sale based on what it has to sell. Sealed-bid sales are reserved for items which appeal to specialized interests, items such as factory equipment or patent rights to inventions, those for which there would only be a limited number of buyers, as in the case of Hakeem Abdul Rasheed's yacht.

Open-bid sales are held to dispose of items that draw a broader public response: Diamond Betsy's goods, the seized stock of a camera store, or someone's car for example. These are the sales the IRS will publicize the most.

Bidding at the IRS auction is done as it is at any ordinary auction, by hand signals usually. Payment is always required in cash, cashier's check, treasurer's check, or money order from the post office or bank and due the day of the auction. If you decide to participate in a sealed-bid sale, you have to send in a percentage of your bid, usually 20 percent, as well. That also has to be in the same form as final

363 (4-14-78)
Sealed Bid Sale

5363.1 (4-14-78)
General

(1) Form 2222. Seized Prop sealed bids. vide that the sealed envel… bears the bic time and pla public notice considered u. Officer condu of the bids. All to the prope…

property will be decl… m…m price for the Ur 5361.1:(3). If th… ncement of the… …ipt of the … …Sealed Bid …

5362.3 (11-20-78)
Auction Procedure

(1) At the time and place set for the sale, the revenue officer should call the prospective bid- ders to order and recite the authority for the sale and the conditions under which the property will be offered. The statement provided in Exhibit 5300-22 should be used, but may be altered as necessary to fit any conditions peculiar to a particular sale. See IRM 5356.1:(7) for instruc- tions related to conditional sales.

(2) The revenue officer will then open the sale, …if it has been determined to announce …before the sale, the revenue …by requesting that …

5363.2 (4-14-78)
Consideration of Bids and Sale of Property

(1) At the appointed time and places sc… uled for the opening … onducting … …er … for the sale, the … the Reve… all the gat… …tement. …ceived a …eized fr… was p… dates …

payment: cash, cashier's check, etc. Sealed-bid payments typically are due in full within ten days of the sale.

Minimum bids: One basic fact about IRS auctions you should know is that the agency sets a minimum bid for what it puts up for auction. It is not always announced and may not be disclosed at the beginning of an auction, but it is there. If the government does not get bids for at least that amount, it will withdraw the lot. By law it must "bid in"—that is, buy the property itself, and credit the account of the tax- payer for that amount of money. At that point the IRS goes from being custodian of the seized property to owner. What the govern- ment does with this bid-in property in the future is up to itself. It will either reoffer it at another auction or try to sell it at a sealed-bid sale.

Liens on auctioned property: Another special feature of the IRS auc- tion is that the IRS does not guarantee that when you buy property from them you are getting free and clear right, title, and interest to the property. Instead, the rights, title and interest you do get are whatever was controlled by the taxpayer whose property was seized. This is seldom anything to worry about if you are buying personal property at an IRS auction, but it can be a factor to consider if you are thinking of getting real property—real estate—at an IRS auction. When you go to an IRS auction, you'll notice that the first thing done before any bidding is the reading of a disclaimer. It states in part:

"The right, title and interest of the taxpayer (named) in and to the property is offered for sale subject to any prior valid outstanding mortgages, encumbrances or other liens in favor of third parties against the taxpayer that are superior to the lien of the United States. All property is offered for sale 'where is' and 'as is' and without recourse against the United States. No guaranty of warranty, expressed or implied, is made as to the validity of the property or its fitness for any use or purpose. No claim will be considered for allowance or adjustment or for recession of the sale based on failure of the property to conform with any expressed or implied representation."

Don't get the impression, however, that shopping at an IRS auction is a total gamble. The IRS does research the financial history of the property it seizes. The more valuable the property, the deeper the research. It does this for its own protection to make sure it has the right to seize, sell, and collect the money from the sales of property. It checks public records to find out who the other lien holders, if any, are on a property.

This gets into a complicated area of tax-lien laws where even the experts can be confused. Essentially the government wants to assure itself that it has priority on liens on a property over everyone else. There may be other judgments against a piece of property, which will be found on file in the county courthouse, but usually if no one has taken the next step of having the judgment enforced through a sheriff's or marshal's office, for example, the IRS claims priority.

Now, the IRS is obliged by law to provide to an interested party the information discovered in researching the public financial history of a piece of property. But it is not obliged to *volunteer* this information, so if you want to know about any other possible claims on a property, you have to ask for it. If you get this far in investigating a piece of real property for sale by the IRS and you do not have expertise in researching and evaluating the financial history you get, what you should do before anything else, according to every IRS expert interviewed for this book, is get a good lawyer, preferably one experienced in real estate transactions, and let his advice guide you in whether you bid and how much.

Redemption by the original owner: One last qualification you should know about when you buy real property from the IRS is what is called the redemption right of the defaulting taxpayer. The previous owner has 120 days from the day of the sale to redeem his property from the government by paying the back taxes owed, plus a penalty. You will be told this at the beginning of a real property auction. Until that period is over, the new owner is given what is called a "buyer's deed." If the 120 days pass and the taxpayer doesn't reclaim his old property, it becomes the new buyer's permanently.

Don't be put off by the fact that either your search or the IRS's search may turn up other liens on the property. You can still get a bargain. IRS agent George Coakley offers one example of how this

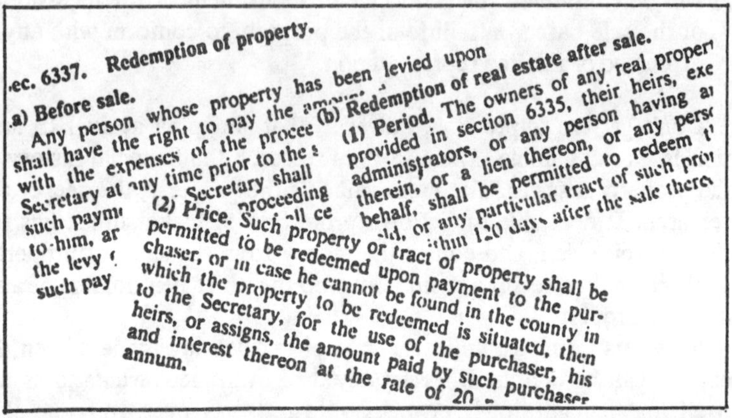

> Sec. 6337. Redemption of property.
>
> (a) Before sale.
>
> Any person whose property has been levied upon shall have the right to pay the amount, with the expenses of the procee[ding] Secretary at any time prior to the s[ale] such payment to him, and the levy [...] such pay[ment ...]
>
> (2) Price. Such [shall ce] permitted to be redeemed [...] chaser, or in case he cannot be [found] which the property to be redeemed [is] to the Secretary, for the use of the [purchaser, his] heirs, or assigns, the amount paid by such purchaser and interest thereon at the rate of 20 [percent per] annum.
>
> Secretary shall [...] proceeding
>
> (b) Redemption of real estate after sale.
>
> (1) Period. The owners of any real proper[ty] provided in section 6335, their heirs, exe[cutors,] administrators, or any person having a[n interest] therein, or a lien thereon, or any pers[on in their] behalf, shall be permitted to redeem t[he property] [so]ld, or any particular tract of such pro[perty, with]in 120 days after the sale there[of ...] or tract of property shall be [...] upon payment to the pur[chaser ...] found in the county in [which the property] situated, then [...]

can work for you. Suppose the IRS is offering at auction a house whose market value is $100,000. Suppose the IRS has set a minimum bid of $50,000 on the house and that your research reveals the house has two liens against it: a $25,000 mortgage and a $5,000 judgment against the property by a home improvement contractor, a debt legally called a mechanic's lien. In total there is $30,000 outstanding against the property.

If you buy the house for the minimum bid of $50,000, then that auction price plus the $30,000 in debts which you assume mean that you have essentially paid $80,000 for a $100,000 house. Even with the complications, it's not a bad deal.

AUCTIONEERS WITH BADGES

Forget about travelling to quaint country auctions or searching out some of the tonier auction parlors for the moment. You may not realize it, but you could have one of the biggest volume auction houses in your own town or city, or at least not very far away. The goods these places put up for bid are not usually antique rugs or 18th-century colonial furniture, not collector's items for the most part. Rather they're down-to-earth bargains in some everyday things you probably have bought not too long ago and in all likelihood will buy again.

It's at these auctions that you could find, for example, a slightly used $200 telephone answering machine for $25; a set of 36 hand-cut Swedish crystal glasses for $75; a $25 pocket calculator for $5; or a $30 tape recorder for $10. Why are these goods so inexpensive? Because they're stolen, most of them. And who is auctioning off hot goods? Your local police or sheriffs or marshals, your local law enforcement officers.

HOW THE LAW BECOMES A "FENCE"

Depending on where you live, one or more of these three types of officers—sheriffs, marshals, and police—will tend to dominate the law enforcement auction field. How they get this role is sometimes a matter of tradition, sometimes a matter of local laws. (The primer on page 155 tells you how to zero in on the various auctioneers in your area); but no matter who they are, they always end up as auctioneers for the simple reason that in the process of doing their jobs they become custodians of millions of dollars of goods. They come by these items in acting in one of two law enforcement roles: as criminal investigators or as officers assigned to enforce the judgment of a court on a city, state, or federal level.

WHO'S IN CHARGE HERE?

Before you find out exactly how various law enforcement officers get their auctionable goods, it might be useful to review very quickly how sheriffs, marshals, and police do and do not differ from one another. Depending on where you live and what your local legal procedures and traditions are, you may be dealing with one or more of them in your auction experience. Since they are more alike than they are different, the task of dealing with the different auctions is not all that difficult.

Sheriffs: The sheriff's job is an ancient one going back as far as the early 8th century in tradition, when each English shire—an early version of the modern county—had a chief law enforcement officer called a reeve. Gradually the term "shire reeve" evolved into the word "sheriff."

Many things have changed since then, but one general aspect of the sheriff's job that has remained constant is the fact that his is usually a law enforcement position for the entire county. By the last tally, according to the National Sheriffs' Association, there were over 3,000 sheriffs in the United States. Some of them work solely for cities, but they are the exception.

A sheriff, usually an elected official, typically holds his job for a four-year term. Exactly what he does in that office will vary from one part of the country to another. In Los Angeles County, for example, the sheriff's office, with jurisdiction over the 81 cities in the county, is *the* most powerful law enforcement agency, transcending even the L.A.P.D. in importance. At the other extreme the city sheriffs of New York City work only within the city limits and their job is exclusively restricted to enforcing judgments for the city court system.

Marshals: There are marshals and there are marshals. The kind most people think of immediately is the U.S. marshal, the federal type. His is a U.S. government position and he is appointed to it by the President. In theory, he holds that job as long as the President "wills" it. In practice, the standard term of office for a U.S. marshal is four years. In the country there are a total of 94 U.S. marshals, one for each Federal Judicial District, and each is an officer of the Federal Judicial Courts. They will get involved with auctions when they are given the job of dispersing property won through a suit in a federal court.

In addition to these federal marshals, some large municipalities may have their own city marshals as well. New York City, for example, is allowed by law to have a total of 83 marshals, all of whom are appointed to their jobs by the mayor for five-year terms. They work for the city's civil court and have the job of enforcing monetary judgments—suits for sums of money—under $10,000. They do other thankless tasks as well, such as enforcing judgments in favor of landlords by evicting tenants.

Typically they will enforce the monetary judgments by income execution, which means collecting part of a debtor's salary every week until the debt is paid, or property execution, which means seizing and auctioning off some belongings of a debtor to pay off the debt.

There is a third kind of marshal, a county marshal who shares the legal domain of the county with the sheriff. Los Angeles County has marshals as well as sheriffs. Although both groups of law enforcement officers are equally qualified to enforce state court judgments and hold auctions, the marshals have come to dominate the area of enforcing judgments. By one official estimate roughly 90 percent of judgment-inspired auctions in Los Angeles County are handled by the marshal's office. Most of the successful civil suits that end up in an auction go through the superior and municipal court system of the state of California, and these, more by tradition than by law, have fallen under the jurisdictional domain of the marshal.

Your local police: Unlike the sheriffs and marshals, police officers generally get involved with auctions solely as a result of their work investigating crimes. Typically the items they end up having to auction fall into four different categories.

One is *evidence,* which would include any items taken by the police in the course of an investigation and, once released by the district attorney, turned over to be sold at auction. A second is *investigative property,* a more general heading which could include anything seized in the course of an investigation. For example, a raid on an empty apartment the police suspect of being a storage dump for hot TV sets could yield a motherlode of ownerless sets that eventually end up on the auction block. Third is *found property,* which could be anything from an unclaimed expensive watch turned in to the police to a stolen car that has gone unclaimed by its owner. The fourth and last category could be called, for lack of a better term, *miscellaneous.* This might include items found on people who end up in the morgue with no next of kin to claim their belongings, or items that are collected as the result of a local quirk in the law. In Nashville, for example, people arrested for drunk and disorderly conduct have to turn in their belongings where they are jailed. When these same people sober up the next day, they sometimes forget to reclaim their belongings and leave jail without them. And if they don't come back and pick them up in 90 days, the law says the items can be eligible for being sold off at an auction. (This tends to happen fairly often in Nashville since the police don't give receipts for the personal items turned in, and without receipts people forget.)

YOUR LAW ENFORCEMENT AUCTION PRIMER

Your telephone and your local newspaper are your two best allies in finding out exactly who handles the bulk of law enforcement auctions in your area. Once you find out this information, the best thing to do is mark it all down—the name of the law enforcement agency, phone number, special title of the person in charge, frequency of the auction—in a small notebook to keep a permanent record of it. The process of getting this information is simple. It will involve three, or at the most, four phone calls.

Sheriffs/Marshals: Check your county directory for a listing of county officials and read down until you find the listing for the sheriff's or marshal's office. Call the office (or offices if you find both) and ask them the following:

* Do they conduct auctions?
* How and where do they post notices of them?
* What do they ordinarily handle at their auctions (land, cars, odds and ends)? Do they have specialized auctions for specific types of items?
* Do they have a schedule of auctions for the near future?
* When and where will the next auction be held?
* Do they have a mailing list and if so how do you get on it?

U.S. marshals: Although they do not tend to have as many auctions as the other officers, the U.S. Marshal's office may be worth a call. You will find your nearest one in the phone book under the general heading of U.S. Government and under the specific heading of Justice Department/U.S. Attorney. All you need to ask them is:

* How they post notice of their auctions?
* What they have auctioned lately, some typical items?
* When and where the next auction is to happen?

Police: Call your local police headquarters and ask for the Property and Evidence Clerk, or Division, or whoever is in charge of handling their auctions. You may find out immediately your police force doesn't handle auctions at all, a possibility if you live in a small town. But if they do, ask:

* How they post notices of their auctions?
* If they have general auctions only or auctions for specific types of items, bicycles and vehicles for example, as well?
* If they have a set schedule for their auction (or auctions)?
* When and where they will be holding their next auction?

Get in the habit of reading the legal notices section in your local paper. This tends to be where law enforcement officers and others as well post many of their auction notices. And lastly check with your local library to see if they receive copies of your county's bar association newspaper. If it does, start taking a look at that publication as well. Get to know its format, specifically where the legal notices are posted in it as well. That is where you are also likely to find news of upcoming law enforcement auctions.

THE AUCTION GOODS

Ask anyone involved in law enforcement auctions what is likely to come up on the block and he'll say "Anything and everything," which is as succinct a description as you'll find. Among some of the items sheriffs, marshals, and police officers interviewed for this book said they have passed under the auctioneer's gavel are: tombstones, toilet seats (new), at least one computer, abandoned because it cost too much to reprogram (new it cost $35,000; at auction it went for $100); anything that can be stolen and resold easily (cars, CB radios, tape recorders, TV sets, stereos, cameras, bicycles); boats; airplanes (at least one DC-3 was mentioned); furniture; cattle; racehorses; show dogs; farm equipment; one ocean liner (the S.S. *America*); cotton still growing in the fields; an interstate trucking license, one hockey team (the Atlanta Flames), and a pair of silver saddles.

Contrary to the image that may pop up in your mind with the hockey team, the auctioneer did not have the whole team with their skates, heavily padded uniforms, and their hockey sticks stand in front of a crowd while people yelled out bids. What actually happened took place in an office and all on paper. The team went bankrupt (and has since ceased to be the Atlanta Flames) but at that time the person owning 87% of the team had bid for the remaining 13% so he could own the whole works. His bid was accepted and the papers were signed under the watchful eye of the sheriff.

The story of the silver saddles comes from the Los Angeles County marshal's office, which was given the job of enforcing a judgment against a particularly slippery defendant. The plaintiff in the case, who was owed $5,000 for some construction work he had done, had trouble fixing on property that could be sold to pay off the debt. The man who owed him money was extremely secretive about his possessions and wasn't about to make the marshal's job any easier.

The plaintiff did have an ace in the hole. It was a pair of silver saddles that the defendant put on his horses which were ridden every year in the Rose Bowl Parade. So the word went out to the marshals: get the saddles at the parade.

As arranged, a deputy from the marshal's office showed up at the beginning of the parade route and tried to claim the saddles. The uproar from parade officials and television people covering the event was so intense he had to back off and promise to wait until later. So he would not lose his man, the deputy walked the whole parade route with his eyes glued to the silver saddles on the horses. Finally, when the parade was over, so was the defendant's ownership of his saddles.

Evidence: This is not to say you will find an elegant pair of silver saddles waiting for your bid at the next law enforcement auction, but you should be ready for anything when you go. Typically the ones that are the best for an individual looking for small items are those that come out of criminal investigations. If you had gone to a typical recent police auction in New York City, for example, you would have been able to get an expensive 10-speed Fuji bike for $120; a 3-speed Raleigh bike for $25; two radial tires for $45; a taxi meter (without the taxi attached) for $5; a new cassette tape recorder for $10; a three-horsepower lawnmower for $40; and a wheelchair for $5.

Bicycles are apt to be real bargains. Very often stolen and unclaimed bikes get auctioned off once in the spring and again in the

No.	Item		No.	Item
230	Calculators		270	Pants
231	CB Radio		271	Projector
232	Typewriter		272	Camera
233	Contact Lens Cleaner		273	Radio Cassette Player
234	Bolt Cutters		274	Camera
235	Elec Calculator		275	Thermos Bottles
236	Taxi Meter 15		276	Cameras
237	Dinnerware 25.00		277	Radio Cassette Player
238	Calculator		278	Auto Radios
239	Antenna 7.50		279	Hearing Aid
240	Records 50.00		280	Radios
241	Cameras 55.00		281	Radio Cassette Player
242	Typewriter 30.00		282	Auto Radio
243	Turntables 60.00		283	Shirts
244	Radio Tape Recorder 30.00		284	Pagecom
245	Helmets 15.00		285	T.V. Set
246	Walkie Talkies 50.00		286	Valves
247	Ladies Tops 22.50		287	Turntables
248	Stereo Set & Stand 40.00		288	Jacket 8L-235
249	Tape Recorder 5.00		289	Jacket
250	Cutlery 45.00		290	Jacket
251	Radios		291	Jacket

fall. Prices are never very steep—running $25 to a high of $150—but you probably do best by waiting for the fall bike auctions since the seasonal interest has passed by then.

JURISDICTION

The way the police get what they auction is relatively straightforward, no corruption, no shady deals. Whatever can be considered lost, stolen or unclaimed by whoever handles the bulk of criminal investigations where you live can end up at an auction if its rightful owner doesn't get it. There is a set way the police, for example, have of processing and eventually disposing of these goods in which the auction may be the last step.

Where procedures can get a little more complicated is where the law enforcement officer, usually a sheriff or marshal, has to enforce some court judgment. What the judgment is and where it comes from can vary, but what the situation boils down to is someone goes to court for help on collecting an overdue debt, usually of some size. By the time a sheriff or marshal has gotten involved, the person owed the money has received permission from the court to take something that belongs to his debtor and sell it off so he can be reimbursed for what is owed him.

Orders from the courts: The authority for what the law enforcement officer does comes from the law and the courts. Police procedure is pretty much a standard routine when disposing of property, but it can get a little more complicated with sheriffs and marshals. For example, Tennessee sheriffs work under six distinct courts: criminal courts, chancery courts, probate court, circuit court, general session courts, and even out-of-county courts for which they will serve papers. In Cook County, Illinois, the bulk of the decisions the sheriff's department is called on to execute come from either the state

chancery courts, which deal mainly in foreclosure actions on behalf of banks and finance companies, or local municipal courts, which decide on what are called personal property cases in which something other than a house—a car or a coin collection, for example—might be seized and sold to pay off a debt. In other areas of the country, such as Los Angeles County or in Fulton County, Georgia, it is the local marshal's office that will handle goods for the same kinds of courts.

The Federal marshals: Of course, the legal situation is a little more uniform for the U.S. marshal, since all the decisions he handles regardless of where he is in the country come through the Federal District Court. In general the U.S. marshal handles fewer auctions than the other law enforcement offices simply because suits that reach federal courts tend to be more complicated and less frequent. Usually federal courts get involved if there is some sort of interstate complication between the plaintiff and defendant—the one suing for the money and the one who owes it—and the matter falls beyond the jurisdiction of county or state courts. Typically the U.S. marshal handles cases where the U.S. government is the plaintiff. Such cases might involve, for example, the Small Business Administration. Trying to recoup money from someone who defaulted on his loan beyond suits, there might also be cases in which the defendant has violated a federal law and there is property involved. In one such case, federal marshals in Chicago seized 30 refuse bins because they did not meet federal health and safety standards for public receptacles.

A CASE IN POINT

Shop your local sheriff: Just for the sake of an example and to give you insight into how a particular piece of property might go from court to an auction, here is how things work in Hennepin County, Minnesota, which includes the city of Minneapolis. According to Lieutenant William Berry of the Hennepin County sheriff's department, the kind of property the sheriff handles at auctions arises from four kinds of legal situations.

The first is *abandoned property,* which includes items left behind at a hospital by someone who never bothered to return and claim them, or the belongings of someone who ends up in the morgue with no next of kin.

Other goods come from what is known as a *possessory lien.* This legal situation arises when someone drops off an appliance for repair and never comes back to get it or puts something in storage and never takes it out. In cases like this, the sheriff is asked by the local merchant to step in and sell off the property in order to cover the repair or storage cost.

A third category of goods is the result of a *warehouse lien*. Typically this includes items such as furniture that belonged to a tenant evicted from his apartment. If the evicted person fails to claim his furnishings, the job of disposing of them is left to the sheriff and the auction. The auction proceeds pay for storage costs.

The fourth and largest category of goods you are likely to run across if you attend a sheriff's or marshal's auction, is *property on execution*. This includes anything turned over to the sheriff as the re-

sult of a suit. Perhaps an individual or an organization (a business, a bank, a finance company) is owed a substantial sum of money, enough to make it worth its while to go after the debtor in court after having tried to collect by less drastic methods. In the jargon of the courtroom the one owed the money is the plaintiff and the "ower" or debtor is the defendant. Each side gets a chance to present his case and the matter may be settled out of court before a judgment is reached. If settlement isn't reached and the court decides in favor of the plaintiff, a default judgment is handed down, meaning the plaintiff is entitled to recoup what he is owed through a court-administered sale of some of the defendant's property.

The next step for the plaintiff is to file a writ of execution, which is a collection of legal documents that restate the court's decision, name the creditor involved, specify how much money is involved, and set a date for the sale of the property. The plaintiff then has to pay the sheriff a set fee to handle the writ of execution. This involves notifying the defendant of the writ—usually by sending a copy of it to the defendant's last known address.

In these cases it is the plaintiff's job to figure out what could be sold to recoup at least part of the debt. Cars tend to be popular items simply because they are so visible and seizable, but depending on what state you live in, even a person's home might be fair game for this action.

Selecting what to seize and sell is not always a simple matter. To protect the defendant against greedy or unscrupulous plaintiffs, states have a variety of local laws governing what may or may not be taken and auctioned off. In Hennepin County, for example, the sheriff is specifically forbidden to seize certain items of personal property such as a family Bible, and he must leave the defendant with a certain basic supply of clothing. Many states also have what is generally termed a Homestead Law, which in essence makes it extremely difficult for the authorities to grab someone's house as part of a court settlement. And on a state-to-state basis there may be even finer distinctions. In Florida a sheriff from the Tampa–St. Petersburg area (Hillsboro County) cannot seize a car if it is jointly owned by a husband and wife and the decision is handed down against only one of them.

If a writ of execution is involved and the sheriff or marshal manages to get hold of whatever it is the plaintiff picks out to be sold, the next step is the auction itself. For every step of the way the law enforcement officer has a series of charges that have to be paid: fees for executing the writ of execution, reimbursement for expenses such as mileage costs (usually set by the state legislature), and the cost of printing up handbills and advertising the auction and so on. Very often these expenses become part of the auction, since the sheriff or marshal must be reimbursed as well as the plaintiff from the sale of the property. Often the total of these expenses becomes the minimum bid, sometimes called the *cost bid* or *bid for cost*. If a minimum bid exists, it is announced or will be volunteered to anyone who asks.

WHEN THEY HAPPEN

It would simplify your life if it were possible to predict here how often law enforcement auctions will be held in your area. It can't be done. Common sense dictates that where there are more people, there will be more auctions. More people means more suits and more crime, and more auctions are the result.

Sometimes the frequency is a factor in how auctionable property is disposed. For example, the sheriff of Hillsboro County, Florida, has two kinds of auctions: one for stolen and/or abandoned property; another for seized property offered as the result of a court decision.

Auctions of stolen and abandoned property happen whenever enough has accumulated to justify a sale; about every two months on the average. Seized-item auctions, on the other hand, are held each Tuesday. And in Los Angeles County the sheriff's department has a special boat auction once a year; as many as 30 boats may end up on the auction block, compliments of the county harbor patrol.

Police auctions don't always make such neat distinctions, and they might be held as seldom as twice a year as in Nashville or as often as once a month as in Chicago.

One last thought worth noting about police auctions is that small town police departments may not have them at all. Generally a police auction is much more common in a city. Smaller police departments often give away or sell off privately, without an auction, the property they accumulate. In some states, police departments are not even allowed to have one if the town isn't big enough. In Illinois, for example, no town under 500,000 in population can legally put on a police auction. The simplest way for you to find out if they are held in your area is to keep an eye on your local paper and call your local police department.

WHERE AND HOW THEY HAPPEN

Sheriff's and marshal's auctions are often held in the general vicinity of the county courthouse: sometimes on the steps, sometimes in an adjacent area such as the courthouse parking lot. The notice posted for the auction will tell you where. What is up for auction may or may not be at the sale. If it's real estate, of course, it won't be; large items such as a tractor trailer truck may not be on site either.

Police auctions are often held in the warehouse where the goods have been stored, or if that is not convenient at the headquarters building itself. Procedure in police, sheriff's and marshal's sales are typical of standard auction procedure; an obvious nod or hand gesture or shout will make your bid known to the auctioneer and put you in the running for a piece of property. Payment is usually by cash or certified check, or occasionally a personal check will be allowed. Be sure to ask first, however. Ordinarily you are also required to pick up whatever you've bought within 24 hours. You may get a longer grace period, but never longer than three days.

The line-up: One very important feature of the law enforcement auction to ask about is whether or not there is a pre-auction viewing period and how long it is. The amount of time allotted to inspecting goods ready for auction can vary from two days before the auction to no time at all. In extreme cases, you might be able to see what is up for auction only as it is being unloaded from a truck into a warehouse. In general you are better off if you see what you are bidding on but, amazingly, there are still law enforcement auctions where you don't have this opportunity.

Make the most of your inspection periods when you have them. Otherwise you could end up with a very expensive bargain. One sheriff recalls the case of a man who bought a car at his auction where you were allowed to look at but not start up the vehicles. The man was pleased with his buy until he tried and failed to start the engine. When he opened the hood of the car, he instantly saw why the car wouldn't start. It had no engine.

Sharing the action: Another feature you should find out about a particular auction is how many people are getting a piece on the final bid. Many police departments hire professional auctioneers with the agreement that the auctioneer will get a percentage of everything he sells. One officer who has worked police auctions for years says that this sometimes drives up the prices, since the auctioneer works hard to get all he can.

There are also instances where the law enforcement officer, usually a sheriff or marshal, may get a cut of the auction proceeds in addition to his usual fees. For example, the New York City marshal legally has the right not only to reimburse himself for fees and expenses involved in executing a court judgment, he is also allowed a 5 percent cut of what money remains. Only after these accounts have been settled will the plaintiff in the suit, the one owed the money, get his fair share. It is in the marshal's interest to get the highest possible price for the property.

If you suspect prices at such an auction are running a little on the high side, your best insurance is to sit back and watch how the bids are going. If they seem stiff, either scratch that auction off your list or be shrewd in what you choose to bid on.

Liens: If you are interested in bidding on a large piece of property such as an expensive boat or some real estate, find out what your liabilities will be once you own it. In every instance when you buy an item at a law enforcement auction you are given title to whatever it is. Once you have paid your bid in full, you become the legal owner. What can happen is that you may also be liable for any liens—debts due—still outstanding on that property. Often the sum total of all known liens become the minimum bid for an item and the law enforcement officials, having made a check into the financial history of an item, cover the liens and make certain all are accounted for.

It occasionally happens that they miss some payments due on a car or boat for example, and they may or may not take responsibility for them. Most police departments, for example, assure you that you will not be liable for liens on a car you buy at one of their auctions. Some sheriff's and marshal's offices, however, make no such guarantee and in effect pass whatever hidden liabilities there might be on to you. If you have any doubts, be sure to ask what the policy of the law enforcement officials is before entering into the bidding.

A BRIEF WORD ON REAL ESTATE

If you see a tempting piece of real estate come up for auction and if you are not an expert in the field yourself, the first thing you should do is find someone who is. It could be a real estate lawyer or even a real estate dealer. Whoever it is should know the field. Buying real estate at an auction can be tricky. You should check out the financial and legal history of the property—let's assume it's a house—so you know if you might be bidding on a real buy or a legal nightmare. You may, again, be buying some liens as well as a house and also, depending on local laws, may not even be able to move in for a long while. Many states grant the defendant whose house is auctioned off what is called a statutory right of redemption, which gives the original homeowner a grace period in which to raise the money to pay off his debts plus interest and regain his home. That period can be a year or even more, and during that time the defaulting owner can legally stay in the home. That is just one complication you can run into in buying real estate at the law enforcement auction.

THE GOING OUT OF BUSINESS CROWD

Liquidation, clearance, and going-out-of-business sales are big business. The yearly gross proceeds from the sale of industrial and commercial property at auction dwarf the figures generated in the art, estate, and private-property business. Sales are carried out on a number of different scales—run by auctioneers and liquidation experts with different sizes of facilities, capital resources, and degrees of specialization and expertise, ranging from neighborhood operations up to international corporations.

Serving the needs of the realm of medium-sized and smaller local businesses, from manufacturers of consumer goods to suppliers, wholesalers, and other distributors, on down to every conceivable sort of large and small retail store and service business, are the general auctioneers that abound in every metropolitan area. Usually operating as commissioned agents, they handle, in addition to occasional voluntary liquidations and inventory disposals, the numerous legal sales—bankruptcies, assignments, security agreement sales, and foreclosures—that are daily facts of life in the world of commerce.

Operating on the other end of the scale, at the highest level of the business, are a handful of huge industrial plant liquidators—organizations with offices in many regions and contacts wherever industry operates. Their business is selling off, for corporations or creditors, the inventories and equipment of large factories. The core of the merchandise they auction off is heavy industrial machinery. They have large staffs, including experts on each type of industry whose inventories and equipment they are commonly called upon to sell.

WONDERS EVERY WEEK

Scan the classified auction ads in any Sunday paper and you will quickly begin to see what I mean.

A paint retailer is being sold out. Going under the hammer in that sale will be 3,000 gallons of interior and exterior paints in a variety of colors and finishes, along with varnishes, spray enamels, rust inhibitors, turpentine, mineral spirits, alcohol, an extensive inventory of emery paper, aluminum oxide production paper, wet and dry sandpapers, steel wool, masking tape, drop cloths, a stock of several thousand brushes.

Across town, the same day, a decorator's supply house is liquidating and selling 5,000 rolls of wallpaper ("offered in lots suitable for all buyers"), wheat paste, premixed vinyl paste, wall sizing, strippers, several hundred paper-hanging kits, five wallpaper steamers.

A dock-building firm is going under and selling, among other assets, a tugboat (no details given). Other offerings in that sale include a barge, a hydraulic crane, and a pile driver. (Be the first kid on your block . . .)

The entire contents of a garment factory (nothing special; there are six or eight of these every week); 4,300 pairs of late-model ski boots; 600 fur and fur-trimmed garments; fixtures of an antique soda shop (I'm sure they would go perfectly in the living room); 300 pieces of gold jewelry; seven assorted pizza parlors, bars, and restaurants over the course of the week; a sale of 20,000 formal-wear outfits—dinner jackets (new and used) in styles from the 1930s to the 1970s, in a variety of colors and fabrics including wools, wool blends, mohairs, poly blends, crushed velvets, velours, etc.—and in the same sale, 15,000 pairs of formal pegged and pleated trousers to match (all with button fly) together with an inventory of 30,000 accessories including ties and ascots of every color and description, cummerbunds, and a large quantity of patent-leather shoes.

I could continue to list hundreds of examples of fascinating and offbeat merchandise sold at liquidation and going-out-of-business auctions virtually every week in every major city in this country. On the practical, workaday side, they are a valuable source of inexpensive goods useful to many kinds of buyers. It takes imagination, planning and determination to get the best out of these opportunities, but the potential bargains are there in abundance.

With this perspective in mind, the way I break it down, there are

four categories of goods that *do* fill the needs and suit the budgets of small private and semiprivate buyers:

★ Inventories of consumer goods that lend themselves to sale in the quantities in which you would normally buy them.

★ Items for which you can find a use (one way or another) in the large auction-lot quantities in which they are offered.

★ Common, incidental equipment, owned by virtually every business, that is of day-to-day use.

★ Specialized equipment or supplies that are of interest to particular people for various individual reasons.

BUYING WHAT'S AVAILABLE BY THE PIECE

Generally speaking, liquidations of small and medium-sized retail businesses offer you the best opportunities for bargain snatching. But for businesses in which the stock consists of many small, relatively inexpensive items—shoes, plants, records, groceries, clothing, cosmetics, etc.—the goods must be sold in fairly large lots in order for the auction to proceed with reasonable speed. The logical buyers for this sort of inventory are jobbers, discount outlet operators, and other small retailers.

The ideal opportunity for the private buyer is the liquidation of the type of business in which the size, value, and number of items in the inventory make it reasonable and practical for the auctioneer to sell out the stock piece by piece or in sets. Of the common consumer goods, furniture fits this description best.

Furniture: An amazing amount of furniture is sold at liquidation or clearance sales. Some weeks, one out of ten auction ads is for new furniture, office or domestic. Most of the firms selling out are small or medium-sized retail dealerships; a few are small manufacturers. But virtually all these sales are fair game for private buyers.

The upholstered chairs, the sofa beds, the bookcases, the sectionals and recliners will be sold off piece by piece. The lamps, end tables, pictures, and twin beds will be sold pair by pair. Suites of bedroom or office furniture, dinette or kitchen sets, and box-spring-mattress-frame sets are knocked down just as they would be sold on the showroom floor.

Appliances: Stores that sell home appliances are likely to be liquidated in much the same manner. Each refrigerator, each garbage compactor, each electric range will be sold as a separate lot. Air conditioners and color TVs will be knocked down one by one. Toward the end of the auction you might get a lot of six steam irons or a dozen Waterpiks, but most of the stock will be sold off unit by unit. Hi-fi/stereo shops are often sold out in much the same way.

Restaurant equipment: Much of a restaurant's assets consist of such things as dishes, glassware, eating utensils, linens, furniture, and so forth that are usually sold off in gargantuan lots, but they also have a significant number of items that will be auctioned piece by piece or in reasonable lots. Most of this merchandise falls into the category of kitchen equipment. The roster of possible bargains in this line includes gas ranges, ovens, warmers, refrigerators, freezers, pots, pans, utensils, mixers, slicers, choppers, serving tables, scales, fans, exhaust hoods, and so on. If you are a dedicated cook or are outfitting a kitchen, restaurant liquidations offer many intriguing possibilities.

The unexpected: There are some unusual and surprising auctions that fit into this category. As an example, not too long ago, I attended a massive clearance of the accumulated unsold odds and ends amassed by five antique shops over a period of years. Despite the fact that the merchandise consisted of the white elephants no one had been willing to buy at retail, it was all knocked down in more or less the same lots in which it would have been put up at a typical auction gallery.

If you don't see it, ask: One important principle to keep firmly in mind in shopping liquidation and clearance auctions is to ask questions beforehand. This can save much wasted time and also alert you to opportunities that seem dubious on the surface. Every auction advertisement carries the auctioneer's phone number. If the sale seems to offer merchandise of potential interest, call the auctioneer's office and inquire about details such as lot sizes. The auctioneer will generally be glad to give out whatever information he can.

BUYING IN QUANTITY—AND MAKING DO

All the above examples are cases in which the auction fits the buyer with no alterations needed. There are numerous other cases in which a bit of cutting, fitting, or piecing may be necessary in order to make a bargain out of an auction offering. This is where auction buying gets to be more adventurous, often calling upon your imagination, ingenuity, and business capacity to make an unlikely possibility pay off.

It may be as simple as picking up a lot of half a dozen umbrellas at the liquidation of a local department store, keeping one for yourself and having five to give to forgetful guests who would otherwise have to trudge off into rainstorms on leaving your house. I often buy up lots of items of which I need or want only one, using the remainder as gifts, formal or informal. The auction price of such goods often makes such seeming extravagance quite reasonable in practice.

There are other instances in which a large auction purchase can be a good long-term investment, assuming that you have the capital up front to get in on the deal. There are lots of possibilities here. It is definitely an excursion outside mainstream economics, but then so is most of this sort of auction buying for private citizens. The buying consortium, *ad hoc* or preplanned, is an arrangement that greatly expands the possibilities for private parties at liquidation auctions. It is an unusual householder who can make reasonable use of 200 dinner plates or a set of four tables and 16 matching chairs from the local restaurant, but a clever and resourceful auction shopper who can put together a deal to divide up such budget-priced prizes among others attending the auction, or with friends by prearrangement, will be rewarded with many money saving buys. Another possibility in such a situation would be to buy large quantities of what you wanted on "spec," in the knowledge that, say, a neighbor is organizing a nursery school and is in need of dishes and furniture for the venture, giving you an opportunity to pass along your surplus at a fair price. In these instances the private buyer is truly acting as a small-scale entrepreneur.

STANDARD ITEMS FROM NONSTANDARD SOURCES

Just as every household inevitably contains certain items—a bed, a table, some chairs, a picture on the wall—so every business possesses items which are neither supplies, inventory, nor equipment of the business per se; they are the basic furnishings and equipment of a place of business. These items are excellent auction prospects for two reasons: they are plentiful, and few of the buyers are interested in them.

To begin with the universals, every business has a desk, a chair, a filing cabinet, a typewriter. If these be among your needs, any business liquidation sale can be of service to you. The commercial buyers who populate liquidation sales have offices that are already fully equipped, so they are generally not interested in such ordinary goods. While you may encounter competition from used office furniture dealers once in a long while, the chances are that if you are the only private party at the sale, you will be the only bidder.

Besides the four items mentioned, most businesses will also have some if not all of the following: adding machines, typing tables, postal scales, wall clocks, chairs, tables, bookcases, sofas, storage cabinets, water coolers, fire extinguishers, fans, air conditioners, refrigerators, vacuum cleaners, waste baskets, steel shelving, safes, heaters, radios, stereo or muzak systems, phone-answering machines, photocopiers, and an endless list of other equipment. All of these things are, at one time or another, sought after by ordinary people for use in their daily lives. All are potential liquidation-sale bargains.

Falling into almost the same category—that is, possessed as an asset by many types of businesses but sought a little more eagerly by the buying public—are vehicles. Cars, vans, and trucks of all sizes are owned by many businesses. When such a business is sold out, the vehicles will be sold along with the rest of the property. Many bargain hunters on the lookout for a good car are on to this, so bidding is likely to be a little more competitive than for an office desk, but values are still good.

SPECIAL ITEMS FOR SPECIAL INTERESTS

Specialized equipment and supplies from small businesses are of use to many kinds of people, and they are buyable at auction at bargain prices. The necessary ingredients for success in this kind of quest are desire, and *careful* reading of the auction ads.

As this category of auction fare is defined by personal needs and idiosyncracies, it is hard to generalize meaningfully about the kinds of goods that might be involved. As examples, then, here are a few particular cases that, I hope, illustrate the possibilities.

At the liquidation of a small photoprocessing lab I bought two large stainless-steel processing sinks, a set of stainless developing tanks with film hangers, and three miscellaneous stainless mixing vessels. The merchandise was well used, but serviceable. It cost me slightly less than one-third what comparable equipment would have cost new. On another occasion, I bid on and very nearly won a graphic arts camera. (A graphic arts camera is nothing like a Brownie. It is a huge machine, designed to be mounted in a special room, used in the publishing and graphic arts trades for a number of tasks such as enlarging or reducing type or artwork in reproduction, and for making halftone renderings of photographs for book printing.) My bidding limit was 50 percent of the price of the new equivalent unit. It went for slightly more.

A potter friend of mine bought 4,000 pounds of clay in 100-pound bags from a commercial giftware manufacturer. Another friend, who used to run a neighborhood newsletter and has a love of printing, bought a small platen printing press and five fonts of movable type at the liquidation of a venerable but obsolete print shop. A neighbor—a cabinetmaker specializing in the restoration of French and English furniture—bought practically an entire shopful of woodworking machinery at auction when a local lumberyard cashed in its chips. The most serious cook I know acquired her much-prized restaurant range and exhaust hood at one of the innumerable restaurant liquidations that take place in this area. And so it goes. Scan the newspaper auction ads and dozens of possibilities will suggest themselves.

TYPES OF LIQUIDATION SALES

What's behind this flood of merchandise? What brings about liquidation sales? Actually, there are a number of different kinds of liquidation sales that come about for a variety of reasons. Up to this point, I have been using the terms for various kinds of liquidations fairly loosely. You will have noticed, if you have looked, that the newspaper ads for the several types of going-out-of-business, clearance, and other liquidation sales carry succinct explanations of the reason for the sale.

VOLUNTARY LIQUIDATIONS

There are several circumstances under which some or all of a business may be sold out at the discretion of the owners, managers, or trustees. Many of the major industrial plant disposals fall into this voluntary category, being the results of corporate decisions to relocate, reorganize, consolidate, modernize, or simply to close down and write off a facility. On the level of the smaller business with a single plant or facility, it may mean the latter—the firm has simply decided to throw in the towel—but it doesn't happen that way very often. A viable small business is far more often put up for sale than voluntarily abandoned and liquidated when the owners want out. The sale price of a going concern is likely to be several times higher than the proceeds.

More relevant to the world of small and middle-sized businesses in terms of voluntary liquidation is the kind of sale known as a *clearance* or an *inventory reduction*. These sales are more likely to be held on behalf of wholesalers, distributors, and retailers—the kinds of businesses that accumulate inventories of goods on a speculative basis—than on behalf of a manufacturer, who produces goods on order. The business holding an inventory reduction could be anything from a men's suit wholesaler to a mail-order retail house to an antique shop—any business in which there is an accumulation of goods that for one reason or another don't sell through normal channels. The dual purpose of the clearance or inventory reduction is to clear operating and storage space and to recover whatever can be realized of the capital investment involved.

The phrase "by order of, and for owner" crops up fairly frequently in liquidation-sale ads. It is an official-sounding phrase that has little or no meaning other than that the owner of the merchandise offered authorizes its sale for his own benefit. One auctioneer friend gave me a little grin when I asked him about that phrase. He suggested that the chances were pretty good that most sales so advertised would turn out to be instances of an auctioneer's having picked up a load of goods somewhere (in one of the myriad ways available to auctioneers) and doing a good business passing it along to the public under the ever-alluring guise of auction sale. In other words, it tends to be a puff phrase, designed to lend a feeling of importance to a sale that probably has none.

LEGAL SALES

Most of the rest of liquidation sales fall into one of the three main categories of legal (i.e., legally forced or mandated) sales. These come about when a person or a business owes creditors more than he or it can pay and property is turned into money in order to satisfy the debt. (Throughout the following discussions I will use the term "business," but the term "person" could be substituted in almost any instance without substantially changing the sense or the validity of the information.)

When a business fails to pay its bills for a long period of time and creditors become impatient for payment, they are likely to seek legal satisfaction. The first step in this process is to seek a court judgment officially acknowledging the debt. The next step in recovering the debt is a further court proceeding in which the creditor seeks to gain the right to attach a bank account or to take title to some tangible asset of the business and sell it to produce the money.

Bankruptcy sales: Bankruptcy means being absolved of one's obligations at the cost of one's assets. The bankrupt business relinquishes title to its assets in return for immunity from any prosecution arising from the debts. Bankruptcy is defined and regulated by federal laws, and a federal bankruptcy court will oversee the proceedings. Once bankruptcy is instituted, the bankruptcy court freezes all claims and proceedings against the bankrupt business that may be pending in any other courts and pools all the assets, appointing a trustee whose job it is to manage and oversee the liquidation of those assets on behalf of the creditors. It is the trustee who selects or appoints an auctioneer to actually dispose of the property.

Auctions are considered the only appropriate and efficient method for the liquidation of property in federal bankruptcy proceedings.

The trustee holds title and interest in the business's assets as agent for the creditors and disposes of them in such a manner as to realize their true market value. Bankruptcy law says that an auction defines true market value in this context.

Some peculiarities of bankruptcy sales: There are some special circumstances brought about by the laws regulating bankruptcy settlements that make the auction sales themselves a bit different from other types of liquidations. The first of these comes from the fact that the creditors have no interest in the debtor's assets beyond the value of their combined claims against him. So, if a return higher than the amount of the debt is made on the sale of the property, the excess or surplus reverts to the bankrupt party. In many cases, the debtor has a right of precedence at the sale itself. If he can somehow scrape together the amount of the debt, he can buy back his property *at the auction,* for the amount of the debt, regardless of how high other bidders are prepared to go.

Another anomaly of bankruptcy sales, when an inventory or aggregation of goods is involved, is the so-called bulk bid. In such sales, the auctioneer must solicit and record bids for the entire proceeds sold as a single item, following which the sale proceeds lot by lot. It is not until the court, as referee and advocate for the creditors, confirms the sale to either the bulk bidder or the "piecemeal" bidders that the final disposition of the merchandise is known. This is done to forestall further litigation—to demonstrate that every possible avenue was explored in the attempt to bring the highest return on behalf of the creditors.

Assignee's sales: Similar in many ways to bankruptcy liquidation is the procedure known as an assignee's (pronounced "ass-uh-*neez*") sale. The correct legal term for this procedure is "assignment for benefit of creditors." Before the federal bankruptcy laws were codified, situations in which a debtor was overwhelmed by his creditors were dealt with under the provisions of this ancient common-law procedure (on which the bankruptcy laws themselves were closely modeled). Assignment for benefit of creditors takes place under the jurisdiction of a state or local court, which *assigns* title and interest in the debtor's assets to a court appointee who acts, like the trustee in bankruptcy, in the interests of the creditors.

There are some procedural differences between the working out of a bankruptcy and an assignee's sale. First, in the case of an assignee's sale, all the parties to the transaction must agree beforehand to this method of dealing with the problem. (Agreement or consensus is *not* a prerequisite to bankruptcy.) Second, in assignment for the benefit of creditors, there are options to auction sale—the assets may be disposed of in part or in whole by outright conventional sale, if the parties agree. Aside from these points, the practical differences between assignment and bankruptcy are negligible.

Security agreement sales: The third major category of legally mandated liquidation sale is the so-called security agreement sale. Such sales arise from the many, many instances in which business or personal assets are put up as security for a loan. In some cases the security offered is the item that the loan is used to buy. Automobile loans are routinely secured in this way, and the repossession and sale of a car for breach of installment contract is one of the most common types of security agreement liquidation.

Many secured loans are arranged under the guidelines of the Uniform Commercial Code (an attempt on the part of several of the states to make their financial laws reasonably consistent with one another) and are hence sometimes referred to in the newspaper as "U.C.C. sales."

The U.C.C. requires that if the terms of repayment are not met, the collateral be sold at auction to satisfy the debt. Probably the most technically correct term for this type of sale (and certainly the most descriptive) is "collateral liquidation." Since the original security agreement usually involves an appraisal of the assets secured as collateral, this is one instance in which the creditor has a good chance of recovering more or less the full value of the debt. Certainly a secured loan is a better business risk for the lender than an unsecured one. In any dispute over title or interest of a debtor's assets, property or assets secured by agreement will go to satisfy that agreement before the remainder is divided up to satisfy the remaining creditors.

Foreclosure sales: The familiar term "foreclosure" is another word that often appears on auction sale ads. "Foreclosure" is a technical legal term for the point at which a secured debt is "called"—the point at which the creditor asserts his right to take possession of the secured property in satisfaction of the debt, brought about by the failure of the debtor to meet the terms of repayment. That is a lawyer's way of saying that if you put up the title of your house or your business assets as security or collateral for a loan and you don't make the payments, the lender has the legal right to take the property and sell it in order to get his money back. Foreclosure is the act of doing this.

For practical purposes, then, a foreclosure sale is just a special kind of security agreement sale.

THE ROLE OF ADVERTISING

As you can imagine, buyers are not numerous. The key to success in this sort of business is advertising—extensive and carefully targeted advertising!

The vehicles for these "crash promotion" programs, as they are known, are major urban newspapers (and it is not unusual to see, for example, a Cleveland sale advertised in a New York newspaper or vice versa), trade papers and journals, and, perhaps most important of all, mailings. Auctioneers that operate in these areas maintain extensive mailing lists for each business or industry they deal in. The lists are constantly updated. They are stock in trade. If a liquidator gets a deal to sell out a factory or distributorship in an industry in which he has little experience or contacts, he will usually buy mailing lists through which to promote the sale.

The closer a business is to the retail end of the spectrum, the less rarefied is the market for its goods and equipment, and hence the less specialized and tailor-made the advertising needed to sell it. Most general auctioneers rely primarily on the major local newspapers to bring in the bulk of their customers. But since they are called upon to do a wide variety of different kinds of sales, most of them keep trade mailing lists and use them whenever appropriate. They understand as well as the big firms the value of properly targeted advertising.

LIQUIDATING YOUR OWN PROPERTY

In the unlikely and unhappy event that you, either as a small businessperson or as a private citizen, should need the services of a liquidator, there are some precautions and procedures that should help you to avoid the many pitfalls and make the best of a bad situation.

The circumstances in which a person goes to a liquidator are in many ways analogous to the circumstances in which most families confront undertakers. It tends to be a time of trouble and severe stress—a difficult time in which to be cautious, thoughtful, and deliberate. Time is likely to seem like an unaffordable luxury. One is likely to feel under considerable pressure to act quickly, but, if circumstances permit, it is definitely one of those times to hasten slowly.

A liquidator should be selected carefully. It is an excellent idea to plan on calling at least four or five before making *any* decision. References, if obtainable, are helpful. In evaluating the input you get, make certain that you *clearly* understand the structuring of all fees involved.

Depending on the size of the transaction, an auctioneer's commissions run between 10 and 20 percent of the gross. Over and above this you will be expected to pay for advertising, labor, and other expenses. Make sure you know what all of these extras are. Understand that money spent on advertising—crash promotion, some auctioneers call it—is money well spent (at least up to a point). By the time you have done this research, you will have a good enough idea of what's what and will be able to proceed in the knowledge that you are doing the best that the situation allows.

LAND AND HOUSES

The nature of the real estate auction business is such that it does not often touch the lives of urban dwellers. For most of us, if we have any awareness of real property auctions at all, what comes to mind is the vague recollection of a scene in a movie about the Great Depression in which a heartless sheriff is knocking down the home and hopes of a weary dust-bowl farmer.

Indeed, auction has always been (and still is) the normal, traditional method of land trading in the farming communities of America, and sale of agricultural land is still the largest single component of the real property auction business, but it is by no means the *whole* business, nor has it been for a long time.

Many, many different types of real property are being sold at auction these days. Such sales are deemed "still uncommon" by some specialists in the field, but one thing on which *all* real estate auctioneers agree is that real estate selling by the auction method is gaining momentum rapidly and can be expected to account for a larger and larger proportion of the overall real estate picture in the years to come. If you are in the market for land for residential, recreational, or investment purposes, auction sale may well open up new possibilities for you. On the other hand, if you have real property to sell, you may want to give serious consideration to disposing of it through an auctioneer.

Real property auctions take place in both the public and private sectors. Some of the public-sector real estate selling is dealt with in the sections on the GSA and sheriff's and marshal's sales. Some I will deal with in this chapter. But since, in my opinion, private auction selling has more to offer the typical buyer, let's start off there.

WHY AUCTION?

The world is full of real estate brokers, so why sell your house or land through an auctioneer? One auctioneer who has been a leading specialist in the field for more than two decades gave me the most succinct answer. "The purpose of a real estate auction is to make an *expedient* sale." Another expert told me modestly that it is simply the *best* way of selling property—quick, clean, and fair. He went on, "It is the simplest method, the surest, and the quickest. It is likely to bring the highest price. It stimulates competition and brings the buyer to the moment of decision."

To expand on these points a bit, most real estate auctioneers offer comprehensive service. That is, once a seller makes the decision to sell, virtually every detail of the transaction that might otherwise occupy his attention is dealt with by the auctioneer. That is simple for the seller. Next, once a piece of property (like any merchandise) is put on the auction block, it *will* sell (unless the *seller* imposes reserves or other restrictive covenants). That is sure. Further, the seller

---

Parcel 4. Approximately 23 acres, 512' road frontage.⅔ level, open fields, ⅓ wooded.

Parcel 5. Approximately 24 acres with 500' road frontage, approximately ⅔ open field, ⅓ wooded.

Parcel 6. 12 acres, with approximately 500' frontage. Grove of trees with open fields.

Note, The property will first be offered in 6 parcels, then the property will be offered in its entirety (Parcels 1 to 6).

---

has the rare luxury of deciding *when* his property will be sold. In a standard brokerage transaction, the normal listing period is 180 days, and properties may remain on the market literally for years before a genuinely interested buyer is found. With auction sale, the owner simply picks a date, and, assuming it is far enough off for the auctioneer to make the necessary arrangements and do sufficient publicity (usually about 30 to 60 days), the property will be sold—that day. Finally, the emotional impact of a well-organized, well-publicized, well-run auction is tremendous. It is a very significant factor in determining the final sale price. If the auctioneer has done his basic job—to bring out interested, qualified buyers—then the true market value of the property will indeed be realized. This value is often greater than even the seller had hoped.

MARKET VALUE

The term and the concept have come up again and again in this book, but nowhere is it mentioned more frequently than by real estate auctioneers. The central argument for selling real property at auction is that the property will bring its true market value. I think it is worth a minute to try to make the notion a little clearer, if it is not clear already. To most of us retail-minded people the conviction that "things" have "objective prices" goes very deep. A lipstick is *worth* $1.50, an automobile is *worth* $15,000. There is a price tag that says so. We don't question it. Land, being unique and irreplaceable, with no cost inherent in its production, is one of those commodities that fall into a different system of valuation.

The only real measure of the value of real property is what people will give for it. (Nowadays, in our economic system, what one usually gives is money.) As one real estate auctioneer pointed out, an appraisal is just an opinion, a guess. It may be an educated opinion, but it's an opinion nonetheless. It is *not* an offer to buy the property at the appraised price. The true definition of the value of a piece of real property can only be achieved by putting the property up for sale—by exposing it in an appropriate marketplace. What it brings under competition from interested, qualified buyers is its true market value.

The reasoning sounds a bit circular, perhaps, but this is one of the concepts basic to our economic system. Its operation seems clearer to me in the realm of real property. At any rate, real estate auctioneers are working very hard to get banks and other financial institutions to accept auction price as the true market value for real property. If they succeed, the operation of their business will become that much easier and their stature in the business community will have risen.

SERVICES PROVIDED BY THE AUCTIONEERS

The real estate auctioneer's primary responsibility to the seller is to make sure that there are interested and qualified buyers in attendance at the auction. This is the core of his business, and a great deal of his stock in trade is likely to be business contacts and, above all, promotional expertise. Spending $10,000 to $50,000 promoting a large land sale is not uncommon at all. Real estate auctioneers like to talk about their advertising genius and their promotional budgets almost as much as they like to talk (in general terms) about their profits. But in addition to this basic function there are a number of additional services provided by conscientious real property auctioneers that expedite and facilitate the sale of property.

SUBDIVISION

One of the most important developments in the real estate business in this country over the past two decades has been the increasing sale of farmland for commercial and residential development. As the potential value of land has risen under pressure from developers, so have tax assessments. Farmers, caught in an economic squeeze, have often ended up selling their land to make a profit, rather than sticking it out under increasingly difficult conditions and continuing to grow food.

The sale of a large tract of land, such as a 1,500-acre truck farm, is not a transaction that many private buyers could hope to participate in. One way to make it accessible to greater numbers of buyers is to subdivide. Auctioneers who specialize in what some call "agra-auction" properties do this regularly. (Of course, a developer would do exactly the same thing—divide the tract into smaller parcels or building lots—but finding a single developer willing and able to buy 1,500 acres is not so easy.) Cutting a huge tract of land down into smaller, logical, legal parcels brings ownership of that land within the reach of many more buyers. In addition, the property not only becomes more salable, it also becomes worth more, as each smaller parcel will tend to sell at a higher price per acre than the whole tract could possibly have brought.

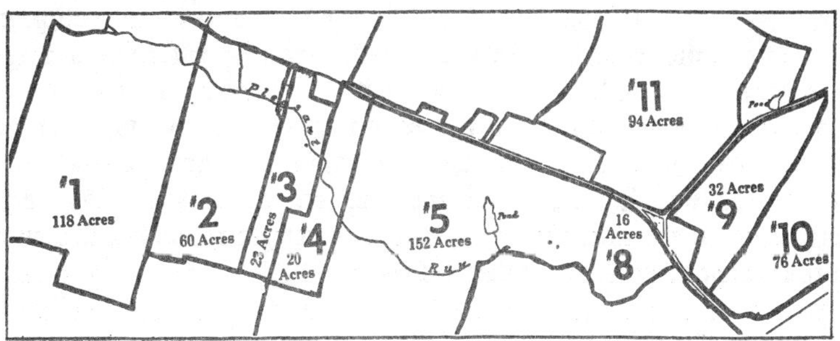

One of the significant aspects of this type of subdivision is that it offers one of the relatively few opportunities for the private buyer to get in as first owner of newly opened land. Once a parcel has passed through the hands of an investor or developer, the price will have risen substantially.

One real estate auctioneer friend held just such a sale recently. The tract, which consisted of four separate but contiguous farms, totaling 1,543 acres, was divided into 18 parcels. The parcels were offered one at a time and then in a variety of different combinations, giving the buyers an opportunity to keep large acreages together by paying a premium over what the individual buyers bid for the individual parcels. (That strikes me as a really creative marketing twist; subdividing to raise the price and offering the opportunity to gang parcels together at a still *higher* price!) The sale went smoothly, with all 18 parcels selling quickly, and one composite being sold at the end. The sale netted something just under $3,000,000.

RESEARCH

Another of the services that the real estate auctioneer frequently provides to his clients is research, information and assistance in handling paperwork. As the auctioneer referred to in the preceding paragraph remarked to me, he likes to have "informed buyers." He researches title history, covenants, easements, and other peculiarities and idiosyncrasies that may come with the deal. "If the buyer knows everything you know about the property and he still wants it, you know you have a sincere buyer. He's not going to come back to you later and try to wiggle out of the deal."

Besides providing or guaranteeing a clear title, the auctioneer will often look into such matters as tax assessments, zoning provisions, drainage patterns, water table testing, rights of access, inspection of houses or other buildings for structural soundness or termite damage and whether parts of the property may be subject to legal restrictions, such as environmental protection statutes. They may even go so far as to survey a property under certain circumstances. And since it is virtually their daily bread, they can and do provide advice and assistance in the drawing up of various legal papers and documents, if they do not actually do it themselves.

FINANCING

One prominent Kentucky real property auctioneer offers the opinion that the key to success in his business is "creative financing." I think the phrase is apt, despite the image it conjures up in my mind of the kind of on-paper wizardry that brought New York City to the very brink of default and financial disaster. Anything the agent (auctioneer) can do to make sure that financing will be available to cover the sale obviously facilitates the transaction.

On the level of conventional financing, auctioneers can negotiate with banks, savings and loan institutions, and other lending and financing agencies on various points having to do with the assumption of existing mortgages, interest rates, and complex financial packages. Indeed, many real estate auctioneers, as trusted and respected members of the business community, hold positions on the boards of these institutions themselves and thus have direct input into loan decisions.

Besides dealing with banks, etc., auctioneers will frequently advise, counsel, and otherwise help to arrange financing of the purchase by the seller. Seller financing, often called a *payment money mortgage* or *time installment sale,* is not unique to auction selling of real estate—it is resorted to in many cases of sale by conventional brokerage, especially in times when credit is tight—but it is very frequently a component of auction deals. Assuming that the seller can and is willing to function as a substitute bank, the arrangement, again, is of benefit to both parties to the sale. Making financing available to buyers who might not, for any number of reasons, qualify for conventional funds brings that many more potential buyers into the ring, which has the inevitable effect of driving the price up.

There are several different arrangements by which a seller can finance a real estate deal, but the two most common should be sufficient to suggest the inherent possibilities. The first and most common is a straight self-amortizing mortgage given by the seller. Buyer and seller negotiate down payment (usually from 15 percent to 30 percent), interest rate (these days likely to be from 10 percent to 20 percent) and repayment time (anywhere from 5 to 20 years). The down payment is made at the time of purchase (either all at auction time, or part then, the remainder at closing). Payments can be scheduled monthly, quarterly, semiannually or yearly.

The other standard way of handling owner financing is called a "balloon" mortgage. It is designed to take advantage of certain IRS provisions. The buyer pays 29 percent of the total purchase price at the outset (at auction, or part at auction, part on closing). That is his total payment for the first year. For a fixed period, usually five years or so, the buyer pays only interest on the remaining 71 percent. At the end of the five (or however many) years he repays the rest of the principal, having, presumably, had time to fix up the property and arrange for other financing. There are numerous variations possible on these agreements, but they all add up to the same thing; if the seller offers financing, he will attract more buyers and get a better price for his property.

WHO AUCTIONS REAL ESTATE?

Virtually every auctioneer is called upon to sell a piece of real property now and then, along with all the other clearance sales, salvage disposals, factory liquidations, etc.

There are also a number of general auctioneers, both in urban centers and in smaller towns or rural areas, that sell quite a lot of real estate, both agricultural and residential, although it is not their exclusive preoccupation.

Finally, there are the real estate specialists or experts. They are really a breed apart. Many are licensed realtors. Some sport degrees in urban and regional planning. Most have large staffs of professionals handling research, legal matters, and promotion and advertising. Real estate auctioneers travel a great deal, talking to others in the trade, exchanging information, keeping on top of developments in real estate generally, and constantly searching out new properties to sell. They are an impressive group from what I have seen and heard of them. They work hard at their trade, and their hard work seems to pay off handsomely.

COMMISSIONS AND FEES

In virtually all real estate transactions, commissions are paid by the seller, rather than the buyer, but there is no set commission or fee structure in the real property auction business comparable to the standard 6 to 10 percent of gross that goes to the conventional real estate broker. Some auctioneers pride themselves on charging a smaller commission than the conventional broker. One midwestern auctioneer I have talked to charges a straight 3 percent on all his auction sales, real estate included. If he doesn't make a sale, he doesn't take a penny. He hastens to point out that that seldom happens, of course. His success rate is very high. Like most real estate auctioneers, he won't take a property unless he feels he has a very good chance of selling it at the owner's upset price. He does a good business by selling a large volume of properties.

Larger, more sophisticated operators are less likely to operate on so small a commission, or such a simple fee structure. They will use a sliding fee scale, related to the size of the transaction. Costs of advertising and promotion may or may not be included in the commission figure. Each deal will be priced on the merits of the specifics involved. After going through all that evasive action, most big-time real property auctioneers will generally tell you that they take, on average, a 10 percent commission, plus expenses. So they are more expensive than a conventional broker, but any one of them would tell you that you would get back the difference several times over. I don't doubt it.

HOW A REAL PROPERTY AUCTION IS RUN

Variations on the procedures described here are many, but the basic terms and rituals are fairly universal.

Offerings are unrestricted; come one, come all. Auctions are either *absolute* (strictly to the highest bidder, regardless of price), subject to a *reserve* or *upset* price (meaning a limit below which the seller will not agree to the sale), or subject to *confirmation* (meaning that the seller has the option of deciding after the auction whether or not to accept the highest bid). Most real property auctions fall into the first two categories. Since most real estate auctioneers like their buyers to know the conditions of sale beforehand, they clearly state reserve or upset prices or at least the fact that property is being sold subject to reserve. Some auctioneers use the sale subject to confirmation as a come-on to induce sellers to list properties with them. Many will not handle that sort of sale, preferring to devote their energies to dealing with sellers who are sure that they want to sell.

Land auctions may be *contingent* or *noncontingent,* depending on whether or not the providing of financing for the buyer is a precondition of the sale. As noted above, providing or arranging financing is one of the most significant services that the auctioneer can provide for the buyer. It is also a service for the seller, since it increases the number of buyers who can compete for the property, and hence tends to raise the selling price.

Real estate auctions are frequently held *in situ,* that is, on the premises being auctioned off. If the property is undeveloped, the auctioneer may provide a tent or other shelter, with seating, display space, projection facilities for showing films or slides of the properties, even refreshments. Alternatives to the tent are houses or other buildings on the property, nearby banks, firehouses, Grange halls, or other institutional halls of appropriate size.

Paying for purchase: Sale is to the highest bidder, subject to the exceptions noted above. By law, a cash deposit, known as *hand money, earnest money,* or *good faith money,* is required from the high bidder at the time of the sale. This may vary from 10 percent to 25 percent or more of the hammer price. At this time, the buyer is also generally required to sign a contract or purchase agreement. Arrangements will be made for a *closing date* anywhere from 30 to 120 days after the auction. The closing is the meeting at which all liens and payments are settled and the deed to the property is transferred to the new owner.

Closing dates more than 30 days after the auction are generally for *noncontingent* sales. This is the time the buyer will spend getting his financing worked out. In the event that a buyer fails to come up with financing within the allotted time, he will generally forfeit the deposit. According to one experienced real estate auctioneer, however, this doesn't happen even once in 100 cases. Most people who buy real property at auction seem to have considerable means or financial backing (or are smart enough to arrange their financing beforehand).

WHAT'S IN IT FOR THE BUYER?

Auctioneers have a lot to say about the advantages of auction sale for buyers of real property—although I must state that in my own opinion the advantages to the *buyer* are somewhat less clear than the advantages to the *seller*.

First, there is the question of services. As mentioned, the auctioneer often provides thorough research, descriptions, and inspections, as well as investigation of title, restrictive covenants, easements, and so forth. He generally offers a *clear* deal to the buyer.

Second, through subdivision and similar activities, the auctioneer often brings large tracts of land onto the market in parcels likely to be within reach of small private buyers—he makes property available that would not be otherwise.

Since most auctioneers prefer to deal with what they call "motivated sellers," people who really want to sell *now,* there *are* bargains to be had. The suggestion implicit in the promotional material I have gotten from several real estate auctioneers—that buyers can get good bargains at the same time sellers are getting the highest prices—defies logic. But off the record, most of these auctioneers will admit (or boast) that while many properties bring more than expected at auction, some do sell for less.

But the clearest, most consistent statement that auctioneers make about the position of the buyer is that auction is the cleanest, fairest method for *everybody;* that the buyer can be confident that he will not pay *more* for a piece of property at auction than it is worth, while through a broker he may well pay too much. "Facing the competition gives the bidder confidence," as one auctioneer put it. The fact that the winning bid is just one bid over the competition is proof that the buyer is operating within a market defined by others' willingness to offer similar prices.

WHAT KINDS OF PROPERTIES ARE AUCTIONED?

If you talk to different auctioneers, you get different answers to that question. Most agree that not all properties are "ideal" auction prospects; but there is little consensus on what *is* the best kind of real estate to sell by this method. If there is one generalization that can be made about real property auctions, it is that the preponderance of what is sold is country rather than city property, and that more of it is destined for private ownership—farming or residential use—than for commercial or industrial purposes. Few real property auctioneers do much business in the line of typical urban or suburban residences.

One of the real property experts I interviewed characterized properties most suitable for auction sale as "end of the spectrum" properties, by which he means either very desirable and costly, *or* very specialized, difficult-to-sell ones. The difficult end of the spectrum consists of what he calls "bastard" realty—parcels or properties with peculiar or especially individual uses or combinations of resources. Examples he offered in this connection were a chicken farm and a Victorian house on 4 acres of land with a barn big enough for 120

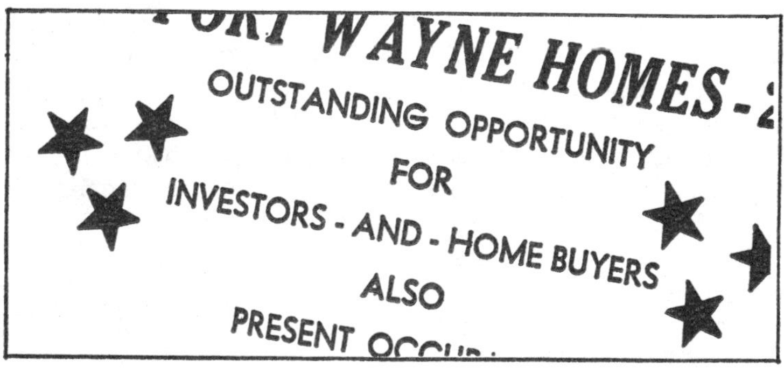

cows. More ordinary, in-between real estate he feels is adequately handled by conventional brokers.

Another specialist, who has been selling real property at auction for 30 years, enumerated his offerings as "residential, commercial/industrial, gentlemen's farms and estates, ranches, family or 'dirt farms' and dairy farms." He sells large quantities of farmland for housing and other development, and was a pioneer in working out this type of auction transaction.

A somewhat different picture is painted by a Florida auctioneer I talked to. He is a generalist, but sells quite a lot of real property including condominiums (which he liquidates for builders and developers when sales have slumped and they need to improve their cash flow), apartment buildings, warehouses, trailer parks, industrial sites and private houses.

WHAT ABOUT PRICES?

Considering the diversity of properties being sold, you can well imagine that prices span a considerable range. Here are a few selected examples that should give you some idea of what's in or out of the ballpark.

For city dwellings, which as I've said aren't a major category of auction offerings, the range runs from a comfortable one-family house in a "changing" neighborhood in Richmond, Indiana, that sold recently at "absolute" auction for $15,000, through a more typical middle-class three-bedroom brick house in a nice neighborhood in Hagerstown, Maryland, that went for $47,500, to a large four-story brownstone on New York's fashionable East Side that brought $400,000.

There are large country estates that go for millions, but more typical of country residential properties is a ten-room Colonial farmhouse (built circa 1760) on 23.5 acres of wooded land, with a swimming pool, that brought $135,000 at auction not long ago. This particular house was part of a larger subdivided property. The rest of the land went in four parcels, at an average price of $4,800 per acre. Depending on size and location, parcels of subdivided farmland are selling these days for between $3,000 and $8,000 an acre.

Rural land sold for farming purposes seems to go for substantially less than development land, so if you are looking to buy a farm, you can do so on a smaller budget. Fairly typical of farm auction sales is a 320-acre farm in eastern Indiana that sold for an even half-million dollars, which works out to roughly $1,500 per acre.

WHEELING AND DEALING WITH CITY HALL

The chances are better than good that every city, town, or county that collects any or all of its revenues by taxing real property will sooner or later find itself reluctantly in the real estate business. Public monies will be spent, therefore taxes must be collected. If you own property, the community will take away your property and sell it to pay your tax bill if you don't pay it. It is one of the areas in which law establishes an order of precedence favoring the needs of the public sector over the rights of the individual. Like a glacier, the processes involved are slow-moving but inexorable. It won't happen quickly, but if things are let go too long, the government must and will act. The process by which a municipality takes title to private property in order to recover its revenue debt is called *in rem* tax foreclosure. (*In rem* is a legalism indicating that the litigation is directed at a thing rather than a person.)

TAX CERTIFICATE SALES

In many localities, the first step the city or county will take in the attempt to balance its tax books is to offer, at auction, what is generally called a *tax certificate*. In a tax certificate auction, bidders vie (oddly enough) for the privilege of paying the delinquent tax bill. In return for this, the buyer of the certificate acquires the right to foreclose on the property in the event that the owner does not "redeem" it by repaying the money within a stipulated period of time—typically two years.

A tax certificate auction is quite different from most of the auctions we have discussed in this book. As mentioned, the bid constitutes a commitment to pay off the delinquent taxes, along with any interest or other penalties that have accrued. But the bid itself takes the form of a percentage of interest—the *per annum* interest that the holder of the certificate will charge the assessee (the owner) for the privilege of having his tax bill financed. In this kind of auction, it is the lowest bid (i.e. the lowest interest rate) that takes the prize.

Redemption: To redeem his property, the owner simply repays the money that the certificate holder has paid out (the back taxes plus penalties), the taxes that have accrued since the sale (also paid by the certificate holder), and the interest on the certificate itself. Local laws vary, but I know of no municipality that gives the owner *less* than two years to settle up.

Foreclosure: If the property owner does redeem his holdings by repaying the debt, the certificate holder will have earned whatever interest on his money he contracted to accept at the auction—probably a modest but reasonable return. The real hope, of course, is that the owner will *not* redeem, in which case, for the same modest investment, he will gain the right to foreclose and take title to (i.e., own) the property. It is definitely a speculator's game.

When there are no takers: The tax certificate route is a very good one for cities and towns. For one thing, it gets them out of the role of the heavy—the party that takes people's property away from them. More important is the fact that the municipality gets its money up front, balances its books, and, above all, keeps the property *on* the tax rolls.

Unfortunately, tax certificates do not always sell. Often there are no takers at all. When this happens, the community itself takes the lien and forecloses on the delinquent property. The laws are usually structured so that the city can foreclose in a much shorter time than a private certificate holder can—six months is typical. As I pointed out, this solution is not so good for the city. The property is no longer on the tax rolls, the revenue has not been recovered, and the city has the added burden of selling off the property in order to gain whatever return can be generated from the transaction.

BUYING REAL ESTATE FROM CITY HALL

Whether they like it or not, cities, towns, and counties do gain title to a considerable number of properties in this manner, and the method of disposing of them is almost invariably auction sale. In the larger cities, disposing of tax-foreclosed property has become such a high priority, in terms of maintaining a viable tax base, that many have begun to devote a lot of creative energy to promoting and facilitating such sales.

The City of New York is a good case in point. New York has real estate sales several times a year. They are held irregularly, at the discretion of the Board of Estimate, but the average is about one every three or four months. Roughly 200 parcels are sold on each occasion. The auctions are highly publicized, and the city publishes a large brochure for each, containing listings and descriptions of all the properties offered, along with an account of any special conditions that might apply to particular parcels, photographs of the more desirable offerings, a full rundown on the terms and conditions of sale, and information about available financing—a virtual auction catalog. New York is genuinely interested in getting private buyers in on this auction. "Your chance to own a piece of New York City," reads the promotional advertising. "Play your part in making it great again . . . and realize potential profit in the process."

The County of Los Angeles is another municipality that takes real estate sales seriously. (In California, real estate taxes are levied at the county level. Tax-delinquent properties are deeded to the state but auctioned by the county as agents for the state.) The county holds its one annual real estate auction each January, offering to the public an attractive promotional brochure on request, and, for a reasonable fee, a complete catalog of all the properties offered. In 1979, Los Angeles County auctioned off more than 11,000 parcels of land. The sale, attended by 2,000 to 3,000 buyers, was held in the L.A. Convention Center and went on for a week and a half. There is truly big-time action to be had in municipal real estate.

ADVERTISING AND PUBLICITY FOR MUNICIPAL AUCTIONS

Like virtually all auctions, municipal sales of real property are invariably advertised in the classified sections of "newspapers of record"—usually the principal newspapers of the area in question. This advertising is generally mandated by law. In addition to that, some cities will place ads more prominently in the main body of the paper (New York, for example, as cited above). Without exception, every municipality I have consulted maintains a mailing list for interested parties.

TYPES OF PROPERTIES SOLD AT MUNICIPAL AUCTIONS

The offerings at municipal real property auctions are a mixed bag. If you have been dreaming, while reading this section, of snapping up a comfortable ten-room suburban house, complete with well-trimmed lawn, forget it. This is not to say that desirable properties do not come up at public auction—they do, but they are the exception rather than the rule. Finding a real prize is likely to be the product of a lot of looking or a lot of luck.

Much of what is sold is a grab bag of vacant lots, some suitable, many unsuitable for building, residential, or commercial use; of odd, substandard strips and chunks of land entirely enclosed by the property of others and without legal access (known as "interior lots"); of

PARCEL NO.	BLOCK	LOT	LOCATION
12	1632	29	North Side of East 104th Street, 175 feet West of 3rd Avenue (Also known as 175 East 104th Street)
			4 Story former Firehouse

The development of and use of the subject property is r... and educational purposes, and any succe... purpose. This Govern...

catch basins, storm drains, pieces that defy description. For example, in New York one 34-by-100-foot parcel was described as 70 percent underwater, and another had the dimensions 3 1/2 *inches* by 112 feet.

Another major and, unfortunately, growing category of auction real estate is that of building lots on which the structures are so deteriorated as to constitute more of a liability than an asset. A typical situation would be an urban dwelling, abandoned by its owner, who is willing to sacrifice his probably minimal investment in the property in order to get out from under the burden of maintenance and taxes. During the time it takes for the municipality to gain title to and control over the property, the building is likely to be subject to considerable vandalism. By the time the city does get hold of it, it may be little more than a shell, or it may be destroyed entirely by fire or neglect. There is seldom enough left to interest the average or even the highly adventurous home buyer. In such circumstances, where besides the cost of acquisition considerable expenses would be incurred just to bring the property into line with codes and minimal safety standards, buyers can be pretty hard to find. Many municipalities will take on the expense of demolishing the building and grading the lot in order to increase its attractiveness and salability and reduce its danger as a public nuisance.

Finally, there are the viable, usable properties: a fair number of commercial buildings and building sites, surplus city or county facilities such as disused firehouses, offices, warehouses, etc., and dwellings of various sorts—one-, two-, and three-family homes, tenement and apartment buildings, and so forth. Some of these properties are in truly fine condition, many require some repair work, a few need substantial or total rehabilitation.

Incentives to buy: The prospects for the urban auction house hunter are reasonable, if not rosy, and getting better all the time. Many cities, large and small, have realized that it lies in their interests as well as those of potential buyers to set up programs that encourage and facilitate responsible ownership and, hence, neighborhood stability. One way of doing this is to set aside the more desirable residential properties, offering them to a select group of buyers under various kinds of contingencies (such as owner-occupation requirements) and with various kinds of inducements (such as subsidized rehabilitation financing). The object is usually to get suitable properties into the hands of owner-occupants—people whose interest in maintaining and improving the property is much more personal than that of a speculator or investor whose only interest is return on investment.

Further, in the cases of the many odd, irregular, substandard parcels, the interior lots, strips, bits and patches that abound in every jurisdiction, many municipalities are making a special effort, through research and personal contact, to encourage owners of adjacent properties to buy them on favorable terms, consolidating holdings and, presumably, ending their orphaned status for good.

PRICES AT MUNICIPAL AUCTIONS

Minimum prices: I know of no municipality that sells its tax-foreclosed properties at "absolute" auction. Virtually every parcel has an upset price. Local laws dictate the method or formula by which upset prices are established, and they vary from place to place, but the goal is generally the same—to strike a balance between bringing a fair return for the municipal treasury and making the value reasonably attractive to buyers.

In some communities, upset prices are established by an assessor or appraiser who actually inspects the property, taking its condition into account in arriving at the final figure. More often, the upset is determined on the basis of the existing tax assessment. The relationship between assessed valuation and actual market value varies tremendously from community to community. As a result, so do formulas for determining auction minimums. In Los Angeles, for example, the minimum acceptable bid is twice the assessed value of the property. Since assessed value is about one-fourth of present market value in California, these upset prices equal about 50 percent of market. In a community where assessed value approaches true market value, the auction upset price would generally be a percentage of the assessment—25 to 75 percent. Whatever the method or formula for fixing them, upset prices in municipal real estate auctions are never secret or confidential, like reserves in an estate auction. They are clearly stated on the listings and advertisements of the properties to be sold.

Sale prices: It is, of course, difficult to generalize about sale prices. Several factors influence the price a property brings at auction: primarily location, condition, and competition. The most I can hope to do here is suggest some limits and some general ball-park figures.

I have never seen any piece of urban property offered at auction with an upset price of less than $100. I'm sure that in large rural counties there are many such parcels. It is probably possible to buy real estate for $10 or less in the country.

The man at the tax assessor's office in Newark, New Jersey, told me that most of his area's vacant properties sell for between $100 and $3,000. Parcels with houses on them run from $5,000 or so for "shells" to upward of $35,000 for one- or two-family houses in reasonable condition. Average house prices there run about $18,000.

Prices for commercial buildings, surplus institutional facilities, and such can run from well below the $39,000 paid for a firehouse in my neighborhood recently up to several hundred thousand for a large warehouse or tract of land suitable for commercial development.

	SIZE	CASH REQUIREMENT*	MINIMUM UPSET PRICE
t, 33 feet North of 4th to 503 Clinton Street)	66 x 75	$8,000.	$40,000.
?t, 350 feet East of the New York City Transit Authority as shown on	222 x 200	$9,800.	$49,000.
150 feet ...			

Again, keep in mind that the prices I am referring to are city prices. In the country, real estate may be considerably cheaper.

WHO CAN BUY? WHO CANNOT?

Municipal real estate sales are public auctions. Presumably anyone can bid. Buyers at these sales are likely to consist in large part of professional speculators, but there are also a good number of sincere, motivated private and commercial buyers—people seeking homes, places of business, or places to build business establishments. As I said, some communities make a special effort to attract responsible private buyers; some do not.

The buyers who are *not* welcome are the sharp dealers and dishonest speculators—people who have histories of unscrupulous dealings. Many municipalities now require all bidders at public real estate sales to register ahead of time and to sign an affidavit swearing that they are acting for themselves alone, that they do not owe back taxes, that they have never had property foreclosed for tax delinquency, that they have never breached a contract for land purchase, and the like.

TERMS, CONDITIONS, AND STIPULATIONS OF SALE

Terms of public real estate sales aren't materially different from those at any other kind of real estate auction. Payment is, as usual, in cash, by certified check, or by personal check with a letter of credit. Some cash deposit is always required at auction time. This may range from total payment (in Los Angeles County, for properties sold for less than $5,000) down to as little as 10 percent. More typical is a deposit of 25 percent (or some arrangement like 10 percent at sale time followed by an additional 15 percent within 72 hours), with the balance to be paid on closing. Closing may be specified within any period from 15 to 120 days after the auction, usually within 30 to 45 days.

All real estate sold at public auction, like most auction goods, is sold *as is*. No credit or allowance is given for defects. In fact, quite the opposite is true. Most of these properties are sold subject to their being brought into compliance with all building and safety codes, usually within a stated period of one to two years.

Some communities make auction sales of real property contingent on confirmation by some ruling body such as the city council or board of managers. In these cases, the review is generally guaranteed to take place within a specified time of the auction. In the event that the sale is not confirmed for any reason, the purchaser's deposit is returned and the entire transaction is nullified.

Finally, as cities and towns have become increasingly concerned with directing and controlling the development of their lands and resources, it is more and more likely that specific stipulations will be attached to the sales of particular plots of land. Some sites may be sold with the provision that they be built on or otherwise developed within specified time limits. A building may be sold with a covenant barring its use for residential purposes. A vacant lot may be offered with the directive that it be used only for nonprofit, community-oriented open space for the residents of the area, and so forth. All such stipulations are clearly spelled out in the printed catalogs of properties offered and are also announced at the time of the auction.

FINANCING AND FINANCIAL AID FROM MUNICIPALITIES

In an effort to attract and cultivate responsible private buyers (as opposed to professional land speculators), some communities are beginning to offer various kinds of financial help. Only in one case that I know of does the municipality offer buyers primary financing—an actual mortgage. That is New York City. It strikes me as a practice that ought to be more widespread. It certainly facilitates sale of many otherwise unsalable properties, and it means income for the city that it otherwise would not be getting. Sure, the accountants would rather have the cash up front, but if the choice is between not selling at all and taking payment over 15 years (with interest), why not the latter? The city is not putting up any cash, after all. Anyway, it is a good deal for potential private buyers without extensive capital, especially in these times of tight money and expensive or unobtainable bank mortgages.

Other cities, large and small, are offering programs of various sorts to assist property owners, sometimes especially including purchasers of tax-foreclosed properties, with the problems of maintaining or upgrading their lots and houses—bringing them up to code standards or making substantial improvements. Programs take the form of free architectural help and planning advice, financing of rehabilitation loans under extremely favorable terms, tax abatements, and the like. They are finding wherever these programs are in effect that they contribute to stabilizing the community, increasing tax ratables, and generally reversing the tendencies that brought the properties to public auction in the first place. If you are considering bidding on properties offered at auction by your city or county, an inquiry about any assistance programs operating in the community might have a profound influence on your final course of action.

HOW DO YOU FIND OUT?

As mentioned, all auctions of publicly held property are advertised (by law) in the classified sections of the local "newspapers of record." If you read the papers regularly, you will know when sales

---

LAND AUCTION

SATURDAY JUNE 14 at 1 p.m.
1/4 mile east of Antioch, Ill. (Lake County) on North Ave.

78.07 ACRES
VACANT LAND

To be offered in 4 parcels, 15 to 23 acres and as 1 parcel. Located 1/4 mile from City limits, sewer and water. 2 1/2 miles west of Rte. 45 on State Line Rd., or 1 1/4 miles east of Rte. 83 on North Ave.

OTTO SPRENGER,
Antioch, Exclusive agent.
For information and brochure, call or write

auctioneer:
GORDON STADE
4312 N. Pioneer Rd.
McHENRY, ILLINOIS (815) 385-7032

are coming up. Also, as mentioned, every municipality in which I have made inquiries maintains a mailing list for interested buyers. Anyone can get on the list. If you just want to *talk* to someone about the real estate auctions in the area, a call to the tax assessor's office will get you in touch, directly or indirectly, with the person who can answer your questions.

ODD AND NOT-SO ODD LOTS

PUBLIC ADMINISTRATOR'S SALES

In most states, the law dictates that the property of decedents without heirs or without wills shall "accede" to the state. The state is not interested in the property itself, of course. It is the *proceeds* of estates that fit neatly into the public coffers, not the books and furniture. So what often happens is that an arrangement is made between the state and the local government by which the local government (usually at the county level) handles the disposal or liquidation of such estates, passing the cash along to the State Treasury.

In many areas of the country this job is done by a public administrator, or a similar official, and the property is sold at public auction. In other areas, the liquidation of maverick estates is handled through the probate courts, which appoint a representative to deal with all such matters. In these cases, the liquidation is likely to be handled through a private auction house. The quickest way to find out whether your community has a public administrator (or a similar official with a different title) is to call the probate court and inquire.

The bulk of what gets auctioned off consists of unremarkable basic household and personal property: appliances, rugs, bookcases, tables, pictures, binoculars, filing cabinets, beds, bathroom scales and the like. So, if you are looking for household items at super bargain prices, this is the kind of auction you should head for without delay.
Just plain folks: The estates that are disposed of by the public administrator for the most part consist of all the ordinary things that most people accumulate in the course of their lives. (Although the estates of some fairly well-to-do individuals do come into the hands of the public administrator from time to time, the chances are much greater that substantial estates will be handled in a safe, lawyerly fashion.)

The goods at these sales tend to be unedited and unsorted. That is to say, the things have been moved out of the home, lock, stock and barrel, and into a warehouse (after a search has been made for objects of special value). Desk drawers and cupboards still hold their original contents. File cabinets are full of tax records and personal correspondence. Wardrobes and dressers are often still full of clothing. This can make for some interesting if slightly depressing shopping.
Prices—none lower: Most of this ordinary household property goes for incredibly little money. At the first public administrator's sale I attended I acquired for a total of $32.65 (including local sales tax),

a decent blender, a steam iron, an orange juicer, a small vacuum cleaner, a floor polisher, and a good dictionary. That's hard to beat. **Treasure hunting:** Jewelry is an important item at these sales. Both retail and wholesale jewelry dealers attend. Competition is fairly brisk, but prices are still dealer prices, which is slightly below wholesale and far below retail. Private buyers are right in there bidding too. It is by no means an exclusive dealer's province.

The recent emphasis on jewelry at such sales has motivated some public administrators to start separating it out from the rest of the property (along with real estate) for disposal in special sales. More and more, the good pieces, the antiques, the artwork, and anything else thought to be worthy of special attention are set aside and sent off to mainstream auction galleries. This would seem to be the wave of the future, since pressure to squeeze the most possible public revenue from any available source is bound to increase.

MANY WARES, MANY BUYERS

The crowd at the local public administrator's sales is mixed. There are many secondhand dealers who will buy virtually anything, from old books and magazines to plant stands to old clothes, as long as they can get it cheaply. (Many lots go for $1 at these sales.) Mixed in with the junk dealers are retail and wholesale jewelry dealers, a smattering of antique shop operators, specialist "collectibles" buyers hunting such things as dolls, toys, paperweights, etc., and many private buyers.

THE TONE OF THE ESTABLISHMENT

The average public administrator's sale is a pretty gritty affair. The auctioneer is usually an independent, working on commission, and usually has a big day's work ahead of him when he starts out. You should be prepared to be assertive at these sales. Get your bids in loud and clear. Fast knockdowns are frequent. The auctioneer doesn't want to waste any time. If you feel that your bid has been ignored, let the auctioneer know.

KEEPING INFORMED

Public administrator's sales are advertised in the newspapers. Since in many areas these sales are held only when needed, most public administrators also maintain mailing lists and would be happy to put you down. Call up your city or county probate court, find the public administrator or his equivalent, and get on the mailing list. It is the easiest way to keep abreast of this rough-and-ready auction action.

PHILATELIC AND NUMISMATIC AUCTIONS

Collectibles have been mentioned frequently in this book, but so far I've failed to mention America's two oldest hobby pastimes: stamp and coin collecting. Both are very much alive.

Although stamps and coins are sold retail at dealers' shops and at philatelic and numismatic shows, the greater part of trading takes the form either of private deals between individuals or of auction sale. According to Frank Campbell, librarian at the American Numismatic Society, "If you consider all the dealers, both the major companies and the small distributions, there are thousands of coin auctions held in the U.S. every year." The same holds true for stamps. There are major dealers and auctioneers of stamps and coins (those grossing $15 million or more in annual sales) in every major urban area and many in smaller towns across the country.

THE QUESTION OF VALUE

Stamps and coins derive much of their value from their condition. In both areas of collecting, tradition has established categories of quality: for coins, fair, good, very good, fine, almost uncirculated, uncirculated, and mint (the last referring to specially made coins with a smoother finish than the standard issue); for stamps, good, fine, very fine, extremely fine, and superb. The value of a specimen of a particular issue will vary considerably depending on the condition classification it falls into. For example, the 1980 Scott postage stamp catalog (the standard price guide) lists the price of the first issue of the U.S. five-cents stamp of 1847, "used" (meaning it has been sent through the mails and has been canceled), at $550, but a specimen of that stamp will run anywhere from $100 to $3,000 at auction depending on its condition. As with the finest art and antiques, there is much competition for the finest stamps and coins.

EASE IN

Dealers who auction stamps and coins universally recommend that potential buyers and collectors familiarize themselves with the fields before attempting to get in on the action. There are a multitude of books on the subjects. The library of the American Numismatic Society houses over 70,000 volumes. Also fairly essential to anyone intending to buy stamps or coins is one of the standard price guides. For stamps, the guide mentioned above, published by the Scott Publishing Co., is considered the bible. For coins, *The Guide Book of U.S. Coins,* published once a year by R.S. Yeoman of Western Publishing, is considered an excellent reference source.

HOW IT WORKS

As far as procedures are concerned, stamp and coin auctions are much like other auctions. Most stamp and coin auctioneers provide detailed catalogs for all their sales. This facilitates the vast amount of "armchair" bidding that goes on in these areas of collecting. In a typical sale there might be 20 bidders on the floor (of whom several are likely to be agents representing one or more absent buyers), but the auctioneer might have as many as several hundred mail-order bids for the same event. It is quite normal for half the lots at a stamp or coin auction to go to mail-order bidders.

Relatively few stamp or coin auctioneers maintain permanent auction galleries, so sales are often held in rented rooms or halls at hotels. In order to make efficient use of such rented space, the auctions tend to be big affairs, often consisting of a series of sessions spread over a period of two or three days. As mentioned, mail-order bids are welcome at virtually all stamp or coin auctions, but order bids must be accompanied by a deposit, generally 50 percent of the bid. Terms of sale for floor bidders are not substantially different from those of the typical general merchandise auction.

The collecting of stamps can be a fascinating and rewarding pastime, and it can be a very lucrative investment, but heed the advice of the experts: Know what you are doing before you get into an auction situation. One of the major stamp dealers has put together a 32-page booklet for buyers and sellers on how to participate in a stamp auction. This should start you out on the right track, and it's anyone's guess where you go from there. Write to: *Jacques C. Schiff,*

Jr., Inc., Schiff Auction Catalogs, 195 Main St., Ridgefield Park, NJ 07660.

VINTAGE MERCHANDISE

Wines are currently one of the hottest items to be sold at auction these days, and as with so many auction goods, prices are climbing. It was only in 1970 that a double magnum (equal to four standard bottles) of 1865 Chateau Lafite first sold for as much as $480. Since that time, feverish wine enthusiasts have spent big money to enjoy the prestige of owning a bottle of superb wine. Prices of rarities have soared. A single bottle of 1806 Lafite, auctioned in London in 1977, went for $14,442. The same wine sold in Chicago two years later for $28,000. Since 1969 Heublein Inc., a major importer and marketer of wines and spirits, has held one of the world's largest public auctions of fine international wines. Rarities offered in recent Heublein auctions have included such exotic items as 19th century Bordeaux, Madeiras, and Ports salvaged from a British ship sunk in 1840—and a rare bottle of Tokay Essence vintage 1746, unearthed from the legendary Dresden cellars of Augustus III, Elector of Saxony and King of Poland.

MORE MODEST FARE

While Heublein prides itself on the extraordinary range of rare wines obtained from private collectors, the majority of offerings are selected from the best of the recent vintages, so there is plenty of wine flowing for the connoisseur with a more modest purse. The detailed catalog that Heublein puts out for the annual event includes price estimates, and a quick scan reveals many modestly priced wines. Currently, a case of Austrian Langenloiser Dechant is estimated to sell for between $50 and $150 (which works out to between $4.50 and $12.50 a bottle). Chateau Beauséjour, 1976, a fine French red, is estimated at $50 to $100 the case (or $4 to $8 a bottle).

BEST-TASTING AUCTION YOU'LL EVER ATTEND

One of the delightful things about the Heublein auction, and one that sets it apart, is that the equivalent of the standard auction exhibition is a "preview tasting." Five of these sessions are offered in the month prior to the sale in various locations throughout the United States plus Bermuda. For those who feel unschooled in the subtleties of wine appreciation, Heublein offers a two-day rare wine seminar, which features selections from the year's auction offerings. The auction catalog, purchased beforehand, serves as admission ticket to both the auction and the preview tasting.

So, for people with a taste for wine, a pilgrimage to San Francisco, Atlanta, New York, or Chicago (the location of the auction changes each year) would be a good bet. Catalogs and further information may be obtained by writing to: *Heublein, Inc., Box 505, Farmington, CT 06032.*

CHARITY AND FUND-RAISING AUCTIONS

Many nonprofit educational and charitable institutions supplement their income by holding auctions. The goods and/or services auctioned off are usually donated by patrons of the institution, and the labor necessary to set up and run the sale is generally provided by volunteers.

Many auction houses conduct charity or fund-raising auctions from time to time. They donate the use of their facilities and mailing list, and they use their staffs to set up and run the sale, with a bit of help from outside volunteers. In return for this public service, they reap a certain amount of free publicity and goodwill.

As long as the organization or institution benefiting from the auction has tax-exempt, nonprofit status, the value of any donation made to the sale is a tax deduction for the donor. This is one of the reasons that auction sales are a good source of revenue. For people in high tax brackets, helping a worthy cause can also be a way of easing their own tax problem.

AUCTIONS OVER THE AIR

Of all the auctions held in this country nowadays, probably none are more visible than the annual fund-raising sales held by the more than 70 television stations of the Public Broadcasting System. The idea of using auctions to raise money for public TV was put into practice a number of years ago. It was quite successful, and it spread quickly throughout the PBS network. These events have become a key element of public television's fund-raising activities, and for the smaller stations especially, the auction income constitutes a significant portion of operating revenues.

The goods and services auctioned off are donated by private individuals, small businesses, and corporations, and a great deal of the labor involved is done by unpaid volunteers—members of the viewing public, for the most part. The local auction businesses get involved, too—donating their services as auctioneers and helping in the organization of the event.

The auction offerings on these televised extravaganzas are as varied as the donors. You can bid on anything from handmade ceramics to gold coins to Joan Crawford's silver compact to a dinner for two at the restaurant of your choice. A minor scandal was brought about by the last item. In 1976, the American Express Company donated a dinner for two, and the winning bid (of $300) went to Craig Claiborne, a well-known New York restaurant critic and author. The restaurant he selected for the event was in Paris. With wines included, the bill came to an incredible $4,000.

Blocks of air time are devoted to the events. During this time, the goods (or pictures and descriptions of them) are shown over the tube, and bids are solicited. Each lot is put up for a specified length of time, with the more important and valuable items remaining on the block for longer periods. Viewers participate by calling in by phone to place their bids. As the auction progresses, the bids on each item are announced, giving people a chance to bid again if their earlier bid has been bettered. After the bidding on each lot closes, the amount of the winning bid and the identity of the winning bidder are announced (unless the bidder wishes to remain anonymous).

These PBS auctions generate a great deal of excitement and fun. Everyone has a good time in the end, despite missing an episode or two of Masterpiece Theater. They are also quite lucrative.

A TRULY DIFFERENT KIND OF FUND-RAISER

If you are in the market for a dream come true, there is an auction you shouldn't miss. It's called the Possible Dreams Auction and takes place each summer in early August on Martha's Vineyard, off the coast of Massachusetts. The auction is held by the Martha's Vineyard General Services Organization to raise money for their various social services, which include a visiting-nurse service, a youth center, a mental-health center, an early-childhood program, a counseling and crisis program for alcoholics, and a thrift shop. What kind of dreams can be bought at an auction? Explains Marcia Shafer, spokeswoman for the Martha's Vineyard GSO, "We auction the things that are not normally available for purchase, things indigenous to this island, experiences you couldn't have elsewhere."

Have you ever wished to be a lobsterman for the day tending lobster traps in the whaling town of Menemsha, or to cruise the islands in a Coast Guard patrol boat, or to be the guest of the captain in the pilothouse of the Martha's Vineyard ferryboat? How about picking beach plums and making plum preserves with the island's jelly-making expert, or touring the Cape Pogue Wildlife Preserve on Chappaquiddick, or blowing the foghorns in the lighthouses that dot the Cape Cod islands? All these fantasies and more were up for bids before the more than 350 people who attended the premiere auction in 1979.

What really drew the crowds, says Ms. Shafer, were the unique "celebrity lots" arranged by the famous persons who vacation on Martha's Vineyard and see the island as a second home. The items donated and services rendered by these celebrities were particularly well received by the enthusiastic crowd of bidders as they sipped complimentary drinks in the courtyard of the Harborside Inn, donated for the occasion by its proprietor, Arthur Young. Sculptor Richard Lee was on hand to present a life mask of Gene Shalit, critic for NBC News. The mask sold for $75. Mia Farrow contributed a jacket worn in one of her films, and it sold for $200. If you were inclined, you could bid for honorable mention in Art Buchwald's Washington *Post* column, or you could opt for an evening of dancing at Carly Simon's restaurant on the island.

Of all the lots auctioned that day the one which drew the most attention was sold to a regular summer resident of the Vineyard, for a bid of $225. The islander won the privilege of a day's sail for two with Mr. and Mrs. Walter Cronkite on their 38-foot ketch.

For further information, write to: *Martha's Vineyard General Services Organization, Inc., P.O. Box 591, Vineyard Haven, Martha's Vineyard, MA 02568.*

AUCTIONING REMNANTS OF THE PAST

Described as "the P.T. Barnum of the auction business," John P. Wilson, a 41-year-old former precision-instruments salesman, switched to the nostalgia business some ten years ago. He holds an annual auction of architectural remnants that is as much a party as it is an auction.

The auction, which offers such desirable remains of old buildings as stained-glass windows, doors, ceilings, entryways, bars, mantels and entire paneled rooms, is an extravaganza which some 1200 people pay $250 each to attend. The $250, which is nonrefundable but applicable to any later purchase, also entitles a person to the fabulously prepared meals that are catered for the three-day event. Other amenities for the buyers include Dixieland bands, shuttle buses, disposable toothbrushes in the restrooms, and simultaneous translation for foreign visitors.

Despite all the fun, the auction is held to make money. The nostalgia business and theme have grown rapidly in recent years with no end in sight, and this sale offers treasure from the past. The buyers range from private individuals looking for some trinket to enhance their home to the restaurant owners searching for the kind of old-fashioned decor that can't be bought new anymore. A restaurateur from Florida relates, "At the first auction I paid forty-five hundred dollars for a real historic bar from Chicago. This year ordinary bars are bringing forty-five thousand. I don't know if it is the total devaluation of the dollar or total inflation or a general dissatisfaction with shoddy material. Some of this is good, beautifully made stuff." If Wilson's auction is good for the buyers, it is also good for the seller. Wilson's gross in 1979 exceeded $7.5 million.

The items offered for sale are collected from all over the world. Some come from afar, such as the interior entryway from Lloyd's of London, some from closer by, such as a stained-glass dome originally made for a San Francisco Elks' hall, which sold in 1979 for $90,000.

AT THE SIGN OF THE THREE GOLDEN BALLS

We are accustomed to thinking of pawnshops as places that offer bargains, but not auction bargains. Nevertheless, in some parts of the country, pawnbrokers do put merchandise on the auction block.

Pawnbrokers have been around for a long time, acting as a kind of neighborhood finance company, lending sums small and large to individuals on tangible collateral.

Although they may be an endangered species (there were more than 130 pawnshops in New York City in 1946—there are only about 20 today), pawnbrokers are still alive and doing business. One of the many laws regulating the conduct of the business deals with the disposal of unredeemed pledges. (The item of collateral that the borrower puts up to secure the loan is called a "pledge," and "redeeming" it simply means paying off the loan, principal and interest, and resuming possession.) In most municipalities, the term of the loan is fixed by law—usually three to six months. At the end of this time, if the borrower hasn't settled the debt, the broker begins to take steps to recover his money.

After various stages of notification, the broker's final recourse is generally to take title to and sell the property to recover his money. In most states, the pawnbroker simply takes the merchandise and puts it in his window with a price tag and waits for the right customer to come along. But in some states, the law mandates that unredeemed pledges be sold at auction. New York is one of those states, and in New York City, there are two auction houses that operate full-time selling pawnshop merchandise.

Most of the unredeemed pawn pledges are items of jewelry; there are, however, odds and ends of other merchandise, and the auction houses that sell for pawnshops hold occasional sales of the typewriters, cameras, binoculars, stereos, musical instruments and other things that make up the 5 percent of miscellaneous pledges. More private buyers tend to show up for these odds-and-ends sales, but there is still a preponderance of dealers.

Prices are medium-low. I have seen television sets sell for between $35 and $125. Manual typewriters sell for as little as $12; electrics for as little as $75. Radios were knocked down for between $5 and $50. One large conga drum sold for $25.

The pawnshop auction is worth checking out. The easiest way to find out if pawn pledges are sold at auction in your area is to give a local pawnbroker a call and ask what he does with his unredeemed items.

CARS, VANS, TRUCKS (A Summary)

Cars (including vans, trucks, motorcycles, etc.) are one of the best auction buys, if not the single best buy, for the private auction shopper. They turn up at an astonishing variety of auction sales, and sooner or later just about any kind of vehicle you could ever want will cross the auction block—probably sooner.

While certain auctions are held exclusively for the sale of automobiles, most cars are sold as part of a larger auction procedure. This is the case for private general merchandise auctions as well as government agency sales. These sales have been mentioned as part of that larger process in the other chapters of this book. What follows is a brief summary of the auto auction market as well as some helpful hints on where and when some specific auctions take place.

CLASSICS

Automobiles are definitely a part of the glitter world of auctions. Both the international giants among auction houses, Christie's and Sotheby's, have automotive sales divisions. Automobile sales held by these international houses and by auto specialists such as Kruse Auctioneers based in Auburn, Indiana, are designed primarily to sell classic vintage cars—collector's items that have been properly cared for or lovingly restored by wealthy owners. In addition, however, they do sell many cars "for use." This category includes many good Rolls-Royces, Bentleys, Daimlers and Mercedes-Benzes that have not quite achieved "classic" status.

For information on "classic" car auctions consult the classified section of your local paper under "Autos." *The Old Cars Newspaper,* published in Iola, Wisconsin, also frequently carries ads for these sales. Finally, *Road & Track Magazine,* published in Newport Beach, California, prints ads in their Marketplace section for "classic" cars and these sometimes include "classic" car auctions. Finally, all three auction houses mentioned above will furnish catalogs and sale notices to interested buyers on written request.

REPOSSESSIONS

Repossessed cars are the stars of the auto auction offerings simply because, of all the cars available at auction, they are likely to be the newest—the normal period for payment of car loans is 36 months. When a bank or finance company, because of defaulted loans, accumulates enough repossessed cars to justify the effort, they hold an auction. The bank either enlists the services of a local auctioneer or runs the auction on their own. Some banks choose to conduct their own auctions because it saves them the auctioneer's percentage. Banks that run their own auctions maintain mailing lists to inform interested parties of the sale schedule. Sales are also advertised in major local papers.

Repossessed cars are sold "as is," but new car warranties are often still in effect when the new owner takes possession. Also, these cars carry a clear title; when you buy, you own free and clear. Inspection is generally limited to starting up the car, kicking the tires, etc.—test driving is seldom allowed. Payment is generally 25 percent in cash or certified check at auction time, and the balance within 3 to 5 days. Financing arrangements are up to you.

144 AUTOMOBILES

PUBLIC AUTO AUCTION BY ORDER OF AVCO FINANCIAL SERVICES, BANK OF NEW YORK, BANKERS TRUST COMPANY, CHASE MANHATTAN BANK, CHEMICAL BANK, CITIBANK, LONG ISLAND BANK, LONG ISLAND TRUST, MANUFACTURERS HANOVER TRUST COMPANY AND UNDER THE

CARS FROM COPS

In the course of duty, police departments accumulate a large number of cars. Many have been stolen and then abandoned. Some are taken in evidence or during an investigation, and many are towed for parking violations. If no one comes forward to claim them, the police dispose of them, generally at auction.

All cars are sold "as is" and "where is"—usually without the keys. (There is often a locksmith on the premises, but his services are definitely an extra.) Typically, inspection is visual only, and the cars are sold subject to minimums determined at the discretion of the auctioneer. Payment is in full in cash or certified check at the time of the auction, and the vehicle must be removed within 24 to 72 hours or storage charges will accrue. You must register the car properly before removal.

Advertising for these auctions is often in the name of the auc-

AUCTION

By Order of the Chicago Police Department

We Will Sell at Public Auction

1974 AUTOMOBILES AND UP

200 AUTOMOBILES MORE OR LESS

Every Automobile to be sold individually

1974 AUTOMOBILES AND UP

THESE CARS WILL BE SOLD INDIVIDUALLY TO THE SUCCESSFUL BIDDER OR BIDDERS AND CERTIFICATE OF PURCHASE WILL BE ISSUED TO THE BUYER. Cars must be removed from Pound within 7 days. After 7 days, $2.50 per car per day storage will be charged to the Buyer.

TERMS OF SALE: All Sales are for cash only. No checks accepted. Payment in full at time of purchase. All cars sold on as is where is basis without any representation as to condition or vintage.

Honorable JANE BYRNE
Mayor

JOSEPH DILEONARDI
Acting Superintendent

PAUL T. DUELLMAN, Director, Department Custodian

ACE AUCTIONEERS & LIQUIDATORS, INC.

ALBERT PALETZ, Auctioneer

321 WEST LAKE STREET

(312) 346-5955

tioneer handling the sale, but you will notice something like "by order of the police department" at the top of the notice. Few police departments maintain mailing lists, but most have a phone number to call for information on upcoming sales. Call your local headquarters and ask for the Property and Evidence Clerk, or the section which handles their vehicle auctions.

BUYING FROM OTHER LAW ENFORCEMENT AGENTS

Sheriffs and marshals also sell automobiles at public auction. Their sales are generally the result of a court proceeding in which an individual, an institution or a government agency is seeking to satisfy a debt. Cars tend to be among the more visible and salable pieces of claimable property.

Automobile auctions run by the sheriffs and marshals do not differ significantly from repossession sales except in terms of the clarity of title that can be offered. If there are liens on the car, the car is sold subject to those liens. In other words, the buyer of the car also buys the obligation to pay off all liens.

There is, then, a certain risk in buying a car at one of these sales, but the prices, especially at parking-violations auctions, reflect this risk—they are low. Look in your local paper under the legal notices section for the sales or call your local sheriff's or marshal's office.

BANKRUPTCY AND LIQUIDATION SALES

Bankruptcies and liquidations are another excellent source for used cars, vans and light trucks. However, sometimes there are liens on vehicles sold at these auctions. You will do well to gather all the facts before you bid. Often an auctioneer will pay off all liens and offer his cars free and clear in order to expedite business. This is an exception, however, not the rule, so you should find out beforehand what the terms and conditions of sale are. Inspect the vehicle very carefully at the viewing and be prepared to pay a 25 percent cash deposit at the time of the auction.

As for questions of where and when, your local paper is the best source—ads in the classified section will list the details, locations and dates.

CAR AUCTION "DEALERSHIPS"

There is a small but growing number of permanent, established businesses which auction off cars to the public and to dealers alike. Vehicles offered for sale include repossessed cars, fleet cars from government agencies, corporations or service businesses, cars from auto dealers and cars owned by private individuals who are anxious to sell them quickly. Sometimes you'll even find fire engines or tractors up for sale.

Sales are generally held weekly. Cars can be inspected visually, sometimes started, but seldom driven. A deposit is required on knockdown, and buyers are usually given seven days to come up with the balance in cash or certified check.

WHEELS FROM UNCLE SAM

The auctions held by the Department of Defense constitute a fair, not great, source of motor vehicles for private use. The chapter concerning the Department of Defense auctions explains why. The GSA auction program, on the other hand, is an excellent source. As suggested in the GSA chapter, get on the mailing list of the district in which you live, and you will receive notices of upcoming sales which give the particulars, including location, date, inspection times and the telephone number for the Interagency Motor Pool facility at which the sale is being held. That phone number is the key to efficient buying at GSA.

Postal Service sales: Each of the many postal districts has a Vehicle Maintenance Facility which cares for the Service's cars, trucks and jeeps. When the "useful life" of each vehicle is deemed at an end—as far as the Postal Service is concerned—they are sold off to the public. They may have plenty of life in them for the private consumer.

While the Postal Service is an excellent source of used cars and trucks, the method of sale is up to the discretion of the local postal district. Most have elected to use a fixed-price sales method for the vehicles they recycle. Only one major postal district, Chicago, employs the auction method for the bulk of its car and truck turnovers.

Postal vehicles are given good care before they are sent out into the private sector. All vehicles are repainted, many are given new tires, tune-ups, new bumpers and such, and all must pass a basic set of safety tests.

Sales are publicized by radio and television advertising, newspaper ads and flyers posted in all post offices. Interested buyers seeking further details should contact the Fleet Operations division of the Vehicle Maintenance Facility for the General Post Office in the city or town where they live.

THE AUCTION PAGES

The listings on the following pages have been selected in order to provide you with a source list to the auction markets. Local and federal government sources of auction information and auction property, private auctioneers, and private auction galleries have been broken down by federal region, by state, and where possible by localities.

The listings of individual auction houses are based on questionnaires which were answered and returned during the making of this book. The mention of these individual auction sources is not intended as a warranty as to a particular individual, organization, or corporation.

Use these sources selectively, and take advantage of the opportunity to get on the various mailing lists for sale announcements and presale catalogs. The information here should prove to be invaluable in expanding your auction shopping experience.

Antiques Magazine
551 Fifth Ave.
New York, NY 10017
(212) 682-8282

Antique Monthly
P.O. Drawer 2
Tuscaloosa, AL 35402
(205) 345-0288

Antiques World
122 E. 42nd St.
New York, NY 10017
(212) 599-6060

Antiques & the Arts Weekly
The Bee Publishing Co.
Newtown, CT 06470
(203) 426-8036

The Antique Trader Weekly
Box 1050
Dubuque, IA 52001
(319) 588-2073

The Gray Letter
P.O. Drawer 2
Tuscaloosa, AL 35402
(205) 345-0288

Art & Auction
50 W. 57th St.
New York, NY 10019
(212) 582-633

The Maine Antique Digest
Friendship Rd.
Waldoboro, ME 04572
(207) 832-7534

Art Newsletter
122 E. 42nd St.
New York, NY 10017
(212) 599-6060

The Southeast Trader
P.O. Box 519
Lexington, KY 29072
(803) 359-9182

The Auction News
Livestock Exchange Bldg.
1600 Genessee
Kansas City, MO 64102
(816) 421-7117

The Tri-State Trader
27 N. Jefferson
Knightstown, IN 46148
(317) 345-5134

AUCTION SCHOOLS

Repperts School of
Auctioneering
Box 189
Decatur, IN 46733
(219) 724-3804

Missouri Auction School
914 Livestock Exchange Bldg.
Kansas City, MO 64102
(816) 421-7117

NEW ENGLAND REGION
CONNECTICUT (CT), MAINE (ME), MASSACHUSETTS (MA), NEW HAMPSHIRE (NH), RHODE ISLAND (RI), VERMONT (VT)

General Services Administration

GSA
(Real Property)
Post Office and Courthouse
Boston, MA 02109
(617) 223-2651

GSA
(Personal Property)
Post Office and Courthouse
Boston, MA 02109
(617) 223-2394

Department of Defense

DoD Surplus Sales
P.O. Box 1370
Battle Creek, MI 49016
(Write to this address to
get on national mailing list)

Defense Property Disposal
P.O. Box 13110
Columbus, OH 43213
(614) 236-2114

Internal Revenue Service

IRS, District Director
P.O. Box 959
Hartford, CT 06101
(203) 244-2791

IRS, District Director
P.O. Box 787
Augusta, ME 04330
(207) 622-1081

IRS, District Director
P.O. Box 9112
JFK Post Office
Boston, MA 02203
(617) 223-6201

IRS, District Director
P.O. Box 720
Portsmouth, NH 03801
(603) 436-7720 x750

IRS, District Director
P.O. Box 6528
Providence, RI 02940
(401) 528-5221

IRS, District Director
11 Elmwood Ave.
Burlington, VT 05401
(802) 895-6355

Customs

U.S. Customs Service
120 Middle St.
Bridgeport, CT 06609
(203) 579-4606

U.S. Customs Service
312 Fore St.
Portland, ME 04111
(207) 780-3326

U.S. Customs Service
2 India St.
Boston, MA 02109
(617) 223-6598

U.S. Customs Service
24 Weybosset St.
Providence, RI 02903
(401) 528-4383

U.S. Customs Service
Main & Stebbins St.
St. Albaud, VT 05478
(802) 524-6527

U.S. Marshals

U.S. Marshal
141 Church St.
New Haven, CT 06504
(203) 643-8107

U.S. Marshal
P.O. Box 349
Portland, ME 04112
(207) 833-3355

U.S. Marshal
P.O. Box 352
Boston, MA 02101
(617) 223-2851

U.S. Marshal
P.O. Box 1435
Concord, NH 03301
(603) 834-4734

U.S. Marshal
P.O. Box 1524
Providence, RI 02901
(401) 838-4305

U.S. Marshal
Elmwood Ave. & Pearl St.
Burlington, VT 05401
(802) 832-6271

Post Office

Procurement Services
Office
Connecticut Valley District
U.S. Postal Service
141 Weston St./Rm. 311
Hartford, CT 06101
(203) 244-2486

Post Master
Dead Parcel Branch
Boston, MA 02109
(617) 223-7534

Procurement Services
Office
U.S. Postal Service
202 South Postal Annex
Boston, MA 02109
(617) 223-5086

State Surplus Departments

State Surplus
Property Center
P.O. Box 298
Wethersfield, CT 06109
(203) 566-7018

Bureau of Purchasing
State Office Bldg./Rm. 211
Station 9
Augusta, ME 04333
(207) 289-3521

Division of Purchase &
Property State Surplus
State House Annex
Concord, NH 03301
(603) 271-3200

State of Rhode Island
Division of Purchasing
301 Promenade St.
Providence, RI 02908
(401) 277-2375

State of Vermont
Purchasing Division
Montpellier, VT 05602
(802) 828-2219

SHERIFFS

Connecticut: BRIDGEPORT—Fairfield County Sheriff's Dept., Main St., Bridgeport, CT 06604 (203) 579-6239 / HARTFORD—Hartford County Sheriff's Dept., 95 Washington St., Hartford, CT 06106 (203) 566-4930
Maine: PORTLAND—Cumberland County Sheriff's Dept., 122 Federal St., Portland, ME 04112 (207) 774-1444
Massachusetts: BOSTON—Suffolk County Sheriff's Dept., Suffolk County Courthouse, Rm. 102, Boston, MA 02108 (617) 227-2541 / SPRINGFIELD—Hampden County Sheriff's Dept., 50 State St., Springfield, MA 01103 (413) 781-8100
New Hampshire: MANCHESTER—Hillsboro County Sheriff's Dept., 300 Chestnut St., Manchester, NH 03101 (602) 623-7259
Rhode Island: PROVIDENCE—Providence County Sheriff's Dept., 250 Benefit St., Providence, RI 02903 (401) 277-3510
Vermont: BURLINGTON—Chittendon County Sheriff's Dept., Box 1042, Burlington, VT 05401 (802) 863-4341

POLICE

Maine: PORTLAND—Portland Police Dept., Property Officer, 109 Middle St., Portland, ME (207) 775-6361
Massachusetts: BOSTON—Boston Police Dept., Property Room, 154 Berkley St., Boston, MA (617) 247-4579
New Hampshire: MANCHESTER—Manchester Police Dept., 351 Chestnut St., Manchester, NH (603) 688-8711

GENERAL MERCHANDISE—ESTATE SALES—COUNTRY AUCTIONS

Connecticut: BRIDGEPORT—Park City Auction Service, 925 Wood Ave. (liquidators, appraisers; Monday night auctions) (203) 333-5251; Stratford Auction Gallery, P.O. Box 1121 (estates) (203)

375-7628 / CANTON–Canton Barn Auctions, 79 Old Canton Rd. (antiques, household furnishings; Saturday 5:00 p.m. auction) (203) 693-4901 / CHESTER–Sage Auction Galleries, Rt. 9A (antiques, home furnishings; no children allowed) (203) 526-3036 / EAST HARTFORD–Col. Rod Clarke Auction Gallery East, Inc., 273 Ellington Rd. (estates, antiques, commercial-industrial liquidations) (203) 289-6165 / NEW MILFORD–Gallery on the Hill, Rt. 109 (fine arts, antiques, estates) (203) 354-4653 / NEW LONDON–Seymour Manheimer, 38 Green St. (industrial-commercial liquidations, bankruptcies) (203) 443-5942 / NORWALK–Fairfield County Estate Liquidators (Robert Ruggiero, Auctr.), 66 Fort Point St., (estates, antiques; country auctions first and third Saturdays at noon–middle & low-quality furniture, appliances, household goods) (203) 838-6541 / SOUTHPORT –William J. Josko & Sons, 5 Pease Ave. (estates, antiques, general merchandise, liquidations) (203) 255-1441 / WETHERSFIELD–Clearing House Auction Galleries, Inc., 207 Church St. (estates, fine arts, antiques) (203) 529-3344

Maine: PORTLAND–Barridoff Gallery, 242A Middle St. (fine arts, antiques; three auctions a year in Spring, Summer, Fall: catalogue for each sale) (207) 772-5011 / ELLSWORTH–Mayo Auctioneers and Appraisers, Inc., Rt. 1, Box 285 (estates, antiques, American furniture; monthly auctions March through November) (207) 667-8062 / FAIRFIELD–Julia's Auction Barn (James Julia, Auctr.), Rt. 201, Skowhegan Rd. (general merchandise) (207) 453-9725

Massachusetts: BOSTON–Phillips, 1 Dock Sq. (fine arts, furniture, silver, collectibles) (617) 227-6145; Sotheby Parke-Bernet, Clarendon St. (fine arts, antiques, silver, collectibles) (617) 247-2851; John S. McGrath and Son, Inc., 99 State St. (real estate, bankruptcies, liquidations, customs) (617) 227-1125; Paul E. Saperstein Co., Inc., 126 State St. (liquidations) (617) 227-6553 / BROOKLINE–Joseph Louis Auction Gallery, Inc., P.O. Box 388 (estates, antiques, furniture, silver) (617) 277-0740 / BOLTON–Robert W. Skinner, Inc., Bolton Gallery, Rt. 117 (estates, antiques, fine arts, furnishings) (617) 779-5528 / EAST DENNIS–Robert Eldred, Box 796 (fine arts, antiques) (617) 385-3116 / HYANNISPORT–Richard A. Bourne, Box 141 (fine arts, antiques, country things) (617) 775-0797 / LAKEVILLE–John Roselle, Rt. 105 (antique furniture) (617) 947-2122 / SEEKONK– Leo Melanson Antiques and Interiors, Auction Division, 288 Fall River Ave. (antiques, furnishings) (617) 336-8063 / AGAWAM–Collectibles Unlimited, 65 Agawam Shopping Center (413) 786-9884 / AMHERST–Amherst Auction Gallery (William Hubbard, Auctr.), Jct. Rts. 116 & 63, N. Amherst, MA (Saturday Auction 10:00 a.m., two book auctions a month, estates) (413) 253-9914 / EASTHAMPTON– George T. Lewis and Assoc., 350 Main St. (estates, antiques) (413) 527-5722 / GREENFIELD–Mark Polon, 54 Hope St. (fine arts, antiques, Friday night auction) (413) 774-3631 / LUDLOW—Anchor Auction Assoc., 438 Center St. (real estate, antiques, equipment, commercial-industrial liquidations) (413) 583-5131 / NORTHFIELD—Ken Miller and Son, Inc., Warwick Ave. (general merchandise) (413) 498-2749 / PALMER—Robert Chaffee and Sons, 1 Auction Pl. (general merchandise) (413) 283-3841

New Hampshire: MANCHESTER—Arthur D. Collins, 342 Bridge St. (estates) (603) 669-8980; Coin and Stamp Shop, 1033 Elm Rd. (603) 624-4400; Hooksett Auction Gallery, Daniel Webster Highway, N. Manchester, NH (estates, business liquidations) (603) 627-4969 / HILLSBORO—Richard Withington, Hillsboro Center (fine arts, antiques, household goods, collectibles) (603) 464-3232 / KEENE—Bruce Amadon, 111 North St. (antiques) (603) 352-0362; Old Road to Boston Antiques, 31 Dartmouth St. (603) 352-3859 / MERRIMACK—Artpro Auctioneering Services (Arthur Provencher, Auctr.), Rt. 3 (estates, business liquidations) (603) 424-9964 / NORTH LONDONDERRY—J.S. Leblanc and Co., Inc., Rockingham Rd. (general merchandise) (603) 432-2597

Rhode Island: PROVIDENCE—Max Pollack and Co., Auctioneers Ltd., 45 Eagle St. (commercial-industrial liquidations, residential liquidations, auctions for federal, state, municipal governments) (401) 331-6950; W.L. Conley Co., 273A Thayer (books) (401) 621-9700; Barnett Carter and Co., Inc., 936 Hospital Trust Building (real estate, general merchandise, machinery, bankruptcies) (401) 521-8844 / CRANSTON—Ocean State Auction Gallery (Margaret Motola, Auctr.), 2166 Broad St. (estates, antiques) (401) 781-6222 / PAWTUCKET—Rhode Island Auction Gallery, 129 Norfolk Ave. (general merchandise) (401) 724-8585

Vermont: BURLINGTON—Arthur H. Smith Auctioneer, Box 86, Ferrisburg, Vt. (estates, appraisals, antiques, household furnishings) (802) 877-3638 / RUTLAND—Tom Whittaker, 1 Franklin St., Box 145, Brandon, Vt. (village and country real estate, farm auctions, appraisals) (802) 247-6633 / BRATTLEBORO—Paul Lawton and Son, Auctioneers, P.O. Box 551 (antiques, good modern furniture, commercial sales; Wednesday evening auction; on location sales in summer; Labor Day auction on the common in Newfane) (802) 254-8969; Rare Books (Ken Leach) P.O. Box 78 (802) 257-7918 / MIDDLEBURY—Forrest and Theo Lowell, 34 Main St. (real estate, personal property, antiques, household furnishings, farm and chattel) (802) 388-2338 / MILTON—K C Auction and Furniture (Leo Hinton, Auctr.), Rt. 7 (general merchandise, furniture) (802) 893-2188 / SHELBURNE—Warren H. Smith, 24 Meadow Lane (antiques, home furnishings, estate and insurance appraisals) (802) 985-2044 / WATERBURY CENTER—Sir Richard's Antique Auction, Box 98 (real estate, personal property) (802) 244-8829

REGIONAL MEDIA

Connecticut: HARTFORD—Hartford Courant (auction ads Sunday) (203) 249-6411 / NEW HAVEN—New Haven Register (auction ads daily) (203) 772-3700 / NEWTOWN—Antiques & The Arts Weekly, published by the Bee Publishing Co., Newtown, CT 06470 (source of auction info. for entire U.S.) (203) 426-8036

Maine: BANGOR—Bangor Daily News (auction ads daily; more Thursday) (207) 942-5246 / PORTLAND—Portland Press Herald (auction ads daily; more Sunday) (207) 775-3151 / TOSPHAM—Maine Times (weekly—comes out Friday) (207) 729-0126 / WALDOBORO—Maine Antique Digest, Friendship Rd., Waldoboro, ME 04572 (source of auction info. for entire U.S.) (207) 832-7534

Massachusetts: BOSTON—Boston Globe (auction ads daily; more Sunday) (617) 929-2000; Boston Herald American (antique auction ads Sunday-Wednesday-Friday-Saturday; other auction ads Sunday) (617) 426-3000 / NORTHAMPTON—Hampshire Gazette (auction ads Thursday-Friday-Saturday) (413) 584-5000 / SPRINGFIELD—Springfield Sunday Republican (auction ads Sunday) (413) 787-5163

New Hampshire: CLAREMONT—The Claremont Eagle Times (auction ads Monday-Tuesday-Thursday-Friday) (603) 542-5121 / KEENE—Keene Sentinel (auction ads Thursday-Friday-Saturday) (603) 352-1234 / MANCHESTER—Manchester Union Leader (auction ads Thursday) (603) 668-4321

Rhode Island: PROVIDENCE—Providence Journal (auction ads Wednesday and Friday) (401) 277-7700

Vermont: BRATTLEBORO—Brattleboro Reformer (auction ads daily; more on weekend) (802) 257-0563 / BURLINGTON—Burlington Free Press (auction ads Thursday and Friday) (802) 863-3441 / RUTLAND—Rutland Herald (auction ads Thursday) (802) 775-5511

MID-ATLANTIC REGION
NEW JERSEY (NJ), NEW YORK (NY), PENNSYLVANIA (PA)

General Services Administration

GSA
(Real Property—NY, NJ)
26 Federal Plaza
New York, NY 10007
(212) 264-2650

GSA
(Personal Property—NY, NJ)
26 Federal Plaza
New York, NY 10007
(212) 264-2034

GSA
(Real Property—PA)
7th & D St., S.W.
Washington DC 20407
(202) 557-1619

GSA
(Personal Property—PA)
7th & D St., S.W.
Washington DC 20407
(202) 557-1619

Department of Defense

DoD Surplus Sales
P.O. Box 1370
Battle Creek, MI 49016
(write to this address to get on national mailing list)

Defense Property Disposal
P.O. Box 13110
Columbus, OH 43213
(614) 236-2114

Internal Revenue Service

IRS, District Director
P.O. Box 939
Newark, NJ 07101
(201) 645-2198

IRS, District Director
Leo W. O'Brien Federal Bldg.
Clinton Ave. & N. Pearl St.
Albany, NY 12207
(518) 472-4453

IRS, District Director
P.O. Box 380, G.P.O.
Brooklyn, NY 11202
(212) 330-7500

IRS, District Director
P.O. Box 60 Niagra Sq. Sta.
Buffalo, NY 14201
(716) 846-5500

IRS, District Director
P.O. Box 3000 Church St. Sta.
New York, NY 10008
(212) 264-2000

IRS, District Director
P.O. Box 12805
Philadelphia, PA 19106
(215) 597-4210

IRS, District Director
P.O. Box 1837
Pittsburgh, PA 15230
(412) 644-5641

Customs

U.S. Customs Service
Airport International Plaza
Newark, NJ 07114
(201) 645-3760

U.S. Customs Service
111 W. Huron St.
Buffalo, NY 14202
(716) 842-5901

U.S. Customs Service
6 World Trade Center
New York, NY 10048
(212) 466-5817

U.S. Customs Service
127 N. Water St.
Ogdenburg, NY 13669
(315) 393-0660

U.S. Customs Service
2nd & Chestnut Sts.
Philadelphia, PA 19106
(215) 597-4605

U.S. Marshals

U.S. Marshal
P.O. Box 186
Newark, NJ 07101
(201) 341-2404

U.S. Marshal
225 Cadman Plaza East
Brooklyn, NY 11201
(212) 656-7493

U.S. Marshal
68 Court St.
Buffalo, NY 14202
(716) 437-4851

U.S. Marshal
1 St. Andrews Plaza
New York, NY 10007
(212) 662-1100

U.S. Marshal
P.O. Box 418
Utica, NY 13503
(315) 952-8108

U.S. Marshal
601 Market St.
Philadelphia, PA 19106
(215) 597-7272

U.S. Marshal
7th & Grant St.
Pittsburgh, PA 15219
(412) 722-3351

U.S. Marshal
P.O. Box 310
Scranton, PA 18501
(717) 592-8306

Post Office

Procurement Services
Office
U.S. Postal Service
Newark, NJ 07102
(201) 645-3333

Post Master
Dead Parcel Branch
New York, NY 10001
(212) 971-7761

Procurement Services
Office
U.S. Postal Service
G.P.O. Rm. 3227
New York, NY 10001
(212) 971-7697

Procurement Services
Office
Empire District
U.S. Postal Service
P.O. Box 72
Rochester, NY 14601
(716) 263-5825/28/29

Post Master
Dead Parcel Branch
Philadelphia, PA 19104
(215) 596-5478

Procurement Services
Office
Delaware Valley District
Susquehanna District
U.S. Postal Service
P.O. Box 7498
Philadelphia, PA 19101
(215) 596-5526/5355/5213

Post Master
Dead Parcel Branch
Pittsburgh, PA 15219
(412) 644-4500

Procurement Services
Office
Allegheny District
Mountaineer District
U.S. Postal Service
P.O. Box 818
Pittsburgh, PA 15230
(412) 644-4704

State Surplus Departments

New Jersey
Distribution Center
1620 Stuyvesant Ave.
Trenton, NJ 08628
(609) 984-2979

Dept. of Treasury
Bureau of Real
Property Mangt.
Div. of Purchase & Property
135 W. Hanover St.
Trenton, NJ 08625
(609) 292-9694

NY State Bureau of Surplus
Personal Property
Bldg. 18/State
Office Campus
Albany, NY 12226
(518) 457-6335

NY State Bureau of Surplus
Real Property
Empire State Plaza,
Tower Bldg.
Albany, NY 12228
(518) 474-1542

Dept. of General Services
2221 Foster St.
P.O. Box 3361
Harrisburg, PA 17125
(717) 787-5940

SHERIFFS

New York: NEW YORK CITY—New York County Sheriff's Office, 31 Chambers St., New York, NY 10007 (212) 374-8223 / BUFFALO— Erie County Sheriff's Dept., 10 Delaware Ave., Buffalo, NY 14220 (716) 846-7600

New Jersey: NEWARK—Essex County Sheriff's Dept., Essex County Courts Building, Newark, NJ 07102 (201) 961-7520 / TRENTON— Mercer County Sheriff's Dept., Mercer County Courthouse, Trenton, NJ 08650 (609) 989-6100

Pennsylvania: PHILADELPHIA—Philadelphia County Sheriff's Dept., City Hall, Rm. 316, Philadelphia, PA 19107 (215) 686-3535 (real estate) (215) 686-3560 (personal property) / PITTSBURGH— Allegheny County Sheriff's Dept., Rm. 111, Allegheny County Court- house, Pittsburgh, PA 15219 (412) 355-4700

POLICE

New York: NEW YORK CITY—New York City Police Dept., Police Dept. Storehouse, 4715 Pearson Pl., L.I. City, NY (general merchandise and auto auctions) (212) 982-2190 / BUFFALO—Buffalo Police Dept., Administrator's Office, 74 Franklin St., Rm. 104, Buffalo, NY 14202 (716) 855-4567 (4568, 4569, 4577)

New Jersey: NEWARK—Newark Police Dept., Property Room, 104 Arlington St., Newark, NJ 07102 (201) 733-6260 / TRENTON— Trenton Police Dept., Evidence Room, Perry and N. Clinton Ave., Trenton, NJ 08608 (609) 989-3924

Pennsylvania: PHILADELPHIA—Philadelphia Police Dept., Public Property Division, Rm. 1300, Municipal Services Building, Procurement Dept., Salvage Division, Philadelphia, PA 19107 (auto auctions only) (215) MU6-4749

GENERAL MERCHANDISE—ESTATE SALES—COUNTRY AUCTIONS—LIQUIDATORS

New York: NEW YORK CITY—Astor Galleries, 1 W. 39th St. (auctions every third Tuesday) (212) 921-8861; Christie, Manson, and Woods International, Inc., 502 Park Ave. (212) 826-2888; Christie's East, 219 E. 67th St. (212) 570-4141; William Doyle Galleries, Inc., 175 E. 87th St. (212) 427-2730; Lubin Galleries, Inc., 72 E. 13th St. (212) 254-1080; Manhattan Galleries, Inc., 1415 Third Ave. (212) 744-2844; Phillips, 525 E. 72nd St. (212) 570-4842, and 867 Madison Ave. (212) 570-4830; Plaza, 406 E. 79th St. (212) 879-1800; Sotheby's Inc., 980 Madison Ave. (212) 472-3400; PB 84, 171 E. 84th St. (212) 472-3583; Tepper Galleries, Inc., 110 E. 25th St. (212) 246-1800

Daley-Hodkin, 150 Broad Hollow Rd., Melville, NY (industrial liquidations: construction, manufacturing plants; cars, trucks) (516) 421-1414; Industrial Plants Corp., 211 E. 43rd St. (industrial liquidations) (212) 661-2550; Samuel Kamins, Foreclosure and Commission Sales, P.O. Box 178, Bay Station, Brooklyn, NY (autos, general merchandise, printing plants, clothing stores, furniture stores) (212) 769-3303; S. Knitzer and Son, 708 Broadway (commercial liquidations; bankruptcies) (212) 254-4020; Henry A. Leonard, 300 Hamilton Ave., White Plains, NY (914) 948-0011; David Strauss and Co. Inc., 150 W. 28th St. (commercial-industrial liquidations; autos) (212) 924-4540 / BUFFALO—American Industrial Auctioneering Co., Inc. (Matt and Chuck Anderson, Auctrs.) 1843 Hertel Ave. (estates, real estate brokers, heavy machinery, vehicles) (716) 836-2311; Lew Bronstein Inc., Auctioneers, 79 Ellicott St. (real estate brokers, estates, farms, liquidations of inventories, equipment; cars auctioned every other Wednesday) (716) 853-5200; Daniel Cutini Auctioneering & Appraising Sales Corp., 695 Longmeadow Rd. (estates, antiques, industrial-business liquidations; Friday 7:30 p.m. auction) (716) 835-2265; A to Z Auction, 2150 William Sloan (antiques, new furniture, household goods) (716) 896-3342 / CHATHAM—John Blaine Warner, Jr., RD 1, Box 39 (antiques, estates, general merchandise) (518) 237-4854 / CLIFTON PARK—Pete Murray, Northway Exchange, Rt. 146 (auto auction) (518) 371-7500 / COPAKE—Friedman's Auctions, Old Rt. 22 (general merchandise) (518) 329-1142 / DURHAM—Durham Auction Barn, Rt. 145 (general merchandise) (518) 239-8475 / TROY—Uncle Sam Auctions, Inc. (Ralph Passonno, Jr., Auctr.), P.O. Box 415 (real estate, commercial liquidations) (518) 274-6464 / WESTCHESTER—Westchester Auction Galleries, 2986 Navajo St., Yorktown, NY (art, antiques, general merchandise) (914) 248-8669

New Jersey: ELIZABETH—Morton S. Kaye, 829 Newark Ave. (business liquidations, bankruptcies) (201) 289-0607 / ENGLEWOOD—Herbert B. Caspert Enterprises, Inc., 333 Sylvan Ave., Englewood Cliffs, NJ (commercial-industrial liquidations) (201) 871-1600 / MIDLAND PARK—Jerry Krawitz, Brownstone Mill, 11 Paterson Ave. (antiques, glassware) (201) 652-6424 / PLUCKEMIN—Max E. Spann, Inc., P.O. Box 253, Rt. (202) 206, Bedminster Township (real estate) (609) 658-3688 / RARITAN—Col. Gerald Sterling, Sterling Auction Gallery, 62 N. Second Ave. (antiques, fine arts, furniture, silver, glass, jewelry; monthly auction) (201) 685-9565 / REPAUPPO—S & S Auction, Repauppo Rd. (furniture, household goods, appliances, tools, antiques, new merchandise; Thursday 6:30 p.m. auction) (609) 467-3778 / TRENTON—Lester and Robert Slatoff, Inc., 777 W. State St. (estates, household furnishings) (609) 393-4848

Pennsylvania: PHILADELPHIA—Samuel T. Freeman, 1808 Chestnut St. (fine art, antiques) (215) 563-9275; John H. Frisk, 1611 Walnut St. (fine art, antiques) (215) 564-3644; Lewis Trainman and Co., 1519 Spruce St. (real estate) (215) 545-4500; Quaker City Auctioneers, 40 S. Second St. (collateral liquidations) (215) 925-0796 / UNIONVILLE—James Boswell, Realtor, Appraiser, P.O. Box 457 (real estate, personal property) (215) 347-2467 / BUCKS COUNTY—Brown Brothers, Box 217, Buckingham, PA (estates, antiques, new furniture, appliances, farm equipment, cars; Saturday auction) (215) 794-7630 / BLUE BALL—Martin Auctioneers, 220 W. Main St. (antiques, carriage auctions) (717) 354-7006 / COGAN STATION—Bob, Chuck, & Rich Roan, Inc., Auction Gallery, R.D. 3, Box 118 (antiques, furniture, jewelry, silver; monthly auction) (717) 494-0170 / NEW HOLLAND—Vernon Martin, Auctioneer, P.O. Box 248 (horses, livestock, buggies, whips) (717) 354-9333 / SCIOTA—Collector's Cove, Ltd., Rt. 33, Box 333 (antiques, toys, collectibles; second Sunday general auction, last Sunday quality antique auction) (717) 421-7439 / SPRING CITY—Bonnie Brae Auction Center (Richard Moyer and Clay Hess, Auctrs.), 2 Bonnie Brae Rd. (general merchandise, estates, antiques, farms; Friday evening auction) (215) 948-8050 / WA-

VERLY—Auctions by Theriault, P.O. Box 174 (doll auctions) (717) 945-3041

REGIONAL MEDIA

New Jersey: NEWARK—Newark Star Ledger (auction ads daily) (201) 877-4242 / TRENTON—Trenton Evening Times (auction ads daily) (609) 396-3232

New York: NEW YORK CITY—Art/World, 1295 Madison Ave., New York, NY 10028 (monthly) (212) 427-2897; New York Law Journal (auction ads daily, except Saturday) (212) 964-9400; New York Times (auction ads daily; more on weekend; marshals auctions Wednesday) (212) 556-1234; Newsday (auction ads daily) (516) 454-2020; The Wall Street Journal (auction ads daily except Tuesday) (212) 285-5000 / BUFFALO—Buffalo Courier-Express (auction ads daily) (716) TL3-8700

Pennsylvania: PHILADELPHIA—Philadelphia Inquirer (auction ads Friday) (215) 854-2510 / PITTSBURGH—The Pittsburgh Press (auction ads daily) (412) 263-1100 / ALLENTOWN—The Allentown Morning Call (auction ads daily; more Friday) (215) 820-6500 / EASTON—The Express (auction ads daily) (215) 258-7171 / BUCKS COUNTY—Advance of Bucks County (subscriptions by mail, comes out Wednesdays), P.O. Box 337, Langhorne, PA (215) 757-6767; Doylestown Intelligencer (auction ads Thursday) (215) 345-3000

EAST NORTH CENTRAL REGION
ILLINOIS (IL), INDIANA (IN), MICHIGAN (MI), OHIO (OH), WISCONSIN (WI)

General Services Administration

GSA
(Real Property)
230 South Dearborn St.
Chicago, IL 60604
(312) 353-6045

GSA
(Personal Property)
230 South Dearborn St.
Chicago, IL 60604
(312) 353-6060

Department of Defense

DoD Surplus Sales
P.O. Box 1370
Battle Creek, MI 49106
(Write to this address to get
on national mailing list)

Defense Property Disposal
P.O. Box 13110
Columbus, OH 43213
(614) 236-2114

Internal Revenue Service

IRS, District Director
P.O. Box 1193
Chicago, IL 60690
(312) 886-4300

IRS, District Director
P.O. Box 1468
Springfield, IL 62705
(217) 525-4040

IRS, District Director
P.O. Box 44687
Indianapolis, IN 46244
(317) 269-6017

IRS, District Director
P.O. Box 32500
Detroit, MI 48232
(313) 226-7198

IRS, District Director
P.O. Box 1818
Cincinnati, OH 45201
(513) 684-2544

IRS, District Director
P.O. Box 99181
Cleveland, OH 44199
(216) 522-3320

IRS, District Director
P.O. Box 495
Milwaukee, WI 53201
(414) 291-3321

Customs

U.S. Customs Service
610 S. Canal St.
Chicago, IL 60607
(312) 353-6100

U.S. Customs Service
477 Michigan Ave.
Detroit, MI 48226
(313) 226-3177

U.S. Customs Service
55 Erieview Plaza
Cleveland, OH 44114
(216) 522-4284

U.S. Customs Service
628 E. Michigan St.
Milwaukee, WI 53202
(414) 224-3924

U.S. Marshals

U.S. Marshal
219 S. Dearborn St.
Chicago, IL 60604
(312) 353-5290

U.S. Marshal
P.O. Box 156
Springfield, IL 62705
F(217) 955-4430

U.S. Marshal
P.O. Box 126
East St. Louis, IL 62202
(618) 277-9363

U.S. Marshal
46 E. Ohio St./Rm. 225
Indianapolis, IN 46204
(317) 331-6566

U.S. Marshal
P.O. Box 4740
South Bend, IN 46624
(219) 332-7246

U.S. Marshal
21 Lafayette St.
Detroit, MI 48226
(313) 226-7754

U.S. Marshal
110 Michigan Ave., N.W.
Grand Rapids, MI 49513
(616) 372-2438

U.S. Marshal
P.O. Box 688
Cincinnati, OH 45201
(513) 684-2904

U.S. Marshal
323 U.S. Courthouse
Cleveland, OH 44114
(216) 293-4346

U.S. Marshal
P.O. Box 1706
Madison, WI 53701
(608) 364-5161

U.S. Marshal
517 E. Wisconsin Ave.
Milwaukee, WI 53202
(414) 362-3707

National Forest Service

U.S. Dept. of Agriculture
Office of Forest Service
Eastern Region
633 West Wisconsin Ave.
Milwaukee, WI 53203

Post Office

Post Master
Dead Parcel Branch
Chicago, IL 60607
(312) 886-2650

Procurement
Services Office
U.S. Postal Service
433 W. Van Buren St.
Rm. 300
Chicago, IL 60607
(312) 886-2699

Procurement
Services Office
U.S. Postal Service
125 W. South/
Rm. 217-A
Indianapolis, IN 46206
(317) 269-6868

Procurement
Services Office
U.S. Postal Service
17500 Oakwood Blvd., BMC
Allen Park, MI 48101
(313) 226-6350

Post Master
Dead Parcel Branch
Detroit, MI 48233
(313) 226-6515

Post Master
Dead Parcel Branch
Cincinnati, OH 45234
(513) 684-5234

Procurement
Services Office
U.S. Postal Service
P.O. Box 1710
Columbus, OH 43216
(614) 469-7390

State Surplus Departments

State & Federal
Property Mgt.
4390 Jeffory
Box 1236
Springfield, IL 62705
(217) 786-6956

Dept. of Administration
State Office Bldg./Rm. 507
Indianapolis, IN 46204
(317) 232-3366

Michigan State Dept.
of Management and Budget
Purchasing Division
P.O. Box 30026
Lansing, MI 48909
(517) 373-0303
(517) 373-6559

Land Division
Dept. of Natural Resources
P.O. Box 30028
Lansing, MI 48926
(517) 373-1250

Investment Recovery
Services
1635 Watkins Rd.
Columbus, OH 43207
(614) 466-2850

Bureau of Procurement
State Property Disposition
101 South Webster St.
Madison, WI 53702
(608) 266-3843

Bureau of Real Estate
Wisconsin Dept. of
Natural Resources
Box 7291
Madison, WI 53716
(608) 266-0202

SHERIFFS

Michigan: DETROIT—Wayne County Sheriff's Dept., Wayne County Court Division, 1711 City Court Building, Detroit, MI 48226 (313) 224-2260

Ohio: CINCINNATI—Hamilton County Sheriff's Dept., 1000 Main St., Rm. 320, Cincinnati, OH 45202 (513) 632-8801 / CLEVELAND— Cuyahoga County Sheriff's Dept., 1215 W. Third St., Cleveland, OH 44113, Attn: Civil Division. (216) 623-6015 / COLUMBUS—Franklin County Sheriff's Dept., 369 S. High St., Columbus, OH 43215 (614) 462-3343

Illinois: CHICAGO—Cook County Sheriff's Dept., 704 Daley Center, Chicago, IL 60602 (312) 443-6463

Indiana: INDIANAPOLIS—Marion County Sheriff's Dept., City-County Building, Rm. 822, Indianapolis, IN 40204 (317) 633-5181

Wisconsin: MILWAUKEE—Milwaukee County Sheriff's Dept., 821 W. State St., Milwaukee, WI 53233 (414) 278-4726

POLICE

Michigan: DETROIT—Police Dept., Public Information, 1300 Beaubien, Detroit, MI 48226 (313) 224-1200 and Police Dept. Auto Pound, St. Jean & Freud Sts., Detroit, MI (313) 224-4210

Ohio: CINCINNATI—Cincinnati Police Dept., Police Property Rm., 222 E. Central Pky., Cincinnati, OH 45201 (513) 352-3000 / CLEVE-LAND—Vehicle Impound Unit, 1300 Ontario, Police Headquarters, Cleveland, OH 44114 (general merchandise auction first wknd. June; bicycles, last Saturday October; autos, every week) (216) 623-5368 / COLUMBUS—Columbus Police Dept. Impounding Division, 120 W. Gay St., Columbus, OH 43215 (614) 462-4620

Illinois: CHICAGO—Chicago Police Dept., Auto Pound Section or Property & Evidence Division, 1121 S. State St., Chicago, IL 60605 (auto (312) 744-5512; P & E (312) 744-6334)

Indiana: INDIANAPOLIS—Indianapolis Police Dept., Property Rm., 50 N. Alabama St., City-County Bldg. Police Wing, Indianapolis, IN 46204 (317) 633-7858

Wisconsin: MILWAUKEE—Purchasing Dept., City Hall, 200 E. Wells St., Rm. 407, Milwaukee, WI 53202 (414) 278-3915

GENERAL MERCHANDISE—ESTATE SALES—COUNTRY AUCTIONS

Michigan: DETROIT—Du Mouchelle Auction Galleries, 409 E. Jefferson (fine art, antiques, collectibles) (313) 963-6255; Park West Galleries, 24151 Telegraph Ave., Southfield, MI (general merchandise) (313) 354-2343; Norman Levy Assoc., Inc., 21415 Civic Center Dr., Southfield, MI (industrial liquidations; appraisers) (313) 353-8640; Midwest Auto Auction & Service, Inc., 14666 Telegraph Ave. (Friday 10:30 a.m. auction) (313) 538-2100 / MARSHALL—Edward L. & Brent H. Belcher, Auctrs. & Sales Managers, 148 W. Michigan (coins, guns, watches, clocks, bronzes, dishes) (616) 781-4258 / TECUMSEH —Spike's Auction Service, Inc., 509 Mohawk (antiques, collectibles, household furnishings; Saturday 6:00 p.m. household auction, second and fourth Sundays 1:00 p.m. antiques auction) (517) 423-6312

Ohio: AKRON—Trade Winds Auction Gallery, 58 Wolcott Rd. (antiques) (216) 836-8669 / CANTON—Richard Kiko, 3656 Werner Church Rd., North Canton, OH (real estate, farms) (216) 494-8541 / CINCINNATI—Allis Co., Inc., 8640 Lynnehaven Dr. (commercial-industrial liquidations) (513) 791-0042; Burke's Auction & Appraisal Service, 2602 Canterbury Ave. (fine art, antiques, estates) (513)

531-3593; Main Auction Galleries, Inc., 137 W. Fourth St. (fine art, antiques, contemporary furniture; Tuesday 10:30 a.m. auction) (513) 621-1280 / CLEVELAND—Fordem Galleries, Inc., 3829 Lorain Ave. (antiques) (216) 281-3563 / COLUMBUS—Action Auction Gallery, 6200 Busch Blvd. (estates, household furnishings, farms, cattle) (614) 846-5500 / DELAWARE—Garth's Auction, Box 315, 2690 Stratford Rd. (estates, antiques, fine art, American furniture) (614) 362-4771 / NEW PARIS—Dave Kessler, 122 W. Main (all types of auctions) (513) 437-7071 / NORTHFIELD—Norm Detrick, 7733 Kitner (commercial-industrial liquidations, household furnishings) (216) 467-8645 / WINTERVILLE—Fort Steuben Auction Co., P.O. Box 2250 (fine arts, antiques) (614) 264-6229

Illinois: CHICAGO—Hanzel Art Galleries, 1120 S. Michigan Ave. (fine art, antiques) (312) 922-6234; Real Estate Auctions, Inc., Subs. of Sheldon F. Good & Co., 11 N. Wacker Dr. (312) 346-1500; Norman Levy & Co., Inc., 6160 N. Cicero (industrial liquidations) (312) 777-0900; House of Williams, 37 S. Wabash Ave. (general merchandise) (312) 236-6320; Sotheby Parke-Bernet, Inc., 700 N. Michigan (312) 280-0185; Arena Auto Auction, 10355 S. Woodlawn Ave. (312) 568-0900; Northwest Book Auction, 231 Burlington, Clarendon Hills, IL (312) 325-4490; Pick Galleries, 886 Linden Ave., Hubbard Woods, IL (antiques) (312) 446-7444; Pace Auctions, 1591 Ellinwood, Des Plaines, IL (antiques, furniture, wicker) (312) 296-0773

Indiana: INDIANAPOLIS—General Auction Co. (Gene Phillips, owner & Auctr.), 2740 Madison Ave. (Wednesday 6:00 p.m. auction) (317) 784-0687 / BROWNSBURG—Richwine Auction House, Rt. 5, P.O. Box 136 (general merchandise; liquidations) (317) 852-4053 / CICERO—Hamilton County Auction Market, 50 W. Buckeye (general merchandise) (317) 984-5772 / DANVILLE—Windy Knoll Auction & Furniture, U.S. 36 (furniture: Friday 7:00 p.m. auction) (317) 745-5166 / AUBURN—Dean Kruse, Kruse Office Building (real estate, estates, classic cars) (219) 925-4004 / FREMONT—Powatomi Museum, Box 631 (Americana, American Indian art auctions) (219) 495-7755

Wisconsin: MILWAUKEE—Milwaukee Auction Galleries, 4747 W. Bradley Rd. (estates, fine art, antiques, new furniture, appliances, rugs) (414) 355-5054; Astor Gallery Victorian Shop, 2630 N. Downer Ave. (fine art, antiques; monthly auction) (414) 964-6780; David S. Gronik, 777 W. Glencoe Pl. (commercial-industrial liquidations; bankruptcies) (414) 273-7144; Travis Auction Galleries, Inc., 1442 Underwood Ave. (fine art, antiques, furniture, collectibles; one 5-session auction a month) (414) 453-0342

REGIONAL MEDIA

Illinois: CHICAGO—Chicago Sun-Times (auction ads daily) (312) 321-2303; The Chicago Tribune (auction ads daily) (312) 222-3232
Indiana: INDIANAPOLIS—Indianapolis Star (auction ads daily) (317) 633-1240 / KNIGHTSTOWN—The Tri-State Trader, 27 N. Jefferson (auction info. of interest for entire Mid-West) (317) 345-5134
Michigan: DETROIT—Detroit Free Press (auction ads daily) (313) 222-6400; Detroit News (auction ads daily; more Sunday) (313) 977-7500 / KALAMAZOO—The Auction Exchange, 5356 Riverview Dr., Kalamazoo, MI 49004 (weekly) (616) 381-1138
Ohio: AKRON—Akron Beacon Journal (auction ads daily) (216) 375-8111 / CINCINNATI—Cincinnati Post (auction ads daily) (513) 421-6300 / CLEVELAND—Cleveland Plain Dealer (auction ads daily) (216) 344-4500 / COLUMBUS—Columbus Dispatch (auction ads daily) (614) 461-5000
Wisconsin: MILWAUKEE—Milwaukee Journal (auction ads daily) (414) 224-2000

WEST NORTH CENTRAL REGION
IOWA (IA), KANSAS (KS), MINNESOTA (MN), MISSOURI (MO), NEBRASKA (NE), NORTH DAKOTA (ND), SOUTH DAKOTA (SD)

General Services Administration

GSA
(Real Property—ND, SD)
Denver Federal Center
Building 41
Denver, CO 80225
(303) 234-3934

GSA
(Personal Property—
ND, SD)
Denver Federal Center
Building 41
Denver, CO 80225
(303) 234-5283

GSA
(Real Property—MN)
230 S. Dearborn St.
Chicago, IL 60604
(312) 353-6045

GSA
(Personal Property—MN)
230 S. Dearborn St.
Chicago, IL 60604
(312) 353-6060

GSA
(Real Property—
IA, KS, MO, NE)
1500 E. Bannister Rd.
Kansas City, MO 64131
(816) 926-7237

GSA
(Personal Property—
IA, KS, MO, NE)
1500 E. Bannister Rd.
Kansas City, MO 64131
(816) 926-7285

Department of Defense

DoD Surplus Sales
P.O. Box 1370
Battle Creek, MI 49106
(Write to this address to get on national mailing list)

Defense Property Disposal
P.O. Box 13110
Columbus, OH 43213
(614) 236-2114
(IA, KS, MN, MO, NE)

Defense Property Disposal
P.O. Box 53
Defense Depot Ogden
Station
Ogden, UT 84401
(801) 399-7388
(ND, SD)

Internal Revenue Service

IRS, District Director
P.O. Box 1337
Des Moines, IA 50305
(515) 284-4293

IRS, District Director
P.O. Box 400
Wichita, KS 67201
(316) 267-6311 x211

IRS, District Director
P.O. Box 3556
St. Paul, MN 55165
(612) 725-7326

IRS, District Director
P.O. Box 5321
Kansas City, MO 64131
(816) 926-5512

IRS, District Director
P.O. Box 1548
St. Louis, MO 63188
(314) 425-4001

IRS, District Director
P.O. Box 1052
Omaha, NE 68102
(402) 221-4186

IRS, District Director
P.O. Box 8
Fargo, ND 58107
(701) 237-5771 x147

IRS, District Director
P.O. Box 370
Aberdeen, SD 57401
(605) 225-0250 x201

Customs

U.S. Customs Service
515 W. First St.
209 Federal Bldg.
Duluth, MN 55802
(218) 727-6692

U.S. Customs Service
110 S. Fourth St.
Minneapolis, MN 55401
(612) 725-2317

U.S. Customs Service
120 S. Central Ave.
St. Louis, MO 63105
(314) 425-3134

U.S. Customs Service
Post Office Building
Penbina, ND 58271
(701) 825-6201

U.S. Marshals

U.S. Marshal
P.O. Box 4740
Cedar Rapids, IA 52407
(712) 863-2417

U.S. Marshal
E. First & Walnut Sts.
Des Moines, IA 50309
(515) 862-4410

U.S. Marshal
444 Southeast Quincy
Topeka, KS 66603
(913) 752-2775

U.S. Marshal
110 South Fourth St.
Minneapolis, MN 55401
(612) 725-2376

U.S. Marshal
811 Grand Ave.
Kansas City, MO 64106
(816) 758-3521

U.S. Marshal
1114 Market St.
St. Louis, MO 63101
(314) 279-4212

U.S. Marshal
215 North 17th St.
Omaha, NE 68102
(402) 864-4781

U.S. Marshal
P.O. Box 2425
Fargo, ND 58108
(701) 783-5443

U.S. Marshal
P.O. Box 1193
Sioux Falls, SD 57101
(605) 782-4351

Post Office

Procurement Services
Office
U.S. Postal Service
4900 Speaker Rd., BMC
Kansas City, KS 66106
(816) 374-4891

Post Master
Dead Parcel Branch
St. Paul, MN 55101
(612) 725-7212

Procurement Services
Office
U.S. Postal Service
3169 Lexington Ave. S./
Rm. 228
St. Paul, MN 55121
(612) 725-3906

Post Master
Dead Parcel Branch
St. Louis, MO 63155
(314) 425-5241

Procurement Services
Office
U.S. Postal Service
1720 Market St./Rm. 243
St. Louis, MO 63155
(314) 425-5843

State Surplus Departments

State Surplus Property
State House
Des Moines, IA 50319
(515) 281-5119

Vehicles
Dispatches Division
State House
Des Moines, IA 50319
(515) 281-5121

Inventory
State Surplus
Property Section
671 N. Robert St.
St. Paul, MN 55101
(612) 296-6131

Director Division
of Purchasing
P.O. Box 809
Jefferson City, MO 65102
(314) 751-3273

GSA/Sales Division
1500 E. Bannister Rd.
Kansas City, MO 64131
(816) 926-7237

State Surplus Property
5001 S. 14th St.
P.O. Box 94901
Lincoln, NE 68509
(402) 471-2694

Dept. of Accounts
& Purchases
State Capitol
Bismarck, ND 58505
(701) 224-2680

Property Management
Office
State Capitol Bldg.
Pierre, SD 57501
(605) 773-3405

SHERIFFS

Iowa: CEDAR RAPIDS—Linn County Sheriff's Dept., P.O. Box 4844, Cedar Rapids, IA 52407 (319) 398-3521 / DES MOINES—Polk County Sheriff's Dept., Polk County Courthouse, Rm. 204, Des Moines, IA 50309 (515) 286-3800

Kansas: TOPEKA—Shawnee County Sheriff's Dept., 200 E. 7th St., Topeka, KS 66603 (913) 295-4444

Minnesota: MINNEAPOLIS—Hennepin County Sheriff's Dept., Rm. 30, Old Courthouse, Minneapolis, MN 55415 (autos & household items (612) 348-3800; foreclosure auctions (612) 348-3730)

Missouri: KANSAS CITY—Jackson County Sheriff's Dept., Rt. 6, Box 93A, Lee's Summit, MO 64603 (816) 524-4302 / ST. LOUIS—Sheriff of City of St. Louis, Civil Court Bldg., Tucker & Chestnut Sts., St. Louis, MO 63102 (314) 622-4841

Nebraska: OMAHA—Douglas County Sheriff's Dept., 505 Courthouse, Omaha, NE 68183 (402) 444-7028
North Dakota: BISMARCK—Burleigh County Sheriff's Dept., P.O. Box 1416, Bismarck, ND 58501 (701) 222-6651
South Dakota: PIERRE—Highes County Sheriff's Dept., Box 186, Pierre, SD 57501 (605) 224-8646

POLICE

Iowa: CEDAR RAPIDS—General Services, 310 2nd Ave., S.W. Cedar Rapids, IA 52404 (319) 398-5115 / DES MOINES—Des Moines Police Dept., Fiscal Property Section or Impounded Vehicles, E. First & Court Sts., Des Moines, IA 50309 (autos (515) 283-4840; general merchandise (515) 283-4850)
Kansas: TOPEKA—Topeka Police Dept., Property Rm., 204 W. Fifth St., Topeka, KS 66603 (913) 354-9551 x311
Minnesota: MINNEAPOLIS—Minneapolis Police Dept., 300 S. Fifth St., Rm. 3, City Hall, Minneapolis, MN 55415 (autos (612) 348-2991; miscellaneous (612) 348-2932)
Missouri: KANSAS CITY—Kansas City Police Dept., Property Rm., 25 Locust St., Kansas City, MO 64106 (autos (816) 221-7928; general merchandise (816) 234-5198) / ST. LOUIS—St. Louis Police Dept., 1200 Clark St., St. Louis, MO 63103 (314) 444-5622
Nebraska: OMAHA—Omaha Police Dept., Vehicle Impound, 1730 Burt St., Omaha, NE 68102 (402) 444-5782; General Merchandise Property Rm., 505 S. 15th St., Omaha, NE 68103 (404) 444-5849
North Dakota: BISMARCK—Traffic Division, Bismarck Police Dept., 700 S. Ninth St., Bismarck, ND 58501 for autos; Administration Combined Law Enforcement Center, 700 S. Ninth St., Bismarck, ND 58501 for general merchandise (701) 223-1212
South Dakota: PIERRE—City Auditor's Office, 222 E. Dakota Ave., Pierre, SD 57501 (605) 224-5921

GENERAL MERCHANDISE—ESTATE SALES—COUNTRY AUCTIONS

Iowa: COUNCIL BLUFFS—Hunter Auction Co., 235 W. Broadway, #4 Ogden Pl. (general merchandise, real estate) (712) 322-2565; Dwane Squibb, Auctr., 722 E. Pierce (antiques, furniture, household goods, appliances, country items) (712) 323-5233 / DUBUQUE—Tri-State Auction & Realty Service, 1598 Central Ave. (antiques, household furnishings, farms, machinery, livestock) (319) 588-4637; Dubuque Auction Service, Inc., RR 4 (antiques, household goods, farms, livestock) (319) 582-5141 / FORT MADISON—Scholl Auction Service (David Scholl & Jerry Cramer, Auctrs.), 813 Avenue H (general merchandise, furniture) (319) 372-7395; barn # (319) 372-6780 / GUERNSEY—Mike & Sandy Hammes' Renaissance Auction, Box 4 (antiques, furniture) (319) 685-4251 / MARSHALLTOWN—Antique Auction Center (Gene Harris, Auctr.), 203 S. 18th Ave. (antiques, household goods, furniture) (515) 752-0600

Kansas: TOPEKA—Topeka Auto Auction, Forbes Field (individuals can sell but not buy cars) (913) 862-1722; Crews Auctions Co., 1212 S.W. 8th St. (general merchandise; Tuesday 6:30 p.m. auction) (913) 232-4632; Kooser Auctioneering Service, 335 Harrison (estates, antiques, household goods, farms, liquidations) (913) 235-1176; B. & B. Auction Service (George Benge, Auctr.), 929 S. Kansas (estates, antiques, household goods, farms, coins) (913) 232-2861; Carlson's Auction Service, 5824 S. Topeka Ave. (estates, household goods, farms, antiques, business liquidations; Monday 6:30 p.m. auction) (913) 862-1110; Stuke Auctions (Susan Stuke, Auctr.), Meriden Rd. N. of 24 Hwy. (estates; Wednesday evening auction) (913) 232-1580 / OLATHE—June Livengood, 504 Kansas City Rd. (antiques; one antique auction a month, one general merchandise auction a month) (913) 764-4009 / FORT SCOTT—Bill Dunn Auction Center, Rt. 1, Box 102, Cattschool Rd. (estates, antiques) (316) 223-3511 / LAWRENCE—Shoemaker's Auction Barn, Rt. 3 (general merchandise; Friday night auction) (913) 841-8067

Minnesota: MINNEAPOLIS—Anderson & Dudlet Auctioneers, 648 Lawry N.E. (industrial liquidations) (612) 788-8693; Central Auction House (Charles Weinberger, Auctr.), 4020 Central Ave., N.E. Minneapolis, MN (estates, farms, bankruptcies; Monday surplus & salvage auction, Tuesday antiques, Thursday general consignments) (612) 789-5025 / ANOKA—Anoka-Fridley, 848 E. River Rd. (general merchandise) (612) 427-6770 / OSSEO—Quickie Auction House, Rt. 3 (new merchandise, antiques, marine, farm) (612) 428-9616 / ROSEVILLE—Rose Galleries, 1123 W. County Rd. (general merchandise; Monday specialty sales, Wednesday antiques) (612) 484-1415 / AUSTIN—Radloff Auction Co., P.O. Box 336 (antiques, collectibles) (507) 437-2366

Missouri: KANSAS CITY—Kenn Kemper, P.O. Box 16932 (antique car auction, classic cars) (816) CLA-SSIC; Ryther Auction & Realty, 1105 N. Jessie James Rd., Excelsior Springs, MO (general merchandise, real estate) (816) 637-5511 / INDEPENDENCE—Independence Auction & Realty Co. (Dale & Carol Vaughn), 1206 W. 24 Hwy. (real estate, household goods, estates) (816) 254-8375; Buckner Auction Center (Dale & Carol Vaughn), Highway 24 & Holly Rd., Buckner, MO (antiques, machinery, construction equipment) / ST. LOUIS—Art Britton Auction Sales, Ltd., 11701 Fallbrook Dr. (general merchandise) (314) 567-5636; M.R. Dugan Auction Co., 11906 Manchester Rd. (general merchandise) (314) 965-2921; Miller & Miller Auctrs. Inc.,

268 Chapel Ridge (industrial liquidations) (314) 731-2079; Benjamin
J. Selkirk & Sons, Genl. Auctrs., 4166 Olive St. (furniture, antiques;
three gallery sales a year of finer furniture, silver, rugs, monthly auction
of other goods) (314) 533-1700; Bob Stovesand & Sons, Auctrs. and
Real Estate Brokers, Cedar Hill (real estate) (314) 285-4525; Ten
Eyck Antique Auctions Ltd., 7438 Leadale (estates, antiques, appraisals) (314) 721-8202; Cockrum Auction, 2701 Hwy. 94N, St.
Charles, MO (estates, real estate, cars; Friday and Saturday 7:00 p.m.
auction, monthly antique auction) (314) 946-7511

Nebraska: OMAHA—Cosgrove Auction, 3805 Levenworth (fine art,
antiques, silver) (402) 342-5254; Dyer's Auction Service, 7071 Maple
St. (estates, furniture, liquidations; monthly auctions) (404) 551-
2889; Guillaume & Sons Auctrs., 3616 Lincoln Blvd. (commercial
liquidations, residential liquidations incl. antiques) (402) 553-8252;
Remains to be Seen, 1034 Howard St. (art, pottery, primitives, general
merchandise) (402) 345-5118; Rine & Rine Auctrs., 525 N. 78th St.
(estates, dealership liquidations, real estate, personal property) (402)
392-1508; Woodring Auction Co., 14685 Grover St. (tool auction)
(402) 334-8422

North Dakota: BISMARCK—Auction Mart, 800 Airport Rd. (general
merchandise) (701) 255-4797; Edmer A. Goetz Realty Co., 203 N.
19th St. (701) 223-1040

South Dakota: SIOUX FALLS—Northwest Auction Co., 326 N. West
(antiques, furniture, appliances; Tuesday 7:30 p.m. auction) (605)
332-4949; Wingler's Furniture & Auction Co., 611 N. Main (furniture;
Thursday 7:30 p.m. auction) (605) 332-5682

REGIONAL MEDIA

Iowa: CEDAR RAPIDS—Cedar Rapids Gazette (auction ads daily;
more Sunday) (319) 398-8211 / COUNCIL BLUFFS—Council Bluffs
Nonpareil (auction ads daily) (712) 328-1811 / DES MOINES—Des
Moines Register (auction ads Sunday) (515) 284-8000 / DUBUQUE
—The Antique Trader Weekly, Box 1050, Dubuque, IA 52001 (source
for auction info. throughout Mid-West) (319) 588-2073

Kansas: TOPEKA—Topeka Capital-Journal (auction ads daily) (913)
295-1122

Minnesota: MINNEAPOLIS—Minneapolis Star-Tribune (auction ads
daily) (612) 372-4141; St. Paul Dispatch (auction ads daily) (612)
222-5011

Missouri: KANSAS CITY—Kansas City Star (auction ads daily; more
Wednesday & Sunday) (816) 234-4000; The Auction News (816)
421-7117 (weekly) / ST. LOUIS—Globe Democrat (auction ads
daily) (314) 342-1212; St. Louis Post Dispatch (auction ads daily)
(314) 622-7000

Nebraska: LINCOLN—Lincoln Journal & Star (auction ads daily; more Sunday) (402) 475-4200 / OMAHA—Omaha World Herald (auction ads daily; more Sunday) (402) 444-1000

North Dakota: FARGO—Fargo Forum (auction ads on special green sheet Friday) (701) 235-7311

South Dakota: SIOUX FALLS—Sioux Falls Argus-Leader (auction ads Sunday) (605) 336-1130

MOUNTAIN REGION
ARIZONA (AZ), COLORADO (CO), IDAHO (ID), MONTANA (MT), NEVADA (NV), NEW MEXICO (NM), UTAH (UT), WYOMING (WY)

General Services Administration

GSA
(Real Property—AZ, NV)
525 Market St.
San Francisco, CA 94105
(415) 556-5314

GSA
(Personal Property—
AZ, NV)
525 Market St.
San Francisco, CA 94105
(415) 556-3623

GSA
(Real Property—CO, MT,
UT, WY)
Denver Federal Center
Building 41
Denver, CO 80225
(303) 234-3934

GSA
(Personal Property—CO,
MT, UT, WY)
Denver Federal Center
Building 41
Denver, CO 80225
(303) 234-5283

GSA
(Real Property—NM)
819 Taylor St.
Fort Worth, TX 76102
(817) 334-2331

GSA
(Personal Property—NM)
819 Taylor St.
Fort Worth, TX 76102
(817) 334-2330

GSA
(Real Property—ID)
GSA Center
Auburn, WA 98002
(206) 833-6500 x264

GSA
(Personal Property—ID)
GSA Center
Auburn, WA 98002
(206) 833-6500 x491

Department of Defense

DoD Surplus Sales
P.O. Box 1370
Battle Creek, MI 49016
(Write to this address to
get on national mailing list)

Defense Property Disposal
P.O. Box 14716
Memphis, TN 38114
(901) 744-5131
(NM)

Defense Property Disposal
P.O. Box 58
Defense Depot
Ogden Station
Ogden, UT 84401
(801) 399-7833
(AZ, CO, ID, MT, NV,
UT, WY)

Internal Revenue Service

IRS, District Director
2120 N. Central Ave.
Phoenix, AZ 85004
(602) 261-3495

IRS, District Director
1050 Seventeenth St.
Denver, CO 80265
(303) 837-5801

IRS, District Director
550 W. Fort St./Box 041
Boise, ID 83724
(208) 384-1300

IRS, District Director
Federal Building
Drawer 10016
Helena, MT 59601
(406) 449-5250

IRS, District Director
P.O. Box 891
Reno, NV 89504
(702) 784-5671

IRS, District Director
P.O. Box 1967
Albuquerque, NM 87103
(505) 766-2751

IRS, District Director
P.O. Box 2069
Salt Lake City, UT 84110
(801) 524-5810

IRS, District Director
308 W. 21st St.
Cheyenne, WY 82001
(307) 778-2472

Customs

U.S. Customs Service
International & Terrace Sts.
Nogales, AZ 85621
(602) 287-4955

U.S. Customs Service
215 First Ave., N.
Great Falls, MT 59401
(406) 453-7631

U.S. Marshals

U.S. Marshal
230 North First Ave.
Phoenix, AZ 85205
(602) 261-3621

U.S. Marshal
C-324 U.S. Courthouse
Drawer 3599
Denver, CO 80294
(303) 327-2801

U.S. Marshal
550 West Fort St.
Boise, ID 83724
(208) 554-1298

U.S. Marshal
316 North 26th St.
Billings, MT 59101
(406) 585-6626

U.S. Marshal
P.O. Box 16039
Las Vegas, NV 89101
(702) 598-6355

U.S. Marshal
P.O. Box 444
Albuquerque, NM 87103
(505) 474-2933

U.S. Marshal
P.O. Box 1234
Salt Lake City, UT 84110
(801) 588-5693

U.S. Marshal
2120 Capitol Ave.
Cheyenne, WY 82001
(307) 328-2196

National Forest Service

U.S. Dept. of Agriculture
Office of Forest Service
Rocky Mountain Region
11177 W. 8th Ave.
Box 25127
Lakewood, CO 80225

U.S. Dept. of Agriculture
Office of Forest Service
Northern Region
Federal Building
Missoula, MT 59807

U.S. Dept. of Agriculture
Office of Forest Service
Southwestern Region
517 Gold Ave., S.W.
Albuquerque, NM 87102

U.S. Dept. of Agriculture
Office of Forest Service
Intermountain Region
324 Twenty-fifth St.
Ogden, UT 84401

Post Office

Procurement
Services Office
U.S. Postal Service
P.O. Box 25009
522 North Central
Phoenix, AZ 85002
(602) 261-4134

Post Master
Dead Parcel Branch
Denver, CO 80202
(303) 837-4251

Procurement
Services Office
U.S. Postal Service
P.O. Box 38100
Denver, CO 80238
(303) 837-5151

Procurement
Services Office
U.S. Postal Service
Main Post Office/Rm. 125
1760 West 2100 South
Salt Lake City, UT 84119
(801) 524-5927

State Surplus Departments

Department
of Administration
Surplus Property Division
312 S. 15th Ave.
Phoenix, AZ 85007
(602) 255-5701

State Surplus Property
4700 Leetsdale Dr.
Denver, CO 80222
(303) 388-5953

Department
of Administration
Bureau of Surplus Property
550 W. State
Boise, ID 83720
(208) 334-3936

Department
of Administration
Purchasing Department
Capitol State
Helena, MT 59601
(406) 777-7253

Nevada State Purchasing
Division
Capitol Complex
Blasbel Bldg./Rm. 104
Carson City, NV 89701
(702) 885-5000

Finance Administration
Procurement Division
Lamy Building
Santa Fe, NM 87503
(505) 827-2626

Department of Finance
State Capitol Bldg./Rm. 137
Salt Lake City, UT 84114
(801) 533-4616

Dept. of Administration &
Fiscal Control
Purchasing Division
Emmerson Bldg./Rm. 301
Cheyenne, WY 82002
(307) 777-7253

SHERIFFS

Arizona: PHOENIX—Maricopa County Sheriff's Dept., 120 S. First St., Phoenix, AZ 85003 (602) 256-1838

Colorado: DENVER—Denver County Sheriff's Dept., Civil Division, 1445 Cleveland Pl., Rm. 304, Denver, CO 80202 (303) 575-5192

Idaho: BOISE—Boise Police & Sheriff's Dept., Attn.: Evidence & Property Division, 7200 Barrister Dr., Boise, ID 83704 (202) 377-6631

Montana: HELENA—Lewis & Clark County Sheriff's Dept., P.O. Box 1685, Helena, MT 59601 (406) 443-1010

Nevada: LAS VEGAS—Clark County Treasurer, 200 E. Carson, Courthouse Bldg., Las Vegas, NV 89101 (702) 386-4011
New Mexico: SANTA FE—Santa Fe County Sheriff's Dept., P.O. Box 1023, Santa Fe, NM 87501 (505) 982-4494
Utah: SALT LAKE CITY—Salt Lake City Civil Division, 437 S. 200 East, Salt Lake City, UT 84111 (801) 535-7525
Wyoming: CHEYENNE—Laramie County Sheriff's Dept., P.O. Box 787, Cheyenne, WY 82001 (307) 634-7931

POLICE

Arizona: PHOENIX—Phoenix Police Dept., Property Room, Rm. B70, 620 W. Washington, Phoenix, AZ 85002 (602) 262-6194
Colorado: DENVER—Property Room B102, 1331 Cherokee St., Denver, CO 80204 (miscellaneous (303) 575-3273), Car Pound, 5160 York St., Denver, CO 80216 (cars (303) 575-3919), Bicycle Bureau, 1200 Broadway, Denver, CO (bikes (303) 575-2954)
Idaho: BOISE—Boise Police Dept., Property Room, 4200 Barrister Dr., Boise, ID 83704 (208) 377-6630
Montana: HELENA—Helena Police Dept., Civic Center, Helena, MT 59601 (406) 442-3231
New Mexico: SANTA FE—Santa Fe Police Dept., P.O. Box 909, Santa Fe, NM 87501 (505) 988-9601
Utah: SALT LAKE CITY—Salt Lake City Police Dept., 450 S. 3 East, Salt Lake City, UT 84111 (801) 535-7193
Wyoming: CHEYENNE—Cheyenne Police Dept., 1915 Pioneer Ave., Cheyenne, WY 82001 (307) 637-6513

GENERAL MERCHANDISE—ESTATE SALES—COUNTRY AUCTIONS

Arizona: PHOENIX—The Arizona Auctioneers, 1832 S. Central Ave. (real estate, liquidations, bankruptcies) (602) 258-6981; John Brunk & Sons, Inc., 4001 N. 7th St. (general merchandise; Wednesday 9:00 a.m. auction, Wednesday 7:00 p.m. auction) (602) 264-3204; Ledbetter's Antique Auction Gallery, 915 N. Central Ave. (antiques, general merchandise) (602) 257-1455; Robert R. Boone Co., P.O. Box 747, Glendale, AZ (estates, real estate, farms, liquidations, personal property, livestock) (602) 841-1596 / HOT SPRINGS—James E. Wilson & Son, Auctrs., 1019 Airport Rd. (antiques) (501) 767-3625
Colorado: DENVER—Estate Liquidators, 4875 E. Evans Ave. (303) 753-9111; Federal Auction, 2575 S. Broadway (303) 777-1550; Rosevall Auction, 1238 S. Broadway (antique and modern furniture, pianos, cars, rugs, storage items; Wednesday 7:00 p.m. auction) (303)

722-4028 / BRUSH—Charles Cumberlin, Pres. of National Auctrs. Assoc., P.O. Box 248 (real estate) (303) 842-2824 / STEAMBOAT SPRINGS—Lockhart-Lee Auction Realty, P.O. Box 305 (real estate, disposal of prop. for govt. agencies) (303) 879-0565

Idaho: BOISE—Boise Auction Hyde Park Furniture, 1501 N. 13 (furniture; Sunday noon auction); Patterson & Assoc., Auctrs., Interstate 80 N. & Franklin Rd., Nampa, ID (real estate, farm machinery, industrial equipment) (208) 466-4007; Garden City Auction, 3831 Chinden Blvd. (new & used furniture; appraisals) (208) 342-0912

Montana: GREAT FALLS—General Auction, 101 57th St. S. (real estate, household goods, livestock; Thursday 7:00 p.m. auction) (406) 453-7666 / BOZEMAN—Mandeville Big Sky Auction Service (John Mandeville, Craig & Lloyd Mandeville) 1121 Mandeville Ln. (real estate, household goods, general merchandise, livestock) (406) 587-7832

Nevada: LAS VEGAS—City Auto Towing, 1701 Western Ave. (702) 384-8902; Las Vegas Auction, 734 N. Nellis Blvd. (storage liquidations, apartments, motels, house liquidations; Friday 7:30 p.m. auction) (702) 453-1018

New Mexico: CARLSBAD—Royce's Auction & Furniture (new furniture, real estate) (505) 887-5073 / CLOVIS—Mennel's Auction, 2021 E. 2nd St. (general merchandise) (505) 762-2581

Utah: SALT LAKE CITY—Johnny's Auctioneer Service, 1136 S. 500 East (antiques, furniture, tools, household goods, autos, livestock) (801) 359-1272; Olson Auction Galleries, 4303 S. Main (general merchandise) (801) 261-4258; Butterfield & Butterfield telephone # in S.L.C. (801) 967-2471

Wyoming: CHEYENNE—Mel's Auction, 4912 Ridge Rd. (general merchandise) (307) 632-8533

REGIONAL MEDIA

Arizona: PHOENIX—Arizona Republic (auction ads Sunday) (602) 271-8000

Colorado: DENVER—The Denver Post (auction ads daily) (303) 825-3377; Rocky Mountain News (auction ads daily) (303) 892-7111

Idaho: BOISE—Idaho Statesman (auction ads on weekend) (208) 377-6333

Montana: HELENA—Independent Record (auction ads daily) (406) 442-7190

Nevada: LAS VEGAS—Las Vegas Sun (auction ads daily) (702) 385-3111

New Mexico: SANTA FE—The New Mexican (auction ads daily) (505) 983-3303

Utah: SALT LAKE CITY—Salt Lake City Desert News (auction ads daily) (801) 237-2100; Salt Lake City Tribune (auction ads Thursday-Friday) (801) 237-2000

Wyoming: CHEYENNE—Wyoming Eagle & Wyoming State Tribune (when there are ads, they appear any day of the week) (307) 634-3361

PACIFIC REGION
ALASKA (AK), CALIFORNIA (CA), HAWAII (HI), OREGON (OR), WASHINGTON (WA)

General Services Administration

GSA
(Personal Property—AK)
P.O. Box 1632
Anchorage, AK 99510
(907) 271-5022

GSA
(Personal Property—CA)
525 Market St.
San Francisco, CA 94105
(415) 556-3623

GSA
(Real Property—CA)
525 Market St.
San Francisco, CA 94105
(415) 556-5314

GSA
(Personal Property—HI)
Federal Bldg.
300 Ala Moana Blvd.
Honolulu, HI 96850
(808) 836-1578

GSA
(Personal Property—
OR, WA)
GSA Center
Auburn, WA 98002
(206) 833-6500 x491

GSA
(Real Property—OR, WA)
GSA Center
Auburn, WA 98002
(206) 833-6500 x264

Department of Defense

DoD Surplus Sales
P.O. Box 1370
Battle Creek, MI 49106
(Write to this address to get
on national mailing list.)

Defense Property Disposal
P.O. Box 58
Defense Depot Ogden
Station
Ogden, UT 84401
(AK, CA, OR, WA)

Defense Property Disposal
Sales Office Hawaii
DPDR-Pacific, Box 211
Pearl City, HI 96782
(808) 477-5252

Internal Revenue Service

IRS, District Director
P.O. Box 1500
Anchorage, AK 99510
(907) 271-4251

IRS, District Director
P.O. Box 391
Los Angeles, CA 90053
(213) 688-4120

IRS, District Director
450 Golden Gate Ave.
Box 36020
San Francisco, CA 94102
(415) 556-5543

IRS, District Director
P.O. Box 50089
Honolulu, HI 96850
(808) 546-8932

IRS, District Director
P.O. Box 3341
Portland, OR 97208
(503) 221-3568

IRS, District Director
P.O. Box 854
Seattle, WA 98111
(206) 442-7417

Customs

U.S. Customs Service
620 E. Tenth Ave.
Anchorage, AK 99501
(907) 271-4043

U.S. Customs Service
880 Front St.
San Diego, CA 92188
(714) 293-5360

U.S. Customs Service
555 Battery St.
P.O. Box 2450
San Francisco, CA 94126
(415) 556-4340

U.S. Customs Service
300 S. Ferry St.
Terminal Island
San Pedro, CA 90731
(213) 548-2441

U.S. Customs Service
335 Merchant St.
Honolulu, HI 96806
(808) 546-3115

U.S. Customs Service
N.W. Broadway & Glisan
Sts.
Portland, OR 97209
(503) 221-2865

U.S. Customs Service
909 First Ave.
Seattle, WA 98174
(206) 442-5491

U.S. Marshals

U.S. Marshal
701 C St., Box 28
Anchorage, AK 99513
(907) 271-5154

U.S. Marshal
312 N. Spring St.
Los Angeles, CA 90012
(213) 798-2485

U.S. Marshal
650 Capitol Mall
Sacramento, CA 95814
(916) 448-2163

U.S. Marshal
450 Golden Gate Ave.
San Francisco, CA 94102
(415) 566-3930

U.S. Marshal
940 Front St.
San Diego, CA 92189
(714) 895-6620

U.S. Marshal
P.O. Box 50184
Honolulu, HI 96850
(808) 546-2150

U.S. Marshal
P.O. Box 871
Portland, OR 97207
(503) 423-2209

U.S. Marshal
1010 5th Ave.
Seattle, WA 98104
(206) 399-5500

U.S. Marshal
P.O. Box 1463
Spokane, WA 99210
(509) 439-3730

National Forest Service

U.S. Dept. of Agriculture
Office of Forest Service
Alaska Region
Federal Office Bldg.
P.O. Box 1628
Juneau, AK 99802

U.S. Dept. of Agriculture
Office of Forest Service
California Region
630 Sansome St.
San Francisco, CA 94111

U.S. Dept. of Agriculture
Office of Forest Service
Pacific Northwest Region
319 S.W. Pine St.
P.O. Box 3623
Portland, OR 97208

Post Office

Procurement
Services Office
U.S. Postal Service
P.O. Box 700
1100 Sullivan Ave.
Daly City, CA 94017
(415) 876-9181

Post Master
Dead Parcel Branch
Los Angeles, CA 90098
(213) 688-2252

Procurement
Services Office
P.O. Box 22220
Los Angeles, CA 90022
(213) 265-0590

Post Master
Dead Parcel Branch
San Francisco, CA 94101
(415) 566-2500

Procurement
Services Office
U.S. Postal Service
415 First Ave. N.
P.O. Box 9268
Seattle, WA 98109
(206) 442-7824

Post Master
Dead Parcel Branch
Seattle, WA 98109
(206) 442-4426

State Surplus Departments

Dept. of Administration
General Services & Supply
Surplus Property
200 N. Wrangle St.
Anchorage, AK 99501
(907) 279-0596

Dept. of Natural Resources
S.E. District Office
Pouch MA
Juneau, AK 99811
(907) 465-2415

Dept. of Natural Resources
S. Central District Office
941 E. Dowling Rd.
Anchorage, AK 99502
(907) 349-4524

Dept. of Natural Resources
N. Central District Office
4420 Airport Way
Fairbanks, AK 99701
(907) 479-2243

Dept. of General Services
Real Estate
Services Division
650 Howe Ave.
Sacramento, CA 95825
(916) 920-6262

Hawaii Dept. of Land
and Natural Resources
Land Mgt. Division
P.O. Box 621
Honolulu, HI 96809
(808) 548-2574

State Surplus
1655 Industrial Dr. N.E.
Salem, OR 97310
(503) 378-4714

Division of State Lands
1445 State St.
Salem, OR 97310
(503) 378-3805

Surplus Property
Central Stores
Revolving Fund
6858 S. 190th St.
Kent, WA 98031
(206) 872-6446

Dept. of
Natural Resources
Public Lands Bldg.
Olympia, WA 98504
(206) 753-5328

SHERIFFS

California: LOS ANGELES—L.A. County Sheriff's Dept., 211 W. Temple St., Hall of Justice, L.A., CA 90012 (213) 974-4211 / SAN DIEGO—San Diego County Sheriff's Dept., P.O. Box 1751, San Diego, CA 92112 (714) 236-2911 / SAN FRANCISCO—San Francisco Sheriff's Dept., City Hall, Rm. 333, San Francisco, CA 94102 (415) 558-4291

Hawaii: HONOLULU—Office of the Sheriff, 33 S. King St. 6th fl., Honolulu, HI 96813 (808) 548-3120

Oregon: PORTLAND—Administrative Services, Fixed Assets-Property Control, 2505 S.E. 11th, Portland, OR 97202 (property); Administrative Services, Property Management, 2505 S.E. 11th, Portland, OR 97202 (real estate) (503) 255-3600 for both offices

Washington: SEATTLE—King County Sheriff's Dept., Civil Division, 516 Third Ave., King County Courthouse, Seattle, WA 98104 (206) 344-3800

POLICE

Alaska: ANCHORAGE—Anchorage Police Dept., Property & Evidence Section, 625 C St., Anchorage, AK 99501 (907) 264-4119

California: LOS ANGELES—L.A. Police Dept., 150 N. L.A. St., L.A., CA 90012 (misc. prop. (213) 485-3196; autos (213) 485-2256) / SAN DIEGO—San Diego Police Dept., Property Room, 801 W. Market St., San Diego, CA 92101 (714) 236-6386 / SAN FRANCISCO—San Francisco Police Dept., Property Control Section, Rm. G25, 850 Bryant St., San Francisco, CA 94103 (415) 553-1377

Hawaii: HONOLULU—Honolulu Police Dept., Evidence Room, 1455 S. Bertania St., Honolulu, HI 96814 (808) 955-8283

Oregon: PORTLAND—police dept. property auctioned by: Property Control, Portland City Hall, 1220 S.W. 5th Ave., Portland, OR 97204 (503) 248-4395

Washington: SEATTLE—Seattle Police Dept., Property Room, Public Safety Bldg., Seattle, WA 98104 (206) 625-2000

GENERAL MERCHANDISE—ESTATE SALES—COUNTRY AUCTIONS

Alaska: ANCHORAGE—Bolt's Quality Auction, P.O. Box 2088 (general merchandise) (907) 276-6804; Hess & Son, 424 N. Klevin St. (real estate, liquidations, trailers) (907) 277-4931 or 272-7734; Pacific Auction, SRA Box 1411 (real estate, general merchandise, cars; weekly auction) (907) 344-1615; Denton Wright Auction Co., 6930 Old Seward Hwy. (general merchandise) (907) 349-6484

California: LOS ANGELES—A.N. Abell, 1911 W. Admas Blvd. (fine art, antiques, rugs, silver) (213) 734-4151; Ames Auction Galleries, 8725 Wilshire Blvd., Beverly Hills, CA (antiques, art) (213) 655-5611; Golden Movement Emporium (architectural remnants auctioned once a year) (213) 726-2345; Arthur Goode, 526 La Cienega (general merchandise) (213) 657-7404; Cliff Harris Real Estate Auctioneer, 5478 Wilshire Blvd. (213) 936-2004; L.A. Horse & Mule Auction, 3226 Gilman Rd., Elmira, CA (tack and horse auction Friday 7:30 p.m.) (213) 448-2608; Repp & Mott Inc., 2501 E. Anaheim, Long Beach, CA (furniture; Wednesday 9:00 a.m. auction) (213) 439-0277; Max Rouse & Sons, 361 S. Robertson Blvd., Beverly Hills, CA (industrial equipment) (213) 655-9300; Sotheby Parke-Bernet, 7660 Beverly Blvd. (213) 937-5130 / SAN DIEGO—Borders' Auction Center (Harold Borders, Owner, Kenneth Glascow, Auctr.), 8205 Ronson Rd. (furniture, antiques, appliances) (714) 279-2070; Buckingham Galleries (Chester J. Whalen, estate Auctr.), 10125 San Diego Mission Rd. (estates, antiques, art) (714) 283-7286; Leo Edge Auction, 3814 El Cajon (general merchandise; Friday 6:00 p.m. auction) (714) 282-5492; Mary's Auction House, 532 28th St. (general merchandise; Thursday 6:30 p.m. auction) (714) 233-3148 / SAN FRANCISCO—Butterfield & Butterfield, 1244 Sutter (fine art, antiques, silver, rugs, collectibles, jewelry) (415) 673-1362 and Auction Warehouse, 660 3rd St. (bankruptcies) (415) 543-9500; J. Canes International, 530 Folsom St. (antiques) (415) 543-7369; La Salle Gallery Inc., 2083 Union (antiques) (415) 931-9200; San Francisco Antiques Gallery, 1217 Sutter St. (415) 441-3800; Trash to Treasures, Personal Property Brokers, 1110 Quintana Rd., Morro Bay, CA (antiques, art, orientalia) (415) 772-7777

Oregon: PORTLAND—Action Auctions, 10025 N.E. Sandy Blvd. (antiques, furniture, storage goods; Monday 7:30 p.m. auction) (503) 256-2299; A-1 Auction (Ormand Hill, Auctr.) 8819 S.E. Powell Blvd. (estates, furniture, appliances, bankruptcies, discontinued stock; Monday night auction, Wednesday night auction) (503) 777-1755; Ash & Assoc., Inc., Auctioneers, 2125 S.W. 4th (industrial equipment, sawmill equipment) (503) 222-9151; Butterfield & Butterfield telephone # in Portland (503) 223-4273; Continental Plants Corp., Georgia-Pacific Bldg. (industrial liquidations) (503) 221-1221; Country Store Trading Post, 3003 Hwy. 101 N., Gearhart, OR (503) 738-5719; Elmer E. Johnson, 3925 S.W. 170th, Beaverton, OR (furniture, appliances, discontinued stock, bankruptcies; Wednesday 7:00 p.m. auction) (503) 649-3753; O'Gallerie, 537 S.E. Ash (fine art, furnishings) (503) 238-0202

Washington: SEATTLE—Alexander's Auction House, 3209 N.E. 4th, Renton Highlands, WA (general merchandise) (206) 255-2862; Bushell's Auction House, 2006 2nd Ave.˙ (estates, antiques, household furnishings) (206) 622-5833; King Auction Service, 8826 N.E. Bothell Way, Bothell, WA (general merchandise) (206) 485-7722

REGIONAL MEDIA

Alaska: ANCHORAGE—Anchorage Daily News (auction ads daily) (907) 274-2561

California: SAN DIEGO—San Diego Union (auction ads daily) (714) 293-1481 / SAN FRANCISCO—San Francisco Examiner (auction ads daily) (415) 777-2424 / LOS ANGELES—Los Angeles Times (auction ads daily) (213) 972-5000

Hawaii: HONOLULU—Honolulu Star-Bulletin & Advertiser (auction ads on Sunday, when there are any) (808) 525-8000

Oregon: PORTLAND—Oregonian & Oregon Journal (auction ads daily) (503) 221-8275

Washington: SEATTLE—Seattle Post-Intelligencer (auction ads Thursday & Sunday) (206) 628-8000; Seattle Times (auction ads Sunday) (206) 464-2111

SOUTH ATLANTIC REGION
DELAWARE (DE), FLORIDA (FL), GEORGIA (GA), MARYLAND (MD), NORTH CAROLINA (NC), SOUTH CAROLINA (SC), VIRGINIA (VA), WASHINGTON D.C. (DC), WEST VIRGINIA (WV)

General Services Administration

GSA
(Real Property—
FL, GA, NC, SC)
1776 Peachtree St., N.W.
Atlanta, GA 30309
(404) 221-5311

GSA
(Personal Property—
FL, GA, NC, SC)
1776 Peachtree St., N.W.
Atlanta, GA 30309
(404) 221-5117

GSA
(Real Property—
DE, MD, VA, DC, WV)
7th & D Sts., S.W.
Washington DC 20407
(202) 557-1619

GSA
(Personal Property—
DE, MD, VA, DC, WV)
7th & D Sts., S.W.
Washington DC 20407
(202) 557-3895

Department of Defense

DoD Surplus Sales
P.O. Box 1370
Battle Creek, MI 49016
(Write to this address to get on national mailing list.)

Defense Property Disposal
P.O. Box 13110
Columbus, OH 43213
(614) 236-2114
(DE, MD, VA, DC, WV)

Defense Property Disposal
P.O. Box 14716
Memphis, TN 38114
(901) 744-5131
(FL, GA, NC, SC)

Internal Revenue Service

IRS, District Director
P.O. Box 2415
Wilmington, DE 19899
(302) 573-6048

IRS, District Director
P.O. Box 35045
Jacksonville, FL 32202
(904) 791-2945

IRS, District Director
P.O. Box 1642
Atlanta, GA 30301
(404) 221-6191

IRS, District Director
P.O. Box 1018
Baltimore, MD 21203
(301) 962-3084

IRS, District Director
320 Federal Place
Greensboro, NC 27401
(919) 378-5306

IRS, District Director
1835 Assembly St.
Columbia, SC 29201
(803) 765-5701

IRS, District Director
P.O. Box 10107
Richmond, VA 23240
(804) 782-2255

IRS, District Director
P.O. Box 1388
Parkersburg, WV 26101
(304) 422-8551 x1201

Customs

U.S. Customs Service
77 S.E. Fifth St.
Miami, FL 33131
(305) 350-4806

U.S. Customs Service
301 S. Ashly Dr.
Tampa, FL 33602
(813) 228-2381

U.S. Customs Service
1 E. Bay St.
Savannah, GA 31401
(912) 232-4321

U.S. Customs Service
103 S. Gay St.
Baltimore, MD 21202
(301) 962-2666

U.S. Customs Service
2094 Polk St.
Wilmington, NC 28401
(919) 343-4601

U.S. Customs Service
200 E. Bay St.
Charleston, SC 29402
(803) 724-4312

U.S. Customs Service
P.O. Box 17423
Gateway Building
Dulles International Airport
Chantilly, VA 22021
(202) 566-8511

U.S. Customs Service
101 E. Main St.
Norfolk, VA 23510
(804) 827-6546

U.S. Marshals

U.S. Marshal
844 King St.
Wilmington, DE 19801
(302) 487-6176

U.S. Marshal
P.O. Box 1489
Jacksonville, FL 32201
(904) 946-2293

U.S. Marshal
P.O. Box 010391
Miami, FL 33101
(305) 350-5346

U.S. Marshal
P.O. Box 1150
Pensacola, FL 32595
(904) 946-5228

U.S. Marshal
75 Spring St./Rm. 1669
Atlanta, GA 30303
(404) 242-6833

U.S. Marshal
Third & Mulberry Sts.
Macon, GA 31202
(912) 743-4693

U.S. Marshal
P.O. Box 9765
Savannah, GA 31412
(912) 248-4213

U.S. Marshal
101 Lombard St.
Baltimore, MD 21201
(301) 922-2220

U.S. Marshal
P.O. Box 59
Asheville, NC 28802
(704) 672-0652

U.S. Marshal
P.O. Box 1528
Greensboro, NC 27402
(919) 699-5354

U.S. Marshal
P.O. Box 25640
Raleigh, NC 27611
(919) 672-4153

U.S. Marshal
1835 Assembly St.
Columbia, SC 29201
(803) 677-5821

U.S. Marshal
P.O. Box 1181
Norfolk, VA 23501
(804) 827-6295

U.S. Marshal
210 Franklin Rd., S.W.
Roanoke, VA 24009
(703) 937-6230

U.S. Marshal
Third & Constitution
Ave., N.W.
Washington DC 20001
(202) 633-1750

U.S. Marshal
P.O. Box 2667
Charleston, WV 25330
(304) 924-1264

U.S. Marshal
P.O. Box 832
Fairmont, WV 26554
(304) 923-1930

National Forest Service

U.S. Dept. of
Agriculture
Office of Forest Service
Southern Region
1720 Peachtree Rd., N.W.
Atlanta, GA 30309

Post Office

Post Master
Dead Parcel Branch
Jacksonville, FL 32201
(904) 791-2669

Procurement
Services Office
U.S. Postal Service
7415 Commonwealth Ave.
Jacksonville, FL 32099
(904) 791-1371

Post Master
Dead Parcel Branch
Atlanta, GA 30304
(404) 221-5456

Procurement
Services Office
U.S. Postal Service
1800 James Jackson
Pky., N.W.
Atlanta, GA 30309
(404) 782-3056

Procurement
Services Office
Maryland/DC District
Virginia District
U.S. Postal Service
P.O. Box 549
Columbia, MD 21045
(301) 997-9088

Post Master
Dead Parcel Branch
Greensboro, NC 27420
(919) 378-5481

Procurement
Services Office
U.S. Postal Service
P.O. Box 27495
Greensboro, NC 27495
(919) 855-4444

Post Master
Dead Parcel Branch
Washington DC 20013
(202) 523-2043

State Surplus Departments

Division of Purchasing
P.O. Box 299
Delaware City, DE 19706
(302) 571-3070

Bureau of State Surplus
Property
324 W. Van Buren St.
Tallahassee, FL 32301
(305) 488-5272

Surplus Property
1050 Murphy Ave., S.W.
Atlanta, GA 30310
(404) 656-3245

Dept. of General Services
Purchasing Inventory
Control
301 W. Preston St.
Baltimore, MD 21201
(301) 383-6148

Dept. of General Services
Land Acquisition/Rm. 1307
301 W. Preston St.
Baltimore, MD 21201
(301) 383-3964

Surplus Property
116 W. Jones St.
Raleigh, NC 27611
(919) 733-3889

State Property
Office (Land)
116 W. Jones St.
Raleigh, NC 27611
(919) 733-4346

Surplus Property
Boston Ave.
W. Columbia, SC 29169
(803) 748-2626

Division of Purchasing
P.O. Box 1199
Richmond, VA 23209
(804) 786-3876

Surplus Property
2700 Charles Ave.
Cunbar, WV 25064
(304) 348-3510

SHERIFFS

Delaware: WILMINGTON—Newcastle County Sheriff's Dept., Public Bldg., 11th & King, Wilmington, DE 19801 (302) 571-7564

Florida: MIAMI—Dade County Sheriff's Dept., Property & Evidence, 95 NW 29th St., Miami, FL 33127 (305) 547-7291 / TAMPA—Hillsboro County Sheriff's Dept., P.O. Box 3371, Tampa, FL 33601 (813) 247-6411

Georgia: ATLANTA—Fulton County Sheriff's Dept., Atlanta, GA 30303 (404) 572-2821 / SAVANNAH—Chatham County Sheriff's Dept., P.O. Box 9604, Savannah, GA 31499 (912) 944-4611

Maryland: BALTIMORE—Sheriff's Dept., Baltimore County, 401 Bosley Ave., Towson, MD 21204 (301) 494-3151

North Carolina: CHARLOTTE—Mecklenburg County Sheriff's Dept., 800 E. 4th St., Charlotte, NC 28202 (704) 374-2543 / RALEIGH—Wake County Sheriff's Dept., P.O. Box 550, Raleigh, NC 27602 (919) 755-6924

South Carolina: CHARLESTON—Sheriff of Charleston County, P.O. Box 605, Charleston, SC 29402 (803) 723-6710 / COLUMBIA—Richland County Sheriff's Dept., 1400 Huger St., Columbia, SC 29201 (803) 779-6100

Virginia: RICHMOND—Richmond Sheriff's Dept., LL1 John Marshalls Courts Bldg., 8th & Marshall, Richmond, VA 23219 (804) 780-8823

West Virginia: CHARLESTON—Kanawha County Sheriff's Dept., Virginia & Court Sts., Charleston, WV 25301 (304) 348-6501

POLICE

Delaware: WILMINGTON—Wilmington Police Dept., c/o Records Division, 1000 King St., Wilmington, DE 19802 (302) 571-4480

Florida: MIAMI—City of Miami Purchasing Agent, P.O. Box 01677, Miami, FL 33101 (305) 579-6350 / TAMPA-ST. PETERSBURG—Tampa-St. Petersburg Police Headquarters, Property & Evidence Division, 1710 Tampa St., Tampa, FL 33606 (813) 223-8181

Georgia: ATLANTA—Atlanta Police Dept., Property Control or Auto Larceny Section, 165 Decatur St., Atlanta, GA 30335 (404) 348-6876

Maryland: BALTIMORE—Evidence Control Section, Baltimore Police Dept., 601 E. Fayette St., Baltimore, MD 21202 (miscellaneous property (301) 396-2048) or Baltimore Police Dept., Abandoned Vehicle Division, 6700 Pulaski Hwy., Baltimore, MD 21237 (autos (301) 396-8175)

North Carolina: CHARLOTTE—Charlotte Police Dept., Property Control, 825 E. 4th St., Charlotte, NC 28202 (704) 374-2378

South Carolina: CHARLESTON—Charleston Police Dept., Supply Division, P.O. Box 98, Charleston, SC 29403 (803) 577-7434 x102 / COLUMBIA—Columbia Police Dept., Property Room, 1401 Lincoln St., Columbia, SC 29202 (803) 733-8367

Virginia: RICHMOND—Bureau of Police, Maintenance Division, 501 N. 9th St., Richmond, VA 23219 (804) 780-5521

West Virginia: CHARLESTON—police dept. property is auctioned by: City Manager's Office, P.O. Box 2749, Charleston, WV 25330 (304) 348-8014

GENERAL MERCHANDISE—ESTATE SALES—COUNTRY AUCTIONS

Delaware: WILMINGTON—Rudnick & Matas, 1908 N. Broom St. (estates, household furnishings) (302) 658-7264; George H. Wilson & Son, 12th St. & Rt. 495 (household goods) (302) 658-6721 / NEW-ARK—Ironhill Auction, Elkton Rd. & Sandy Brae (household goods, general merchandise, tools, guns, furniture, appliances) (302) 453-9138 / HOCKESSIN—John J. McGrellis, Box 217 (estates, antiques, household furnishings) (302) 239-7244

Florida: MIAMI—Auction Co. of America, Inc. (Jim Gall, Auctr.), 7302 N.W. 54th St. (estates, condominiums, moving & storage auctions, general merchandise) (305) 266-8800; J. Wayne Taylor Inc., 3848 Bird Rd. (estates, antiques) (305) 446-0142; Richard H. Thomas, 5524 N.E. 7th Ave. (real estate, household goods, antiques, equipment, liquidations, appraisals) (305) 757-1736 / PALM BEACH—Sotheby Parke-Bernet, Inc., 155 Worth Ave. (305) 659-3555; Trosby Auction Galleries, 905 N. Railroad Ave., W. Palm Beach, FL (fine art, antiques) (305) 659-1755 and Trosby Auction Galleries, 2506 Ponce de Leon Blvd., Coral Gables, FL (305) 446-3436 / ST. PETERSBURG-TAMPA—St. Pete Auto Auction, 14950 Roosevelt Blvd., Clearwater, FL (Thursday night auction) (813) 531-7717; Sun Coast Auction Assoc., 1529 Missouri Ave. S., Clearwater, FL (estates, appraisals) (813) 441-1132; Vince Runowich Auctions, 2312 4th St. N. (household goods) (813) 895-3548; Col. Luther D. Bynum, 1437 Central Ave. (real estate) (813) 898-5392; Nigel's, U.S. 19 & St. Rd. 584, Palm Harbor, FL (antiques, household furnishings) (813) 784-1122; Col. Marty Higgenbotham, 1702 Edgewood Dr., Lakeland, FL (real estate, liquidations) (813) 688-6094 / BROOKVILLE—Airport Mart, 1155 Spring Hill Blvd. (general merchandise, tools; Friday and Saturday 7:30 p.m. auctions) (904) 796-0268

Georgia: ATLANTA—Atlanta Galleries, 2050 Hills Ave. N.W. (antiques: Thursday afternoon & evening auction) (404) 355-0755; Bishop Brothers Auto Auction, 2244 Stewart Ave. S.W. (Monday, Wednesday, & Saturday 7:30 p.m. auctions) (404) 761-6736; Gold's Antiques & Auction Gallery, 1149 Lee St. S.W. (404) 753-1493; Kennedy Antiques, 1088 Huff Rd. (404) 351-4464 / AVONDALE ESTATES—ABCD Auction Gallery, 1 N. Clarendon Rd. (antiques; Wednesday auction) (404) 294-8264 / ROME—J. L. Todd Auction Co., 531 Broad St. (real estate, estates, industrial properties, machinery, liquidations, cattle) (Atlanta Telephone #) (404) 577-2634 / TALMO—Pardue's Antique Auctions, Hwy. 129 (estates, furniture; first & third Fridays 7:00 p.m. auctions) (404) 693-2500

Maryland: BALTIMORE—A.J. Billig & Co., 16 E. Fayette St. (general merchandise, personal property, autos, bankruptcies) (301) 742-8440; Austin Bohn, Auctrs. Mount Airy Furniture & Appliances, 118 S. Main St. (estates, household goods) (301) 795-9222; Alex Cooper, 345 N. Charles St. (liquidations) (301) 752-4868; Michael Fox, Charles Center S., Suite 1915 (autos, liquidations) (301) 332-1333 / RISING SUN—Hunter's Sale Barn, Rt. 276, Box 427 (furniture, tools, farm equipment, cows, chickens, eggs, produce) (301) 658-6400

North Carolina: CHARLOTTE—Ralph Williams, Auctr., 1408 Deplaza (antiques; monthly auctoin) (704) 332-5990 / LENOIR—Ben Griffin Auction Co., 361 Calico Rd. (surplus equipment, school furnishings) (704) 754-9973 / GREENSBORO—Joe Byerly, Auctr., Rockingham Rd. (antiques) (919) 299-3835 / GOLDSBORO—L. E. Warrick, Jr., Auctr., P.O. Box 974 (estates) (919) 735-4648 or 735-6061

South Carolina: CHARLESTON—Dual Lane Furniture Auction Co., 3918 Rivers Ave. (803) 744-5850; Haskell P. Wagers, Office 6893 Rivers Ave. (real estate, equipment) (803) 553-7134 / FLORENCE—William Yonce & Co., Inc., 1513 W. Evans St. (real estate) (803) 665-6060 / GREENVILLE—P.L. Bruce & Co., 912 Poinsettia Hwy. (autos, livestock, special sales) (803) 242-3090; Auctioneer Co. (Ted Bruce, Gene Batson, Rick Bruce, Auctrs.) (general merchandise) (803) 271-8640 / ORANGEBURG—Caroline Auction & Land Co., Inc., Gramling Lane (real estate, farm equipment) (803) 534-8022

Virginia: RICHMOND—Bill Grindstaff, 428 Rochelle Rd. (antiques) (703) 784-5740; Valentine Auction, 1345 W. Broad St. (general merchandise; weekly auction) (703) 353-0439 / A Thieve's Market, 7704 Richmond Hwy., Alexandria, VA (fine art, antiques, household furnishings) (703) 360-4200; Laws Auction & Antiques, 7209 Centerville Rd., Manassas, VA (antiques, furniture) (202) 631-0590 / AXTON—Ray

A. Lambert Auction Co., Rt. 2 Box 270D (general merchandise) (703) 650-2542 or 650-2347

Washington, D.C.: American Auction Corp., 4310 St. Barnabas Rd., Marlow Heights, MD (real estate) (301) 423-0504; Arcade Auction Inc., 733 15th St. N.W. (general merchandise) (202) 393-3480; Atlantic Auctions Inc., 1370 W. North Ave., Baltimore, MD (vehicles) (Washington telephone #) (202) 737-3453; The Middle Man, Auctioneer & Liquidator, 6527 Chillum Pl., N.W. (202) 829-5445; C.G. Sloan & Co., Inc., 715 13th St., N.W. (fine art, antiques, collectibles) (202) 628-1468; Adam A. Weschler & Sons, 905-909 East St., N.W. (estates, fine art, antiques, collectibles; Tuesday auctions) (202) 628-1281

West Virginia: ELKVIEW—Atlas Furniture & Auction Co., Inc., Three Gables (furniture, general merchandise) (304) 965-6191

REGIONAL MEDIA

Delaware: WILMINGTON—Wilmington News Journal (auction ads daily) (302) 573-2000 / NEWARK—Weekly Post (302) 738-7200

Florida: MIAMI—Miami Herald (auction ads daily) (800) 327-6566 / ST. PETERSBURG—St. Petersburg Times (auction ads daily) (813) 893-8111 / TAMPA—Tampa Tribune & Times (auction ads daily) (813) 272-7500

Georgia: ATLANTA—Atlanta Journal-Constitution (auction ads daily) (404) 572-5151

Maryland: BALTIMORE—Baltimore Sun (auction ads daily; more Sunday) (301) 332-6000

North Carolina: CHARLOTTE—The Charlotte Observer (auction ads daily) (704) 377-5555 / GREENSBORO—Greensboro Daily News & Record (auction ads daily) (919) 373-7000

South Carolina: CHARLESTON—The Charleston News & Courier (auction ads Friday) (803) 722-6500 / COLUMBIA—The Columbia State (auction ads on weekend) (803) 771-6161

Virginia: RICHMOND—Richmond Times Dispatch (auction ads daily) (804) 643-4414

Washington, D.C.: Washington Post (auction ads daily) (202) 223-6000

West Virginia: CHARLESTON—Charleston Gazette & Daily Mail (auction ads on weekend) (304) 348-5140

EAST SOUTH CENTRAL REGION
ALABAMA (AL), KENTUCKY (KY), MISSISSIPPI (MS), TENNESSEE (TN)

General Services Administration

GSA
(Personal Property)
1776 Peachtree St., N.W.
Atlanta, GA 30309
(404) 221-5117

GSA
(Real Property)
1776 Peachtree St., N.W.
Atlanta, GA 30309
(404) 221-5133

Department of Defense

DoD Surplus Sales
P.O. Box 1370
Battle Creek, MI 49016
(Write to this address to get
on national mailing list.)

Defense Property Disposal
P.O. Box 14716
Memphis, TN 38114
(901) 744-5131

Internal Revenue Service

IRS, District Director
2121 Eighth Ave., N.
Rm. 1232
Birmingham, AL 35203
(205) 254-1257

IRS, District Director
P.O. Box 1735
Louisville, KY 40201
(502) 582-5331

IRS, District Director
100 W. Capitol St.
Jackson, MS 39201
(601) 960-5083

IRS, District Director
P.O. Box 1107
Nashville, TN 37202
(615) 251-5731

Customs

U.S. Customs Service
250 N. Water St.
Mobile, AL 36602
(205) 690-2106

U.S. Marshals

U.S. Marshal
1800 N. 5th Ave.
Birmingham, AL 35203
(205) 229-1712

U.S. Marshal
10½ St. Joseph St.
Box 343
Mobile, AL 36601
(205) 534-2841

U.S. Marshal
P.O. Drawer 4249
Montgomery, AL 36101
(205) 534-7401

U.S. Marshal
P.O. Box 30
Lexington, KY 40501
(606) 355-2513

U.S. Marshal
600 W. Broadway
Louisville, KY 40202
(502) 352-5141

U.S. Marshal
911 Jackson Ave.
Oxford, MS 36655
(601) 234-6661

U.S. Marshal
P.O. Box 959
Jackson, MS 39205
(601) 490-4444

U.S. Marshal
Main & Walnut Sts.
Knoxville, TN 27901
(615) 854-4577

U.S. Marshal
801 Broadway
Nashville, TN 37203
(615) 852-5417

U.S. Marshal
167 N. Main St.
Memphis, TN 38103
(901) 722-3304

Post Office

Post Master
Dead Parcel Branch
Memphis, TN 38101
(901) 521-3451

Procurement
Services Office
U.S. Post Office
1921 Elvis Presley Blvd.
Memphis, TN 33136
(901) 521-4564

State Surplus Departments

Finance Department
Services Division
Surplus Property
432 Jefferson St.
Montgomery, AL 36130
(205) 832-3445

Division of Property
234 New Capitol Annex
Frankfort, KY 40601
(502) 564-2213

Bureau of Public Property
Capitol Annex/Rm. 105
Frankfort, KY 40601
(502) 564-4313

Property Control
P.O. Box 956
Jackson, MS 39205
(601) 354-6012

Surplus Property
6500 Centennial Blvd.
Nashville, TN 37209
(615) 741-1711

Dept. of Finances
& Admin.
Real Property Division
Commercial Union Bank
Bldg.
Nashville, TN 37219
(615) 741-2315

SHERIFFS

Alabama: BIRMINGHAM—Jefferson County Sheriff's Dept., 716 N. 21st St., Birmingham, AL 35202 (205) 325-5721 / MOBILE—Mobile County Sheriff's Dept., P.O. Box 113, Mobile, AL 36601 (205) 690-8011

Kentucky: LOUISVILLE—Jefferson County Sheriff's Dept., 604 Sifical Court Bldg., Louisville, KY 40202 (502) 585-3660

Mississippi: JACKSON—Hinds County Sheriff's Dept., Civil Process Dept., P.O. Box 1452, Jackson, MS 39205 (601) 969-6800

Tennessee: MEMPHIS—Shelby County Sheriff's Dept., Civil Division, 140 Adams, Shelby County Courthouse, Rm. 208, Memphis, TN 38103 (901) 382-1050 / NASHVILLE—Davidson County Sheriff's Dept., 506 2nd Ave. N., Nashville, TN 37201 (615) 259-6241

POLICE

Alabama: BIRMINGHAM—Birmingham Police Dept., City Hall, 1710 & 19th St. N., Birmingham, AL 35204 (miscellaneous (205) 254-2075); Birmingham Police—South Precinct, 325 Finley Ave., Birmingham, AL (auto (205) 254-2801); Fencing Dept., 20th St. & Hyland Ave., Birmingham, AL (bike (205) 254-2606) / MOBILE—Mobile Police Dept., Detective Bureau, 51 Government St., Mobile, AL 36601 (205) 438-7201

Kentucky: LOUISVILLE—Louisville Police Dept., Property Room (for miscellaneous) or Tow-in Lot (for autos), 7 Jefferson St., Louisville, KY 40202 (502) 581-2578

Mississippi: JACKSON—Jackson Police Dept., Recovered Property Section, P.O. Box 17, Jackson, MS 39205 (601) 960-1221

Tennessee: MEMPHIS—Memphis police dept. auctions held at: Purchasing Dept., City Hall, 125 N. Main St., Memphis, TN 38103 (901) 528-2683 / NASHVILLE—Nashville Police Dept., Property & Evidence Division or Tow-in Lot, 505 2nd Ave., N. Nashville, TN 37201 (property & evidence (615) 259-6276) (tow-in lot (615) 259-5345)

GENERAL MERCHANDISE—ESTATE SALES—COUNTRY AUCTIONS

Alabama: BIRMINGHAM—Clark & Co. Liquidations & Auctions, 2054 Lomb Ave. W. (business liquidations, machines, furniture, fixtures) (205) 786-5231; American Real Estate & Auction Co., Inc., 1210 20th St. S. (estates, residential-commercial-business liquidations, farms) (205) 933-2580 / HUEYTOWN—Rex Realty & Auction Co., Inc., 3067 Warrior River Rd. (real estate, estates, antiques, businesses, personal property, classic cars) (205) 491-4131 / HUNTSVILLE—John Horton Realty & Auction Co., 111 4th St., S.W. (estates, houses, farms, furniture, commercial equipment) (205) 536-7497

Kentucky: LOUISVILLE—Abel Auction of America, 3516 Dutchman's Lane (estates, business, liquidations) (502) 454-5663: Gribbins Auction House, 3026 Taylor Blvd. (antiques, furniture, appliances, tools; Tuesday & Saturday night auctions) (502) 637-1770; Martin Auction Co. (Joe Martin, Auctr.), 1401 Melody Lane (estates, farms, personal property, autos) (502) 366-1881; Pound Auction & Realty, Inc., 10 107 Watterson Trail (estates, farms, liquidations) (502) 267-1743 / BOWLING GREEN—Tommy Hunt, P.O. Box 3440, 1411 Scottsville Rd. (real estate) (502) 781-1234 / LEXINGTON—Keeneland Association, P.O. Box 1690 (thoroughbred horse auctions; four annual auctions: 1) January horses of all ages sale; 2) July selected yearling sale; 3) September yearling sale; 4) November breeding stock sale) (606) 254-3412

Mississippi: JACKSON—Southland Auction Co. (Harry Upton, Jim Brown, Auctrs.), Deposit Guaranty Plaza (estates, real estate, antiques, farm equipment, business liquidations) (601) 355-3695

Tennessee: CHATTANOOGA—Northgate Antique & Auction Gallery, 5520 Hwy. 153 (furniture, porcelain, china, rugs, clocks, silver; first Saturday auction) (615) 877-6114 / MEMPHIS—Delta Auction & Real Estate Co., Inc., 4990 Poplar, First Tennessee Bank Bldg., Suite 301 (real estate, antiques, estates, farms, machinery, commercial-industrial liquidations) (901) 761-5080, evening 386-9261; Tri-State Auto Auction, Inc., 8390 Hwy. 51 N. (901) 393-7909; Volunteer Auction & Real Estate Co. (Col. Virgil Nutt & M.F. Harris, Auctrs.), 2552 Poplar Ave., suite 412 or 1903 N. Locust St., Lawrenceburg, TN (real estate, personal property, equipment, liquidations) (901) 458-8204 / MURFREESBORO—Hubert Songer, 1602 Jones Blvd. (general merchandise, commercial liquidations) (615) 896-4067; Estate Gallery Auction Co., 115 W. Vine St. (drugstore & old general store items, antiques; gallery auctions twice a month) (615) 890-2067

REGIONAL MEDIA

Alabama: BIRMINGHAM–Birmingham News (auction ads daily) (205) 252-1411 / MOBILE–Mobile Press-Register (auction ads Sunday) (205) 438-2541 / TUSCALOOSA–Antique Monthly, P.O. Drawer 2, Tuscaloosa, AL 35402; The Gray Letter, P.O. Drawer 2, Tuscaloosa, AL (weekly) (205) 345-0288

Kentucky: LOUISVILLE–Louisville Courier-Journal (auction ads daily; more Sunday) (502) 582-4011 / LEXINGTON–The Southeast Trader (monthly) (803) 359-9182

Mississippi: GREENVILLE–Greenville Delta-Democrat-Times (auction ads daily) (601) 335-1155 / JACKSON–Jackson Clarion-Ledger (auction ads on weekend) (601) 961-7100

Tennessee: MEMPHIS–Memphis Commercial Appeal (auction ads Sunday) (901) 529-2700 / NASHVILLE–Nashville Tennessean (auction ads daily; more Sunday) (615) 255-1221

WEST SOUTH CENTRAL REGION
ARKANSAS (AR), LOUISIANA (LA), OKLAHOMA (OK), TEXAS (TX)

General Services Administration

GSA
(Real Property)
819 Taylor St.
Fort Worth, TX 46102
(817) 334-2331

GSA
(Personal Property)
819 Taylor St.
Fort Worth, TX 46102
(817) 334-2330

Department of Defense

DoD Surplus Sales
P.O. Box 1370
Battle Creek, MI 49016
(Write to this address to
get on national mailing list.)

Defense Property Disposal
P.O. Box 14716
Memphis, TN 38114
(901) 744-5131

Internal Revenue Service

IRS, District Director
P.O. Box 3778
Little Rock, AR 42203
(501) 378-5338

IRS, District Director
P.O. Box 66
Oklahoma City, OK 73101
(405) 231-4411

IRS, District Director
P.O. Box 30309
New Orleans, LA 70190
(504) 589-2431

IRS, District Director
1100 Commerce St.
Code 400
Dallas, TX 75242
(214) 749-2291

IRS, District Director
P.O. Box 250
Austin, TX 78767
(512) 397-5201

Customs

U.S. Customs Service
600 South St.
New Orleans, LA 70130
(504) 589-6353

U.S. Customs Service
1100 Commerce St.
Dallas/Ft. Worth, TX 75242
(214) 749-3704

U.S. Customs Service
Bridge of Americas
(POB9516)
Building B/Rm. 134
El Paso, TX 79985
(915) 543-7435

U.S. Customs Service
P.O. Box 570
Galveston, TX 77550
(713) 763-1211

U.S. Customs
701 San Jacinto St.
Houston, TX 77052
(713) 226-4316

U.S. Customs
Mann Rd. & Santa Maria
P.O. Box 758
Laredo, TX 78040
(512) 723-2956

U.S. Customs
Fifth & Austin Ave.
Port Arthur, TX 77640
(713) 982-2831

U.S. Marshals

U.S. Marshal
6th St. & Rogers Ave.
Box 1572
Fort Smith, AR 72902
(501) 740-3423

U.S. Marshal
5th & Gaines Sts.
Little Rock, AR 72203
(501) 740-6256

U.S. Marshal
707 Florida St.
Baton Rouge, LA 70801
(504) 687-0364

U.S. Marshal
500 Camp St./Rm. 600
New Orleans, LA 70130
(504) 682-6871

U.S. Marshal
P.O. Box 53
Shreveport, LA 71161
(318) 493-5257

U.S. Marshal
P.O. Box 738
Muskogee, OK 74401
(918) 736-2523

U.S. Marshal
200 N.W. 4th St.
Oklahoma City, OK 73101
(405) 736-4206

U.S. Marshal
P.O. Box 1097
Tulsa, OK 74101
(918) 736-7738

U.S. Marshal
P.O. Box 111
Beaumont, TX 77704
(713) 527-4791

U.S. Marshal
1100 Commerce St.
Dallas, TX 75242
(214) 749-2432

U.S. Marshal
P.O. Box 61608
Houston, TX 77208
(713) 527-4791

U.S. Marshal
655 E. Durango St.
San Antonio, TX 78206
(512) 730-6540

Post Office

Procurement
Services Office
U.S. Postal Service
P.O. Box 220030
Dallas, TX 75222
(214) 948-2850

Post Master
Dead Parcel Branch
Fort Worth, TX 76101
(817) 334-2981

State Surplus Departments

Dept. of Finance
& Administration
Office of State
Purchasing, Marketing &
Redistribution
P.O. Box 2940
Little Rock, AR 72203
(501) 371-1865

Land Commissioner's
Office
State Capitol
Little Rock, AR 72203
(501) 372-1896

Division of
Administration
State Property Control
1502 N. 17th St.
Baton Rouge, LA 70804
(504) 342-6849

Board of Affairs
Central Purchasing
Division
306 State Capitol
Oklahoma City, OK 73105
(405) 521-2115

Purchasing Division
Box 13047
Capitol Station
Austin, TX 78711
(512) 475-3433

SHERIFFS

Arkansas: LITTLE ROCK—Pulaski County Sheriff's Dept., 2900 S. Woodrow, Little Rock, AR 72204 (501) 664-3800

Louisiana: NEW ORLEANS—Civil Sheriff of New Orleans Parish, 421 Loyola Ave., Rm. 403, New Orleans, LA 70112 (504) 523-6145

Oklahoma: OKLAHOMA CITY—Oklahoma County Sheriff's Dept., 321 Park Ave., Oklahoma City, OK 73102 (405) 236-1717 / TULSA—Tulsa County Sheriff's Dept., Civil Division, 500 S. Denver, Tulsa, OK 74103 (918) 585-1261

Texas: DALLAS—Dallas County Sheriff's Dept., 600 Commerce, Dallas, TX 75202 (214) 749-8810 / HOUSTON—Harris County Sheriff's Dept., 301 San Jacinto, Houston, TX 77002 (713) 221-6000

POLICE

Arkansas: LITTLE ROCK—Little Rock Police Dept., Property Desk, 700 W. Markham St., Little Rock, AR 72201 (501) 371-4643

Louisiana: NEW ORLEANS—New Orleans Police Dept., auctions are held at: Bureau of Purchasing, Rm. 4W02, City Hall, 1300 Dereido St., New Orleans, LA 70112 (504) 586-5151

Oklahoma: OKLAHOMA CITY—Oklahoma City Police Dept., Property Room or Auto Theft Dept., 200 N. Shantel St., Oklahoma City, OK 73106 (miscellaneous, bikes) (405) 232-5311 x407; (autos) (405) 232-5311 x361

Texas: DALLAS—Dallas Police Dept., Property Room, City Hall, 1000 Throckmorton St., Dallas, TX 76102 (817) 870-6425 / HOUSTON—Houston Police Dept., Surplus & Salvage, City Treasury Dept., 5711 E. Tex-Freeway, Houston, TX 77026 (713) 692-6837

GENERAL MERCHANDISE—ESTATE SALES—COUNTRY AUCTIONS

Arkansas: LITTLE ROCK—The Auction Center (B.R. Tucker, Auctr.) 10624 New Benton Hwy. (real estate, estates, farms, household goods, commercial-industrial liquidations) (501) 455-3103; Baseline Auction (John Campbell, Auctr.) 3510 Base Line Rd. (new & used merchandise; Sunday 2:00 p.m. auction) (501) 565-9590; Bill & Janet's Auctions (Buddy Watkins, Auctr.) Crystal Hill Rd., N. Little Rock, AR (general merchandise) (501) 753-6265 / BATESVILLE—Col. Paul Kelly Auction Service, Rt. 7, Box 631A (estates, antiques, farm, household goods) (501) 793-6507 / CENTERTON—American Business Auctrs. (Col. Roy Henson, Auctr.) Box 187 (general merchandise) (501) 273-7970

Louisiana: NEW ORLEANS—Morton's Auction Gallery, P.O. Box 30380 (fine art, antiques, silver collectibles) (504) 561-1196; Sotheby Parke-Bernet, Inc. (represented by Samuel Farnsworth Ltd.) 300 Board of Trade Pl. (504) 525-4211; Hampshire House Auctions, 4618 Cleveland Ave. (estates, antiques, hotels, liquidations) (504) 486-3248; Sanchez Uptown Antiques, 4730 Magazine St. (504) 524-0281; Senecore Inc. Auction Services, 8220 Old Gentilly Rd. (estates, liquidations, autos) (504) 241-9393 / KENNER—John Henson, Auctr., 705 Williams Blvd. (estates, antiques, household furnishings; monthly auction) (504) 722-3240

Oklahoma: OKLAHOMA CITY—A-1 Auto Auction, 1800 S. Western (Wednesday 7:00 p.m. auction) (405) 631-6726; Don's Furniture Auction, 3405 N.E. 23rd (Sunday 1:30 p.m. auction) (405) 427-1668; Col. Roy F. Georgia, 4722 S.E. 29th (real estate, classic car auctions) (405) ENterprise 5-3430 / EL RENO—Sam's Auction (Sam Driggers, Auctr.) 1930 E. Hwy. 66 (estates, machinery, business liquidations; antique consignment auction first Saturday 7:00 p.m.) (405) 262-5471 / TULSA—Brandon Auction, 12835 E. 11th (furniture, appliances) (918) 437-2937

Texas: DALLAS-FORT WORTH—Clement's Auction Co., P.O. Box 727, Forney, TX (fine art, antiques) (214) 226-1520 or 226-3044; Joe Small Auctioneers, 3114 Garden Brook, Dallas, TX (general merchandise) (214) 241-1912; Paul Smith, Empire & Assoc., Inc., P.O. Box 9653, Fort Worth, TX (general merchandise) (817) 332-4401; Oak Hill Auction (Alven B. Wilson, Auctr.) E. Hwy. 175, Dallas, TX (antiques, general merchandise; Thursday & Saturday 8:00 p.m. auction, second Monday 8:00 p.m. antiques auction) (214) 286-2610; Ralph Segars Assoc., 5924 Royal Lane, Dallas, TX (real estate, equipment, livestock) (214) 369-8252 / HOUSTON—Bogan's Auction Barn (Harold E. Bogan, Auctr.) Hwy. 35 betw. Pearland & Alvin, Rte. 3, Box 707, Alvin, TX (general merchandise, furniture) (713) 482-6983; Laporte Antique Auction House, P.O. Box 1456, LaPorte, TX (Saturday auction in LaPorte, Sunday auction in San Marcos, Monday auction in Dallas) (713) 471-1313; James Fletcher Galleries, Inc., 518 Shepherd Dr. (antiques, fine accessories; third Thursday & Friday auctions) (713) 527-0822; Miller & Miller, 25518 Wingfield (construction, trucking, oil field, logging, and all industrial machinery) (800) 792-2226; Joe Presswood Co., Inc., 1702 Washington (real estate, antiques, household goods, business & industrial liquidations) (713) 223-9453; Sotheby Parke-Bernet, Inc., 5015 Westheimer (713) 623-0010; Big H Auto Auction, 701 N. Shepherd (713) 869-6485; Regency Auction House, 3902 San Jacinto (general merchandise) (713) 528-1652 / SAN ANTONIO—San Antonio Auction Gallery (J. Kahn & Assoc. Auctrs., John Jones, Auctr.) 5096 Blanco (general merchandise; Friday 7:00 p.m. auction) (512) 342-3800; Barnes Auctions, 2601 S. Hackbury (Wednesday Auction) (512) 532-6641; Lister's Auction Gallery, 9159 S. Presa (second-hand furniture) (512) 633-0340; McKelvery's Antiques, 10302 1H 35 North (512) 654-7272; Peyton Auction Gallery, 435 Isom (general merchandise) (512) 344-7125

REGIONAL MEDIA

Arkansas: LITTLE ROCK—Little Rock Arkansas Gazette (auction ads daily; more Sunday) (501) 371-3700

Louisiana: NEW ORLEANS—New Orleans Times Picayune (auction ads daily) (504) 821-1455

Oklahoma: OKLAHOMA CITY—Oklahoma City Times (auction ads daily; more Sunday) (405) 232-3311 / TULSA—Tulsa World (auction ads daily) (918) 583-2161

Texas: HOUSTON—Houston Chronicle (auction ads daily) (713) 220-7171 / DALLAS—Dallas News, Communications Center (auction ads daily) (214) 745-8256